REVOLUTIONIZ

Many scholars have turned to the groundbreaking critical research methodology, youth-led participatory action research (YPAR), as a way to address both the political challenges and inherent power imbalances of conducting research with young people. *Revolutionizing Education* makes a unique contribution to the literature on adolescents by offering a broad framework for understanding this research methodology. With an informative combination of theory and practice, this edited collection brings together student writings alongside those of major scholars in the field. While remaining sensitive to the methodological challenges of qualitative inquiry, *Revolutionizing Education* is the first definitive statement of YPAR as it relates to sites of education.

Julio Cammarota is Assistant Professor in the Bureau of Applied Research in Anthropology and the Mexican-American Studies and Research Center at the University of Arizona.

Michelle Fine is Distinguished Professor of Social Psychology, Urban Education, and Women's Studies at the Graduate School and University Center, City University of New York.

Critical Youth Studies

Series Editor: Greg Dimitriadis

Beyond Resistance! Youth Activism and Community Change: New Democratic Possibilities for Practice and Policy for America's Youth

Edited by Shawn Ginwright, Pedro Noguera, and Julio Cammarota

Youth Learning On Their Own Terms: Creative Practices and Classroom Teaching

Leif Gustavson

Youth Moves: Identities and Education in Global Perspective

Edited by Nadine Dolby and Fazal Rizvi

Youth Culture and Sport: Identity, Power, and Politics

Edited by Michael D. Giardina and Michele K. Donnelly

Next Wave Cultures: Feminism, Subcultures, Activism

Edited by Anita Harris

Revolutionizing Education: Youth Participatory Action Research in Motion

Edited by Julio Cammarota and Michelle Fine

REVOLUTIONIZING EDUCATION

Youth Participatory Action Research in Motion

edited by Julio Cammarota
and Michelle Fine

NEW YORK AND LONDON

First published 2008
by Routledge
270 Madison Ave, New York, NY 10016

Simultaneously published in the UK
by Routledge
2 Park Square, Milton Park, Abingdon, Oxon OX14 4RN

Routledge is an imprint of the Taylor & Francis Group, an informa business

Typeset in Minion Pro, Franklin Gothic, and Trade Gothic by
The Running Head Limited, www.therunninghead.com
Printed and bound in the United States of America on acid-free paper
by Walsworth Publishing Company

Library of Congress Cataloging in Publication Data
Revolutionizing education : youth participatory action research in motion / edited by Julio Cammarota and Michelle Fine.
p. cm.
Includes bibliographical references and index.
ISBN 978–0–415–95615–4 (hb : alk. paper)–ISBN 978–0–415–95616–1 (pb : alk. paper)–ISBN 978–0–203–93210–0 (ebook) 1. Action research in education—United States. 2. Youth development—United States. 3. Critical pedagogy—United States. 4. Educational innovations—United States. I. Cammarota, Julio. II. Fine, Michelle.
LB1028.25.U6R48 2008
370.72—dc22
2007033796

ISBN10: 0–415–95615–3 (hbk)
ISBN10: 0–415–95616–1 (pbk)
ISBN10: 0–203–93210–2 (ebk)

ISBN13: 978–0-415–95615–4 (hbk)
ISBN13: 978–0-415–95616–1 (pbk)
ISBN13: 978–0-203–93210–0 (ebk)

Contents

Series Editor's Introduction

As Arjun Appadurai (2006) recently argued,[1] the ability to conduct research on one's social surround should be considered a basic human right. By the "right to research," Appadurai means "the right to the tools through which any citizen can systematically increase that stock of knowledge which they consider most vital to their survival as human beings and to their claims as citizens" (168). *Revolutionizing Education*, by Julio Cammarota and Michelle Fine, is best seen in this light, as an important step in what will undoubtedly be a long-term struggle to assert this fundamental right for all young people around the globe. In particular, this volume evidences, explores, and expands upon the very best impulses of participatory action research (PAR)—research conducted "with" as opposed to "on" youth, around the issues they find most important in their lives. *Revolutionizing Education* is, quite simply, a transformative text.

In positing research as a human right—and I believe it is—Appadurai works toward two self-professed and interconnected goals. The first is substantive. Full citizenship today demands the ability to make "strategic" and "continuous" inquiries on a range of issues—AIDS, riots, labor market shifts, migration paths, prisons, among them (168). Clearly, while neo-liberal logics continue to unfold around the world, they "land" in unpredictable ways in particular communities. As the editors and authors in this volume make clear, we cannot *a priori* predict the issues and concerns young people face. The chapters take us across a range of such issues—from the value of the general educational development (GED) credential to the gentrification of New York City neighborhoods to racial segregation in Tucson, Arizona, and beyond. Critically interrogating these issues with youth allows us all sharper perspective on them—allows us to see that they can be otherwise. This is a capacity often denied youth, though it is necessary for a vibrant public sphere—for a democracy (to echo Michael Apple) worth its name.

The second goal is what Appadurai calls "rhetorical." By opening up the notion of "research," we "de-parochialise" it, taking these tools out of the hands of an elite group of specialists and professionals, making it a "much more universal, elementary and improvable capacity" (168). As the editors and authors of this text make clear, PAR is intimately concerned with extending the notion of the so-called "expert" to encompass a wider range of stakeholders. At its very best, PAR opens up a space for a critical, multi-generational dialogue about research itself—one that looks beyond rarified university walls. This is a fundamental challenge to the ways that research is traditionally conducted and knowledge is traditionally stratified. It too is necessary for universities to meaningfully engage in democratic dialogue in these new and uncertain times.

None of this is easy work. As the editors and authors argue, PAR forces us to abandon the categories often used to sort, classify, and essentialize youth. These categories can be deployed by both conservatives and progressives. The former often treat young people as a pathological problem to be managed—"at risk" as defined by adults. The latter often treat young people as incipient radicals, "resisting" dominant culture through everyday cultural practices. Working with youth, in distinction, means seeing young people as partners in struggle, as resources to be drawn upon in common cause. As Cammarota and Fine make clear in their excellent introduction, PAR does not allow us to "freeze" young people in such fashion. PAR treats young people as agents in ongoing, critical struggles.

As *Revolutionizing Education* makes clear, PAR blurs the lines between pedagogy, research, and politics. Yet, as we see in the chapters that follow, each does not extend from the other in seamless fashion. Each demands specific competencies and skills, both on their own and when taken together. If nothing else, PAR is an invitation to a long-term struggle that forces us to operate in these "in between" spaces. This is a site of intense possibility as well as uncertainty. It is one best seen in its specificity and detail, as the volume's contributors make clear. At stake here is what Appadurai calls the "capacity to aspire," the capacity to imaginatively link one's own personal problems and issues to a broader set of social, political, and economic forces and pressures—and to work to transform them (176). This, again, should be a basic human right—a point evidenced on every page of *Revolutionizing Education*.

Greg Dimitriadis
University at Buffalo,
State University of New York

Note

1 A. Appadurai (2006). The right to research. *Globalisation, Societies, and Education* 4(2), 167–77. Special thanks to Bob Lingard for alerting me to this article.

CHAPTER 1

Youth Participatory Action Research

A Pedagogy for Transformational Resistance

JULIO CAMMAROTA AND MICHELLE FINE

In the film *The Matrix*, Morpheus, played by Laurence Fishburne, places Keanu Reeves' character Neo in a chair to tell him face to face about the real truth of his experience. Morpheus shows Neo a red pill in one hand and a blue one in the other, describing that the red pill will lead him "down the rabbit hole" to the truth while the blue pill will make him forget about their conversation and return everything back to "normal." Neo looks confused and worried, hesitates for a moment, and then reaches to grab and then swallow the red pill. The "blue and red pill" scene in *The Matrix* serves as an excellent metaphor for the relationships some educators/activists have with their students, and the kinds of choices we ask them to make. The critical educational experience offered might lead the student "down the rabbit hole" past the layers of lies to the truths of systematic exploitation and oppression as well as possibilities for resistance. After he ingests the red pill, Neo ends up in the place of truth, awakening to the reality that his entire world is a lie constructed to make him believe that he lives a "normal" life, when in reality he is fully exploited day in and day out. What is "normal" is really a mirage, and what is true is the complete structural domination of people, all people.

This book, *Revolutionizing Education*, literally connects to the metaphorical play on chimera and veracity forwarded by the narrative in *The Matrix*. Examples are presented throughout in which young people resist the normalization of systematic oppression by undertaking their own engaged praxis—critical and collective inquiry, reflection and action focused on "reading" and speaking back to the reality of the world, their world (Freire, 1993). The praxis highlighted in the book—youth participatory action research (YPAR)—provides young people with opportunities to study social problems affecting their lives and then determine actions to rectify these problems. YPAR, and thus *Revolutionizing Education*, may extend the kinds of questions posed by critical youth studies (Bourgois, 1995; Fine and Weis, 1998; Giroux, 1983; Kelley, 1994; Macleod, 1987; McRobbie, 1991; Oakes et al., 2006; Rasmussen et al., 2004; Sullivan, 1989; Willis, 1977). How do youth learn the skills of critical inquiry and resistances within formal youth development, research collectives, and/or educational settings? How is it possible for their critical inquiries to evolve into formalized challenges to the "normal" practices of systematic oppression? Under what conditions can critical research be a tool of youth development and social justice work?

The Matrix infers revolution by showing how Neo learns to see the reality of his experiences while understanding his capabilities for resistance. The YPAR cases presented in this book also follow a similar pattern: young people learn through research about complex power relations, histories of struggle, and the consequences of oppression. They begin to re-vision and denaturalize the realities of their social worlds and then undertake forms of collective challenge based on the knowledge garnered through their critical inquiries. As you will read in this volume, the youth, with adult allies, have written policy briefs, engaged sticker campaigns, performed critical productions, coordinated public testimonials—all dedicated to speaking back and challenging conditions of injustice.

What perhaps distinguishes young people engaged in YPAR from the standard representations in critical youth studies is that their research is designed to contest and transform systems and institutions to produce greater justice—distributive justice, procedural justice, and what Iris Marion Young calls a justice of recognition, or respect. In short, YPAR is a formal resistance that leads to transformation—systematic and institutional change to promote social justice.

YPAR teaches young people that conditions of injustice are produced, not natural; are designed to privilege and oppress; but are ultimately challengeable and thus changeable. In each of these projects, young people and adult allies experience the vitality of a multi-generational collective analysis of power; we learn that sites of critical inquiry and resistance can be fortifying and nourishing to the soul, and at the same time that these projects provoke ripples of social change. YPAR shows young people how they are consistently subject to the impositions and manipulations of dominant exigencies. These controlling interests may take on the form of white supremacy, capitalism, sexism, homophobia, or xenophobia—all of which is meant to provide certain people with power at the expense of subordinating others, many others. Within this matrix or grid of power, the possibilities of true liberation for young people become limited. Similar to the film *The Matrix*, the individual, like Neo, may be unaware of the inflections of power fostering oppression. The dawning of awareness emerges from a critical study of social institutions and processes influencing one's life course, and his/her capacity to see differently, to act anew, to provoke change.

Critical youth studies demonstrate that the revolutionary lesson is not always apprehended in schools; sometimes, young people gain critical awareness through their own endogenous cultural practices. Such is the case of Willis' (1977) Lads in *Learning to Labor*. Working-class youth attain insights about the reproductive function of schools through their own street cultural sensibilities. However, they use these insights to resist education en masse by forgoing school for jobs in factories. Scholars (Fine, 1991; Solórzano and Delgado-Bernal, 2001) identify this form of resistance as "self-defeating," because the students' choice to forgo school for manual labor contributes to reproducing them as working class. Although the Lads resist the school's purpose of engendering uneven class relations, their resistance contributes to this engendering process by undermining any chance they had for social mobility.

Young people also engage in forms of resistance that avoid self-defeating outcomes while striving for social advancement. Scholars (Fordham, 1996) identify this next level of resistance as "conformist"—in the sense that young people embrace the education system with the intention of seeking personal gains, although not necessarily agreeing with all the ideological filigree espoused by educational institutions. They use schooling for their own purposes: educational achievements that garner individual gains with social implications beyond the classroom, such as economic mobility, gender equality, and racial parity.

Solórzano and Delgado-Bernal (2001: 319–20) contend that students may attain another, yet more conscious form of resistance, which they call "transformational resistance." A transformational approach to resistance moves the student to a "deeper level of understanding and a social justice orientation." Those engaged in transformational resistance address problems of systematic injustice and seek actions that foster "the greatest possibility for social change" (ibid.).

Although Solórzano and Delgado-Bernal (2001) provide a useful typology (self-defeating, conformist, and transformational) that acknowledges the complexities of resistance, the education and development processes leading to resistances are somewhat under-discussed. Apparently, the production of cultural subjectivities (Bourgois, 1995; Levinson et al., 1996; Willis, 1977) is related to resisting ideological oppressions. However, these cultural productions tend to occur in more informal settings (non-institutional, non-organizational) such as peer groups, families, and street corners.

The work presented in this volume agitates toward another framework—where youth are engaged in multi-generational collectives for critical inquiry and action, and these collectives are housed in youth development settings, schools, and/or research sites. With this series of cases, we challenge scholars, educators, and activists to consider how to create such settings in which research for resistance can be mobilized toward justice.

A key question is whether resistance can develop within formal processes (pedagogical structures or youth development practices). If this question is left unattended, we risk perceiving youth resistances as "orientations" as opposed to processes. In other words, the kinds of resistances, whether self-defeating, conformist, or transformational, will be identified as emerging from some inherent fixed, cultural sensibility. This perspective of young people sustains the ridged essentialization trap that has plagued studies of youth for years (Anderson, 1990; Newman, 1999; Ogbu, 1978). The traditional essentialized view maintains that any problem (poverty, educational failure, drug and alcohol abuse, etc.) faced by youth results of their own volition, thereby blaming the victim for the victim's problems.

Critical youth studies goes beyond the traditional pathological or patronizing view by asserting that young people have the capacity and agency to analyze their social context, to engage critical research collectively, and to challenge and resist the forces impeding their possibilities for liberation. However, another step is needed to further distance critical youth studies from essentialized perspectives by acknowledging that resistances can be attained through formal processes in "real" settings, through multi-generational collectives, and sometimes among youth alone. YPAR represents not only a formal pedagogy of resistance but also the means by which young people engage transformational resistance.

PAR in Education

Participatory action research (PAR) (Fals-Borda and Rahman, 1991; McTaggart, 1997; Selener, 1997) has long been associated with revolutionary pedagogical projects. The history of popular education (Kane, 2001; La Belle, 1987; Wanderley et al., 1993) reveals that PAR has often served as the research arm, so to speak, of many popular education programs. Similar to PAR, popular education (Torres and Fischman, 1994) seeks to engage people in a learning process that provides knowledge about the social injustices negatively influencing their life circumstances. The knowledge about social injustice includes understanding methods for change and thus organizing skills necessary to remedy the injustice. Highlander, the most recognized popular education school in the United States, trained civil rights organizers with this pedagogical approach, including most notably civil rights leader Rosa Parks.

PAR follows popular education by focusing the acquisition of knowledge on injustice as well as skills for speaking back and organizing for change. However, the pedagogy is specifically research such that participants conduct a critical scientific inquiry that includes establishing key research questions and methods to answer them, such as participant observation, qualitative interviews and questionnaires, film, and speak outs. PAR follows and extends principles of validity and reliability by challenging, for instance, where "expert validity" and "construct validity" live—in conversations with those who experience oppression, not simply those who decide to study social issues. Our projects seek new forms of reliability, including theoretical and provocative generalizability, trying to understand how youth research in East Los Angeles schools (see Morrell, this volume) confirms and challenges similar work undertaken by and on high school push outs in New York City (Tuck et al., this volume). In and across sites, we work to craft research designs to dig deeply into local youth politics and also speak across sites and historic moments to understand the long reach of injustice and resistance over time and place. In many ways, PAR challenges and extends "traditional" research such that problems or conditions are analyzed through a rigorous, systematic process.

Herein lie the differences. The first and most important difference is the "researcher." In most PAR projects, the researcher is not a lone investigator but individuals in a collective. Together, or individually in the group, they are systematically addressing the same problem (high-stakes testing, inadequate conditions in schools, anti-immigration policies, push-out practices, violence against women) with a lens that may be crafted individually or collectively. Researchers engage in ongoing conversation and reflection with others, across generations, similarly poised to inquire and act. Research is therefore a collective process enriched by the multiple perspectives of several researchers working together. Second, the researcher, or more appropriately, researchers, are more or less "insiders" in a given situation. In other words, they are the stakeholders within a particular institution, organization, or community. For example, a PAR project in prisons would include prisoners as researchers, or a school project might include student researchers as well as push outs, educators, university professors.

Stakeholders should not be narrowly defined or limited. In any given situation, there might be different types of stakeholders with different interests. Education-based PAR projects feasibly could include policy makers, teachers, administrators, parents, students, push outs and the public, since they all are stakeholders.

Third, stakeholders participating in PAR projects tend to be critical race researchers, adhering closely to the Critical Race Theory (CRT) tenet of intersectionality (Delgado and Stefancic, 2001). Although understanding that race and racism are formative processes within their social contexts, PAR stakeholders look to analyze power relations through multiple axes. Thus, race intersects with gender, class, and sexuality within typical PAR inquiries.

Fourth, the knowledge gained from the research should be critical in nature, meaning that findings and insights derived from analyses should point to historic and contemporary moves of power and toward progressive changes improving social conditions within the situation studied.

Finally, PAR knowledge is active and NOT passive (i.e. mere facts and figures organized for storage). Research findings become launching pads for ideas, actions, plans, and strategies to initiate social change. This final difference distinguishes PAR from traditional research by pointing to a critical epistemology that redefines knowledge as actions in pursuit of social justice.

Although YPAR includes everything described above as participatory action research, we believe that YPAR is also explicitly pedagogical, with implications for education and youth development. The pedagogical philosophy on which YPAR is based derives from Freire's (1993) notion of praxis—critical reflection and action. Students study their social contexts through research and apply their knowledge to discover the contingent qualities of life. Thus, the important lesson obtained from engaging in this pedagogical praxis is that life, or more specifically the students' experiences, are not transcendental or predetermined. Rather, praxis reveals how life experiences are malleable and subject to change, and the students possess the agency to produce changes. The praxis aspects of YPAR inspire profound education and development outcomes.

Through participatory action research, youth learn how to study problems and find solutions to them. More importantly, they study problems and derive solutions to obstacles preventing their own well-being and progress. Understanding how to overcome these obstacles becomes critical knowledge for the discovery of one's efficacy to produce personal as well as social change. Once a young person discovers his or her capacity to effect change, oppressive systems and subjugating discourses no longer persuade him or her that the deep social and economic problems he or she faces result from his or her own volition. Rather, the discovery humanizes the individual, allowing him or her to realize the equal capabilities and universal intelligence in all humans, while acknowledging the existence of problems as the result of social forces beyond his or her own doing.

Although YPAR provides the opportunity for young people to recognize how social constructions mediate reality, the praxis of YPAR allows them to perceive the human machinations behind these constructions and thus encourages recreative actions to produce realities better suited to meet their needs and interests. The knowledge that human agency constructs reality is power—a power that has very specific education and development outcomes. Young people possessing critical knowledge of the true workings of their social contexts see themselves as intelligent and capable. Thus, academic capacities should increase along with problem-solving abilities.

In the end, YPAR represents a fundamental, critical strategy for youth development, youth-based policy making and organizing, and education. The cases presented in this book provide a striking contrast to the many failed pedagogical and youth development approaches purporting to enhance the capacities of traditionally under-served youth. By providing the opportunity to study the reasons for under-service, youth excel personally and also address the root causes maintaining traditions of negligence and dispossession. The two strands of personal and contextual are obviously linked, and engaging youth in processes that address both lead to more profound education and development outcomes. YPAR is a process that situates an individual's learning in his or her socio-historical context—the basis of what some scholars believe is sound pedagogical practice (Lave and Wenger, 1991; Moll, 1990).

The chapters in this book speak more directly to how YPAR is transformative for individuals and the social context in which they are situated. Youth researchers along with adult researchers contribute to the authorship of this book. Thus, *Revolutionizing Education* represents a multi-generational collaboration for the advancement of educational practices. The youth contributors originate from different cities, and the adult researchers have multiple ties to anthropology, sociology, psychology, education, and linguistics. Therefore, the collaboration offers a unique range of generational, geographical, and inter-disciplinary perspectives on education, youth development, and participatory action research. Following the YPAR cases are senior scholars commentating on the transformative potential of the particular pedagogical approach. Sandy Grande, Maxine Greene, Pauline Lipman, Luis Moll, and John Rogers contribute senior scholar commentaries.

Shawn Ginwright contributes the next chapter and discusses in detail the critical politics of democracy, dissent, and analysis. YPAR is a prime methodology, with extensive potential for "art and imagination," for preparing and engaging youth in democratic processes as well as providing young people with a systematic way to analyze the oppressive circumstances within various institutional settings. Ginwright argues that YPAR teaches young people to be active citizens willing and ready to expand their democratic rights and take responsibility for sustaining and promoting democracy. He also adds that YPAR is the best example of democratic and political education in the current realm of youth development programs and approaches for enhancing civic engagement among young people.

Torre and Fine et al. highlight deep participation and how YPAR represents an important example of critical epistemology. They provide examples of deep participation from *Echoes of Brown*—a project in which students participated in a series of "research camps," each held for two days at a time in community and/or university settings. Deconstructing who can "do" research, what constitutes research, and who benefits, they were immersed in methods training and social justice theory. The students learned how to conduct interviews, focus groups, and participant observations; to design surveys and organize archival analyses. They explore the methodological implications of elevating youth knowledge as an explicit engagement and interrogation of power and difference. Their chapter concludes with reflections on performance as a critical and provocative outcome of YPAR.

Tuck et al. present a youth participatory action research project in New York, Collective of Researchers on Educational Disappointment and Desire (CREDD), and their research endeavor, the Gate-ways and Get-aways Project. This project focuses on the overuse of general educational development (GED) credential to push students out of the New York City school system.

Cahill et al. describe the YPAR project of the Fed Up Honeys, a group of young womyn of color studying the effects of gentrification in their New York City neighborhoods. For the Fed Up Honeys, YPAR achieved individual and social transformation by "seeing the world through different eyes, coupled with a desire to open others' eyes." The Fed Up Honeys help us understand the power of their sticker campaign, where they placed stickers all over the Lower East Side to challenge dominant stereotypes about young womyn of color.

Romero et al. document YPAR within the Social Justice Education Project (SJEP), a social science curriculum designed to empower Latina/o students to find solutions to educational disparities. SJEP students conduct research on racial segregation in schools located in Tucson, Arizona. Findings are presented to school officials to determine the best strategies for remedying educational injustices and promoting greater equity within the school system. The students create video documentaries, presentations, and newsletter/reports based on their research findings. These products of PAR become tools for organizing necessary institutional changes within Tucson schools.

Ernest Morrell discusses a YPAR project for IDEA—UCLA's Institute for

Democracy, Education, and Access. IDEA is a network of scholars, students, professionals in schools and public agencies, advocates, community activists, and urban youth. IDEA's mission is to challenge the pervasive racial and social class inequalities in Los Angeles and in cities around the nation, with a special focus on high-quality schooling. IDEA's YPAR project is the summer Youth Summit that features research by youth from all over Los Angeles with the intention of ameliorating conditions in public schools.

Chiara Cannella provides a concluding chapter, which discusses PAR and its connections/tensions with educational theory, practice, and national policies. In particular, Cannella writes about how the educational approaches of the YPAR cases presented in the book contend with the NCLB climate of high-stakes testing and standardization. She discusses the differences between PAR and NCLB, and explains how PAR might achieve the objectives of NCLB, perhaps more effectively. PAR is examined in relation to the achievement gap, academic skills, accountability, and evaluation, areas for which NCLB purports to have effective systems. The discussion of PAR and NCLB exposes potential flaws and incorrect assumptions of current national policies and theories.

Michelle Fine ends our collection with an epilogue written in the form of a fictional letter recommending Assistant Professor H. for tenure and promotion. In this epilogue, she answers the following questions about YPAR: Is this scholarship rigorous? Is there an intellectual tradition within which this work is situated? What about bias? Why are so many of the articles co-authored with high school students? Isn't this just community service? These questions are in reality excuses, not necessarily questions, usually presented by ivory tower institutions to trivialize PAR in comparison to more "traditional" research methods. By answering these questions/excuses, Fine sets the record straight by arguing that YPAR contributes to serious scholarship through rigorous and valid research inquiries. Although most forms of scholarship are hesitant to make this claim, YPAR fosters the kinds of intuitional changes needed for more equitable social relations.

The YPAR projects presented in this book are located throughout the country (Arizona, California, and New York) and cover a range of educational settings—after-school programs, NGOs, and state-mandated US history courses. The diversity of locales and settings allows the reader to comprehend how to conduct similar YPAR projects in different locales (local neighborhoods, city centers, and summer camps) and different situations (classrooms, institutions, and organizations).

Most importantly, the reader should carefully attend to how YPAR represents a systematic approach for engaging young people in transformational resistance, educational praxis, and critical epistemologies. By attaining knowledge for resistance and transformation, young people create their own sense of efficacy in the world and address the social conditions that impede liberation and positive, healthy development. Learning to act upon and address oppressive social conditions leads to the acknowledgment of one's ability to reshape the context of one's life and thus determine a proactive and empowered sense of self. The intended consequence of YPAR is praxis and thus changes of consciousness that allow the young person to perceive him/herself as capable of struggling for and promoting social justice within his or her community.

Finally, many young people involved in YPAR projects could be classified—in the traditional sense—as "marginalized" or "at risk." The standard school system was failing them; they were doing poorly in their classes and were planning to drop out. However, the YPAR project in which they participated inspires new meanings of education. The projects engender educational experiences that are rigorous, relevant, and meaningful for them. They, in turn, excel academically and have reason to not only graduate from high school but also enroll in college. For the first time, education is something students do—instead of something being done to them—to address the injustices that limit possibilities for them, their families, and communities. Consequently, education in YPAR projects includes more than learning skills and abstract knowledge, but also the acquisition of intellectual resources through which students initiate revolutionary projects to transform themselves and the worlds which they inhabit. Similar to the concluding scene in *The Matrix*, PAR is the metaphorical phone booth that allows young people to dial into the systems of domination to inform the "powers that be," like Neo, that they are here, ready to resist.

References

Anderson, E. (1990). *Streetwise: Race, Class, and Change of an Urban Community*. Chicago: Chicago University Press.

Bourgois, P. (1995). *In Search of Respect: Selling Crack in* el barrio. Cambridge: Cambridge University Press.

Delgado, R., and J. Stefancic (2001). *Critical Race Theory: An Introduction*, New York: New York University Press.

Fals-Borda, Orlando, and Anisur Rahman (1991). *Action and Knowledge: Breaking the Monopoly with Participatory Action-Research*. New York: Apex Press; London: Intermediate Technology Publications.

Fine, M. (1991). *Framing Dropouts: Notes on the Politics of an Urban Public High School*. Albany: State University of New York Press.

Fine, M., and L. Weis (1998). *The Unknown City: Lives of Poor and Working-Class Young Adults*. Boston: Beacon Press.

Fordham, Signithia (1996). *Blacked Out: Dilemmas of Race, Identity, and Success at Capital High*. Chicago: University of Chicago Press.

Freire, P. (1993). *Pedagogy of the Oppressed*. New York: Continuum.

Giroux, Henry A. (1983). *Theory and Resistance in Education: A Pedagogy for the Opposition*. South Hadley, MA: Bergin and Garvey.

Kane, Liam (2001). *Popular Education and Social Change in Latin America*. London: Latin American Bureau.

Kelley, Robin D. G. (1994). *Race Rebels: Culture, Politics, and the Black Working Class*. New York: Free Press.

La Belle, T. J. (1987). From consciousness raising to popular education in Latin America and the Caribbean. *Comparative Education Review* 31(2): 201–17.

Lave, J., and E. Wenger (1991). *Situated Learning: Legitimate Peripheral Participation*. New York: Cambridge University Press.

Levinson, B., D. E. Foley, and D. C. Holland, eds. (1996). *The Cultural Production of the Educated Person: Critical Ethnographies of Schooling and Local Practice*. Albany: State University of New York Press.

MacLeod, J. (1987). *Ain't No Makin' It: Aspirations and Attainment in a Low-Income Neighborhood*. Boulder, CO: Westview.

McRobbie, A. (1991). *Feminism and Youth Culture: From* Jackie *to* Just Seventeen. Basingstoke: Macmillan.

McTaggart, Robin (1997). *Participatory Action Research: International Contexts and Consequences*. Albany: State University of New York Press.

Moll, Luis C. (1990). *Vygotsky and Education: Instructional Implications and Applications of Sociohistorical Psychology*. Cambridge and New York: Cambridge University Press.

Newman, K. S. (1999). *No Shame in my Game: The Working Poor in the Inner City*. New York: Vintage Books.

Oakes, Jeanne, John Rogers, and Martin Lipton (2006). *Learning Power: Organizing for Education and Justice*. New York: Teachers College Press.

Ogbu, J. U. (1978). Variability in minority school performance: A problem in search of an explanation. *Anthropology and Education Quarterly* 18: 312–24.

Rasmussen, Mary Louise, Eric E. Rofes, and Susan Talburt (2004). *Youth and Sexualities: Pleasure, Subversion and Insubordination in and out of Schools*. New York: Palgrave Macmillan.

Selener, D. (1997). *Participatory Action Research and Social Change*. Ithaca, NY: Cornell Participatory Action Research Network.

Solórzano, Daniel G., and Dolores Delgado-Bernal (2001). Examining transformational resistance through a critical race and Latcrit theory framework: Chicana and Chicano students in an urban context. *Urban Education* 36(3): 308–42.

Sullivan, M. L. (1989). *"Getting Paid": Youth Crime and Work in the Inner City*. Ithaca, NY: Cornell University Press.

Torres, Carlos A., and Gustavo Fischman (1994). Popular education: building from experience. *New Directions for Adult and Continuing Education* 63: 81–93.

Wanderley, L. E., M. Gadotti, and C. A. Torres (1993). *Educación Popular: Crisis y Perspectivas*. Buenos Aires: Miño y Dávila.

Willis, P. (1977). *Learning to Labor*. New York: Columbia University Press.

CHAPTER 2

Collective Radical Imagination

Youth Participatory Action Research and the Art of Emancipatory Knowledge

SHAWN GINWRIGHT

Introduction

Not long ago, I explained to one of my colleagues that I was feeling somewhat restricted by the confines of social science frameworks to describe, explain, and really capture a more nuanced understanding of youth's engagement with civil society. I explained to my colleague that I wanted the freedom to describe young people's experiences without romanticizing their capacity for social change, but also I wanted to avoid the static deterministic frames which ultimately leave us with a view of youth as victims of the "big bad" systems of oppression.

I vaguely remembered an essay titled "The Creative Process," by James Baldwin, from an undergraduate course years ago. After re-reading this essay, I was inspired and reminded of my role as a scholar as it relates to social change. Baldwin, in his eloquent and relentless precision for which his writing is known, gives us a blueprint for the role of an artist. He says, "The precise role of the artist, then, is to illuminate that darkness, blaze roads through the vast forest, so that we will not, in all our doing, lose sight of its purpose, which is after all, to make the world a more human dwelling place" (Baldwin, 1985).

This statement poses an interesting challenge for those of us who study and advocate for youth. Namely, in what ways does our work move beyond simplistic explanations, descriptions, and prediction of youth behaviors? How can our work both inform and inspire youth to engage in selfless social critique? I am becoming more convinced that the role of a scholar should be more closely aligned with Baldwin's conceptualization of an artist. That is, our role should be not only to inform, but also to inspire and to foster a collective imagination about how to make the world a more human dwelling place. Robin Kelley reminds us that our collective imagination may be the most revolutionary power available to us, "and yet as intellectuals we have failed miserably to grapple with its political and analytical importance" (Kelley, 2002).

Making the world a more human dwelling place, however, requires that our research and advocacy create space to foster a collective imagination among youth. While rare, these spaces hold the possibilities to reframe and re-imagine the type of world in which we choose to live. These spaces, however, are not open to the public and are frequently hidden beneath the layers of the "youth problem" tropes so frequently used to describe young folks' lives. Unfortunately, research and public imagination of young people's lives remain restricted to static conceptualizations of development, rigid frames about work and family life, and distorted notions of behavior, which all fail to capture the mosaic of experiences and textured realities of young people's lives.

Participatory action research (PAR) is one way to create these vital spaces for young people. With an emphasis on democratizing knowledge, fostering critical inquiry of daily life and developing liberatory practices, PAR is both an art and method to engage youth in democratic problem solving. Here the role of the academic and the artist converge in order to form new pedagogical possibilities. Some may frown upon my use of the term "art" to describe a rigorous methodological approach to social scientific inquiry. My point here, however, is to provoke a deeper intellectual curiosity about our capacity as researchers, youth advocates, and teachers to use participatory action research to provide a method of understanding that transgresses the current boundaries of social scientific knowledge. For example, how do we measure, predict, or even describe the meaning of hope among groups of people without resources and access to power? What practices sustain hope and faith among oppressed people? Thomas Kuhn argued in *The Structure of Scientific Revolutions* (1962) that paradigmatic shifts in thinking do not come from simply accumulation of facts, but rather from broader social, economic, political opportunities available to inform new thinking about a phenomenon. While gathering facts and describing social problems are indeed important, this use of scholarly energy is grossly insufficient. PAR as a methodology connected to transforming young people's lives must move beyond restrictive notions of scientific inquiry.

We can point to a number of scholars whose ideas and methods were at first unorthodox and outright rejected, then seriously considered and finally integrated into mainstream thinking. Cheikh Anta Diop's (Diop, 1974) seminal work on the African origins of civilization; Huey P. Newton's discussion of revolution (Hilliard and Weise, 2002; Newton, 1973): action research has multiple beginnings, one of which can be found among scholars of color.

Building from Kuhn's analysis and from activist scholars such as DuBois, Fredrick Douglas, James Baldwin, Zora Neal Hurston, then, how can our scientific knowledge come to bear on explaining the abandonment experience that millions of blacks felt in the wake of the Katrina disaster? How can our scholarship give meaning to rage, anger, and Kanye West's bold and courageous statement on national television "George Bush does not care about Black people"? How can scientific knowledge give meaning to my own and thousands of other black folks'—deeply felt (fist waving in the air)—response to his statement? Perhaps there are tender and precious elements of art that may free us to think beyond our disciplinary boundaries and training to open us to more radical notions of *objectivity*, *validity*, and *generalizability*.

This chapter explores the role of PAR in fostering civic engagement and community change among youth of color. Drawing from youth PAR projects from six cities who participate in the Research Collaborative on Youth Activism, I illustrate how the participatory process involves the intersection of art, science, and imagination. I argue that equal in importance to the analytical skills developed through participatory action research, youth develop a collective radical imagination that is vital for community and social change. I describe the PAR process for these groups and focus on a three-day retreat in which the six groups from around the country came to share their research, learn from each other's struggles and develop a collective imagination about a more human world. By documenting their daily lives, creating new stories about their lived realities and envisioning new social and civic possibilities, PAR forces researchers to re-examine what constitutes research, and shatters the brittle barriers that separate the scholar and artist in each of us.

Research Collaborative on Youth Activism

In 2005, Dr. Julio Cammarota at the University of Arizona and I formed the Research Collaborative on Youth Activism (RCYA) in order to create a community of scholars who work collaboratively with youth to address a common set of research questions under a common conceptual framework. The RCYA is an interdisciplinary network of researchers who study and work collaboratively with young people in their schools and communities. Housed at San Francisco State University's César Chávez Institute for Public Policy, the purpose of the RCYA is to create a learning community of researchers who are engaged in research about youth activism. The aim is to organize information and facilitate the dissemination of relevant research findings to policy makers, practitioners, and researchers in order to increase support for youth activism and social change activities. We also agreed that an understanding of youth rights would be an important ingredient in facilitating the policy change we envisioned. By introducing the idea that all youth in our society should be entitled to certain liberties and protections, we raised questions about the role of youth in our democracy. For example, what rights do young people have in a democratic society? In what ways do young people of color conceptualize their rights? Do youth enjoy the same constitutional protections as adults?

To answer these questions, we invited six adult/youth PAR teams to engage these questions in their local schools and communities.[1] Each of these groups was asked to document school, neighborhood and community problems, provide research about the root and systemic causes of these issues, and develop a set of civic entitlements or rights they believed necessary to redress the problems they identified. Our collective goal was to develop and distribute a Youth Bill of Rights that both served as an assessment tool to examine the extent to which six local communities support youth rights, as well as to provide a common framework for youth activists around the country to articulate their collective work.

The Youth Bill of Rights is to be used in three primary ways. First is to conduct an annual Youth Rights Report Card in the six participating cities. The report card is an assessment of the extent to which youth rights are supported in local schools and communities. The report card assessment is a web-based evaluation tool that provided data about how youth perceive and experience educational and civic life in their respective cities. After providing information about youth rights, each youth is asked to score or grade their city on how well their school or city supports particular youth rights. We anticipate that each research team will recruit approximately 20 youth from each of the six cities (approximately 120 youth) to participate in Youth Rights Report Card. These scores will be aggregated and used for subsequent data analysis.

Second was to develop a "youth rights" handbook, which is a document for practitioners about how youth development programs can integrate activities that promote youth rights into the curriculum in schools and community-based organizations. The youth rights handbook will provide a copy of the Youth Bill of Rights with an explanation of how the document was produced. Additionally, the handbook includes strategies, examples of activities, discussion topics, and curriculum used by the six participating groups in the process of developing the Youth Bill of Rights. For example, the handbook includes how youth in Tucson, who were prohibited from participating in immigrant rights protests, used text messages and MySpace to organize one of Arizona's largest mass protests in history.

Third is to leverage local and state legislative support for a Youth Bill of Rights through the use of data collected in the Youth Rights Report Card in the six participating cities and states. For example, in 2001 the Institute for Democracy, Education, and Access (IDEA) at UCLA used a similar process, which resulted in a State Assembly Bill (AB–2236) sponsored by State Assembly member Judy Chu. While the bill never received enough votes to pass, IDEA's Student Bill of Rights addressed the education California students needed in order to be prepared for a four-year state university, a living wage job, and active participation in civic life. Similar to the Institute for Democracy, Education and Access (IDEA) at UCLA, we will use the report card data to encourage local and/or state legislators to adopt a Youth Bill of Rights. We anticipate that this process will occur after two years of data have been generated from the Youth Rights Report Card.

Imagining a Youth Bill of Rights through PAR

The status of youth rights in the United States is somewhat nebulous. Despite the fact that children and youth have been extended rights under the Constitution, the Bill of Rights did not entirely consider the rights of children and youth. In fact, until recently, children and youth were regarded as property of their parents or wards of the state (Sussman, 1977). Our understanding of youth rights is further complicated by two dominant perceptions of youth in America. The first is the general perception of youth as passive consumers of the democratic process who need protection from laws and policies that could be harmful to their development (Berman, 1997; Wyn and White, 1997). The second is the perception of youth as threats to social and civic order. For example, young people's involvement in the struggle for civil rights was largely viewed by policy makers as unjustified rebellion (Gitlin, 1969; Piven and Cloward, 1979).

These two seemingly contradictory views of youth have rendered young people relatively powerless to adults. For example, in 1990, 191 nations around the world adopted the International Convention on the Rights of the Child. The Convention outlined a vision for the safety and well-being of children and youth around the world and specified national strategies that should be enacted to protect the rights and dignity of children in developed and developing nations. The Convention now serves as a legal instrument to protect children from issues ranging from participation in armed conflict to the use of child labor. As of 2002, the United States was one of only two developed nations in the world that had not ratified the Convention on the Rights of the Child. The United States' refusal to adopt the Convention raises serious questions about its commitment to extending human rights to children and youth who reside in the United States.

A number of scholars have argued that in many ways children and youth in American society are relegated to second-class citizenship through Jim Crow-like laws and policies (Males, 1996; Polakow, 2000). For example, over the past seven years, 43 states have enacted legislation to lower the age at which juveniles can be prosecuted as adults, and have facilitated the transfer of children to adult court (Males and Macallair, 2000; Poe-Yamagata and Jones, 2000). The adoption of these laws reflects the court's departure from the longstanding belief that rehabilitation should be the goal of criminal justice policies toward juveniles and that special protections were necessary to protect children and youth from the effects of the adult penal system. Not surprisingly, the harsher sentencing policies have had a disproportionate impact on poor, urban youth of color. Between 1985 and 1990, the number of African-American and Latino state prisoners under the age of 18 increased by almost 10 percent, while the incarceration rate for white youth declined by 11 percent (Males and Macallair, 2000; Poe-Yamagata and Jones, 2000).

Fostering a Radical Collective Imagination through PAR

When Dr. Cammarota suggested that we should convene these six groups at the Alex Haley Farm in Knoxville, Tennessee to discuss these issues and present their initial reports on youth rights, I could not imagine a more appropriate place. I had only heard about "The Farm" from other people who had returned and painted vivid pictures for me about the Farm's enchanting 150 acres of relaxing southern beauty. In April 2007, all six groups, 17 adults and 25 youth, met for three days at the Alex Haley Farm to deliver a preliminary report on their findings and respond to the following guiding questions:

- What are the social and economic conditions that limit possibilities and opportunities for young people in your community?
- How do young people work with public institutions to improve the quality of life for youth in your communities?
- What are the rights necessary for young people to become active citizens in their communities and society?

- How would specific rights for youth help you in your job to ensure the well-being of youth, children, and their families?

In response to these questions, there were a number of valuable insights about the participatory action research process as well as the role and meaning of the researcher. First, despite the fact that these youth had never met one another and came from vastly different cities—Paseo Boricua neighborhood in Chicago, or the desert of Tucson, Arizona—the PAR process highlighted remarkable commonalities among each of the groups. Each presentation disturbingly illustrated the lived experience of second-class citizenry. For example, students from East Oakland, California, provided a remarkable presentation about not having a voice in evaluating the quality of their school. In response to the California Department of Education School Accountability Report Card, which is supposed to provide the general public an accurate snapshot of the quality of a school using standard indicators, grade point averages, attendance rates, and standardized test scores, these students developed their own School Accountability Report Card that included both quantitative and qualitative data about their school. By training the youth in both quantitative and qualitative methods, the Oakland team designed a tool to help the school identify areas of strength and areas for improvement.

By engaging key stakeholders, students, parents, and teachers, the student-driven school accountability report card provided an opportunity for students and parents to be authentically included in the school evaluation process. Using a participatory research model, students were able to articulate and document aspects of the school experience that are frequently overlooked by standardized evaluation procedures. For example, clean and sanitary bathrooms, and quality of school lunches are key aspects of students' experiences of schooling that may not be included in state evaluations.

For students in Oakland public schools there are few large-scale victories for students or educators. In fact, in 2003, the district was placed in receivership by the California State superintendent to help remedy its fiscal crisis. In addition to school closures, which were supposed to help solve the district's financial issues, East Oakland had experienced a rise in youth-related homicides, some of which occurred near the high school. However, rather than simply documenting the conditions of everyday life for these youths, Dr. Andrade trained youth to document assets and positive aspects of their communities that are rarely seen by the outside. The local park where youth spend summers playing basketball and soccer and a neighborhood youth center that offers aspiring hip-hop artists studio time to record a track are two examples of how PAR can both train students for serious analytical engagement, while at the same time fostering a sense of appreciation of the beauty of their own neighborhoods.

Building a collective radical imagination among youth through participatory research requires the researcher to embrace both art and science. In responding to the questions posed to each of the six groups, I found that PAR facilitates a collective radical imagination among youth through what Aimé Césaire called "poetic knowledge."

Citing Aimé Césaire, Robin Kelley (2002) writes, "Poetic knowledge is born in the great silence of scientific knowledge." Poetic knowledge to Kelley, as for Césaire, is that form of knowledge that, for a moment, allows us to transcend the immediate everyday realities that confine our capacity to dream, imagine, and hope. For Kelley, poetic knowledge is an "emancipation of language and old ways of thinking" that ruptures banal and mundane experience of struggle and in doing so reveals insight and ways to imagine a new social order.

But "poetic knowledge" rarely is gained in the confines of traditional school curriculum. More often, poetic knowledge is fostered through the experience of oppression, developed by learning to name oppression, and sustained by transforming oppressive conditions. The Batey Urbano Youth Center in Chicago is one place where poetic knowledge is sustained and developed. Using the spoken word, youth are exposed to political and cultural ideas that support the surrounding Puerto Rican community. Over the past ten years, the City of Chicago had launched an aggressive redevelopment initiative in the Humbolt Park neighborhood. Ultimately, the redevelopment began to displace longstanding residents and threatened to change only the Puerto Rican community in Chicago. Concerned about the impact of gentrification in their community, young people began to integrate the experience of gentrification into their spoken word. "What happened to the café? Now it say's Starbucks!" Their concern to save their neighborhood led them into participatory action research in which they learned how to document the impact of gentrification, informed residents about what they could do to save their community, and joined forces with adult allies to organize residents to stop the developers' plans to redevelop the area.

Through participatory action research, young people developed a poetic knowledge about gentrification as it relates to their community. Gentrification threatened things in their neighborhood that they once had taken for granted, such as visiting a favorite neighborhood bakery, the sounds of salsa when walking down the main street, the smell of fresh Puerto Rican food. Through participatory action research, youth imagined their lives without the vibrant Puerto Rican community, but more importantly, they also imagined how to strengthen their community. In March 2002, the Batey Urbano was created in order to foster poetic knowledge among Puerto Rican youth in the Paseo Boricua neighborhood. Through the spoken word, young people learn how to describe and name joy, pain, frustration, and hope. Buttressed by PAR, young people transform these important forms of knowledge to action, skills, and ultimately community change.

Conclusion: New Directions for PAR

We learned a great deal about the impact of PAR from our three days in Knoxville. We initially envisioned discussions about youth rights, but to our surprise, we learned more about each other through stories of local struggles, frank conversations about wanting to give up, and intimate sharing about our fears, hopes, and dreams. More importantly, we learned about the power of developing and sustaining a collective radical imagination. None of this would be possible of course without a participatory methodology. I will leave the discussion of rigor and reliability to my colleagues in this volume—I am sure they have a good deal to say about the many ways that PAR's methodology should be more widely embraced. I, for one, am more interested in developing a deeper understanding about the role that PAR plays in fostering hope, imagination, and action in neighborhood conditions that appear permanent.

My observations of these groups leave me with a great deal of hope and optimism about my work and the potential ways that scholars can ground their work in local struggles—emancipatory research which is unapologetically engaged and committed to distribution of power in order to improve the quality of life for marginalized communities. My own work with African-American youth in Oakland teaches me that research is most useful when young people develop skills both to explain systemic causes of issues that shape their lives and to act to transform those conditions. Therefore, emancipatory research will also require us to move beyond our universities and professional associations to build new infrastructure that can facilitate the free exchange of ideas, tools, and people needed for the greater democratization of knowledge.

For youth in low-income communities of color, PAR presents a host of unique opportunities to enhance and strengthen emancipatory research. Broader thinking about what constitutes scholarship and research also needs to be informed by the usefulness of research to transform oppression, and its capacity to create a higher quality of life. Perhaps through an appreciation and relentless practice of PAR we can realize the potential of emancipatory research to yield the type of poetic knowledge given us by Paulo Freire, Audre Lourde, and even Marvin Gaye. In so doing, we move beyond the rather static and restrictive notions of methodology to a broader and richer understanding of how our bold imaginations, dreams, and visions can lead us to revolutionary forms of participatory action research.

Note

1 Each of the groups was led by an adult researcher at the following sites. Dr. Jeff Duncan Andrade, San Francisco State University (students from Oakland, California), Dr. Antwi Akom, San Francisco State University (students from Berkeley, California), Dr. Ben Kirshner, University of Boulder, Colorado (students from Denver), Dr. María Elena Torre (New School New York, students from Brooklyn), Dr. Nilda Flores-Gonzalez, University of Illinois, Chicago (students from Chicago), Dr. Julio Cammarota (students from Tucson).

References

Baldwin, J. (1985). The creative process. In *The Price of the Ticket*. New York: St. Martin's Press/Marek.

Berman, S. (1997). *Children's Social Consciousness and the Development of Social Responsibility*. Albany: State University of New York Press.

Diop, C. A. (1974). *The African Origin of Civilization: Myth or Reality*. Westport, CT: Lawrence Hill.

Gitlin, T. (1969). On line at San Francisco State. In *Black Power and Student Rebellion*, ed. J. McEvoy and A. Miller. Belmont, CA: Wadsworth: 12–30.

Hilliard, D., and D. Weise (2002). *The Huey P. Newton Reader*. New York: Seven Stories Press.

Kelley, R. (2002). *Freedom Dreams: The Black Radical Imagination*. Boston: Beacon Press.

Kuhn, Thomas (1962). *The Structure of Scientific Revolutions*. Chicago: University of Chicago Press.

Males, M. (1996). *The Scapegoat Generation: America's War on Adolescents*. Monroe, ME: Common Courage Press.

Males, M., and D. Macallair (2000). *The Color of Justice*. Washington, DC: Building Blocks for Youth.

Newton, H. P. (1973). *Revolutionary Suicide*. New York: Writers and Readers Publishing.

Piven, F., and R. Cloward (1979). *Poor People's Movements: Why They Succeed, How They Fail*. New York: Vintage.

Poe-Yamagata, E., and M. Jones (2000). *And Justice for Some*. Washington, DC: National Council on Crime and Delinquency.

Polakow, V., ed. (2000). *The Public Assault on America's Children*. Teaching for Social Justice. New York: Teachers College Press.

Sussman, A. (1977). *An American Civil Liberties Union Handbook: The Rights of Young People*. New York: Avon Books.

Wyn, J., and R. White (1997). *Rethinking Youth*. London: Sage.

CHAPTER 3

Participatory Action Research in the Contact Zone

MARÍA ELENA TORRE AND MICHELLE FINE WITH NATASHA ALEXANDER, AMIR BILAL BILLUPS, YASMINE BLANDING, EMILY GENAO, ELINOR MARBOE, TAHANI SALAH, AND KENDRA URDANG

> Teaching is possibility in dark and constraining times. It is a matter of awakening and empowering today's young people to name, to reflect, to imagine, and to act with more and more concrete responsibility in an increasingly multifarious world . . . The light may be uncertain and flickering; but teachers in their lives and works have the remarkable capacity to make it shine in all sorts of corners and, perhaps, to move newcomers to join with others and transform.
>
> **(Maxine Greene, 2003: 72–3)**

Maxine Greene writes on the possibilities of teaching, the provocation of aesthetics and the capacity to "join with others and transform." We have had the privilege of learning with and from Maxine, and we take her teachings seriously in our participatory action research (PAR) with youth, a form of activist pedagogy. We write this chapter as a very diverse collective of (once) high school students, college faculty, artists, poets, writers, graduate students, and college students. We form a collective interested in activist research designed to challenge the injustices of public education and the prison industrial complex. In our work, we add a dimension that is typically not discussed in PAR; that is, we seek to open up a conversation about PAR inside a *contact zone*.

By framing our PAR collective as a contact zone, we create a politically and intellectually charged space where very differently positioned youth and adults are able to experience and analyze power inequities, together. Privileged youth who otherwise might opt out of such work (as it potentially challenges a system which benefits them) ally with historically marginalized youth, who also might not have joined the research collective (as they have learned well that change is slow and promises are rarely kept). As a collective, we have *used* our differences (rather than ignoring them) to further thinking, research, writing, and speaking on educational equity and change. In the following pages, we will describe in detail the Opportunity Gap Project and the *Echoes* Arts and Social Justice Institute that led to the creation of *Echoes of Brown: Youth Documenting and Performing the Legacy of* Brown v. Board of Education.

In this chapter, in particular, we concentrate on how we *work on and through power inequities*, and *across and through differences*, and how this affects the consciousness and the political engagements of youth researchers. While we all speak throughout this chapter, the second half focuses explicitly on youth researchers' analyses and poetry about the political, aesthetic, emotional, and intellectual opportunities of PAR in the contact zone:

- to connect "personal struggles" with historic struggles for justice (see Mills, 1959; DuBois, 1990);
- to convert individual experiences of pain and oppression into structural analyses and demands for justice;
- to interrogate the unfairness of privilege; and
- to link activist research to youth organizing movements for social justice.

Designing Research in a Contact Zone

We borrow the language of contact zones from María Elena Torre (2006), who draws on the writings of Mary Louise Pratt (1991) and Gloria Anzaldúa (1987). Pratt first introduced the term "contact zone" to describe "social spaces where disparate cultures meet, clash, and grapple with each other, often in highly asymmetrical relations of power" (Pratt, 1991: 4). Torre extends the notion into the psychology of inter-group relations, suggesting that within contact zones psychologists can witness a textured understanding of human interaction *across* power differences. Analytically, this provides us an opportunity to "push our psychological theorizing beyond simplified binaries such as oppressor/oppressed or colonizer/colonized and understand relations between" (Torre, 2006: 2). By interrogating social relations in contact zones, we can collectively examine what Anzaldúa (1987) calls "the borderland." A contact perspective "foreground[s] the interactive, improvisational dimensions of colonial encounters so easily ignored by diffusionist accounts of conquest and domination . . . [It] emphasizes how subjects are constituted in and by their relations to each other . . . in terms of co-presence, interaction, [and] interlocking understandings and practices" (Pratt, 1991: 5). Theorizing PAR as a contact zone, thereby underscores the ways subjects are constituted "in and by their relations to each other," and also the multi(ple/peopled) constructions of knowledge and research (Torre, 2006).

> Participating in something like *Echoes* and the Arts and Social Justice Institute was the first time where I had to work as closely and as intensely as I did with people who were so different from me. The project brought youth from very different racial, economic, academic, and social backgrounds into one space to be creative and to most importantly just be themselves. The comfort and safety that was established in the very beginning was instrumental in allowing for the work to get done and for the performance to be shaped and constructed.
>
> **(Emily Genao)**

As Emily describes, the *Echoes* project brought together an intentionally diverse group of young people—by gender, race, ethnicity, class, sexuality, (dis)ability, "track"; by experiences with racism, sexism, homophobia, school administrators, social service agencies, "the law"; by (dis)comfort with their bodies, dance, poetry, groups, etc. In spring 2003, we recruited youth who were interested in writing, performing, and/or social justice from public schools and youth programs in the greater New York metropolitan area, including northern New Jersey.[1] In doing so, we consciously created a "contact zone," a messy social space where differently situated people "meet, clash, and grapple with each other" across their varying relationships to power (Pratt, 1991: 4). With an important sense of purpose, our contact zone was organized around creating a performance of research, poetry and movement that would contribute to the commemoration of the fiftieth anniversary of *Brown v. Board of Education*.

Structuring a research space as a contact zone invites a textured understanding of human interaction across power differences. In such a setting, questions of "history and politics," power, privilege, and oppression can be interrogated across lines of race, age, religion, gender, sexuality, and generation. As youth researcher Kendra Urdang explains:

> What I found most remarkable about *Echoes* was that it gathered a group of youth—all from completely different backgrounds and at

> completely different stages in their lives—and engaged them in discussion about history. Not only do so few people my age care about history and politics, but when they do, few adults care to listen to what we have to say. No matter our age, religion, race, gender, or sexual preference, *Echoes* gave us the opportunity to converse honestly about race, politics, discrimination, and our place in it all, past and present. Furthermore, it was adults who encouraged us to do so in the first place. Rather than having to create a safe space for and by ourselves, each week we found ourselves being pushed by adults to reevaluate our comfort zones, be them political, social, or poetic. I felt that by the end of the almost year-long *Echoes* project, there were no barriers among us. We talked freely about ourselves, our ideas, and our ambitions, and understood which differences between us were valuable, and which were also irrelevant.
>
> **(Kendra Urdang)**

We created a space for contact, but we know that contact carries with it a complicated dialectic. While it can be improvisational and generative, it can also be unwanted and invasive (Tuck in conversation with M. Fine, 2007). That is, under the name of contact, wars, imperialism, colonialism, and rape have been waged.

So have coalitions for social justice.

Thus, in creating the *Echoes* space, we took seriously issues of power, privilege, oppression, participatory action research, and responsibility. Fed by the writings of Linda Thuwai Smith, Nancy Fraser, Amartya Sen, bell hooks, and others, we sought to create a context in which high school and college students would come together with graduate students, activists, faculty, lawyers, writers, and poets—all importing very distinct situated knowledges, within very differently marked bodies, carrying heavy and light loads of biography, privilege, and oppression of racial injustice into spaces we call school.

We began with an awareness that even before we entered the room, power dynamics were already in play, needing to be gracefully deconstructed if we were going to collaborate across zip codes, ethnic biographies, communities, and generations, with trust (see Nancy Fraser, 1990, on the bourgeois public sphere).

> I just want to be honest with you guys, after the first day in the group, my mother warned me about what to expect. She said "Natasha, I want you to just be aware that sometimes White folks, when they are working with you, are caught up in a White man's burden kind of thing. They're wrapped in guilt and just want to do good for Black

> and Latino students, like make things right in school. Sometimes you might run across this." So I kind of had this in mind when we started. But then it changed. I saw that people here weren't really like that . . . It's hard to say how it changed for me, I guess it was by the kinds of conversations we had. The way you talked about high and low power groups, and how we weren't just talking about race. And then when we were talking about some groups wanting schools for just one kind of people, how Michelle said that although she really believes in integration, some of us in the room might feel strongly about the need for separate spaces. And that she'd be willing to work for low power groups to have spaces of their own—like a school for African American students, or all girls—but that she wouldn't do it for a high power group. That they wouldn't really need her help.
>
> **(Natasha Alexander)**

These are the very issues of power that contact zones insist on engaging. PAR in the contact zones opens up such rich avenues for analysis about injustice "out there" but also "in here." Purposely creating *Echoes* as a contact zone, we took on the responsibility to carve out a context that was strategically infused with issues of power, rather than naively pretending it was one "vacated" by power. We did this not simply by remedial means—that is, by giving "voice" to those "oppressed" or simply by counter-hegemonic challenge—encouraging those with privilege to express guilt and responsibility and redeem themselves. Instead, we created a common project for analyzing the patterns of social (in)justice, generated with youth, sculpted from the clay of social history, participatory research, and the personal experiences of the young people present.

The Opportunity Gap and *Echoes of Brown: Youth Documenting and Performing the Legacy of* Brown v. Board of Education

To ground our conversation, we introduce a multi-site project of participatory action research (PAR) launched with youth—street and suburban, Advanced Placement Program (AP) and special education, African-American, Latino, Asian-American, immigrant and White American, wealthy and poor—to map the political economy and social psychology of educational injustice in the United States today. Organized as *doubled resistance*, the Opportunity Gap Project was designed to reveal the presence of deep, historic, and sustained injustice in schools, as well as the clever, creative, and exhausting ways that youth of poverty—and privilege—every day resist and negotiate these injustices. Further, this project was designed to provoke action in discrete and linked sites.

In fall 2001, a group of suburban school superintendents of desegregated districts gathered to discuss the disaggregated Achievement Gap data provided by the states of New Jersey and New York. As is true nationally, in these desegregated districts, the test score gaps between Asian-American, White American, African-American, and Latino students were disturbing. Eager to understand the roots and remedies for the gap, Superintendent Sherry King of Mamaroneck, New York, invited Michelle and colleagues from the Graduate Center to join the research team. We agreed, under the condition that we could collaborate with a broad range of students from suburban and urban schools, to create a multi-year participatory action research project. We understood well Anisur Rahman's belief that:

> Liberation, surely, must be opposed to all forms of domination over the masses . . . But—and this is the distinctive viewpoint of PAR—domination of masses by elites is rooted not only in the polarization of control over the means of material production but also over the means of knowledge production including, as in the former case, the social power to determine what is valid or useful knowledge.
>
> **(Anisur Rahman, 1985: 119)**

Over the course of three years of youth inquiry, through a series of "research camps," more than 100 youth from urban and suburban high schools in New York and New Jersey joined researchers from the Graduate Center of the City University for a PAR project to study youth perspectives on racial and class based (in)justice in schools and the nation. We worked in the schools long enough to help identify a core of youth drawn from all corners of the school to serve as youth researchers—from special education, English as a Second Language (ESL), the Gay/Straight Alliances, discipline rooms, student councils, and AP classes. We designed a multi-generational, multi-district, urban–suburban database of youth and elder experiences, tracing the history of struggle for desegregation from *Brown* to date, and social science evidence of contemporary educational opportunities and inequities analyzed by race, ethnicity, and class (see Fine, Bloom, Burns, Chajet, Guishard, Payne, Perkins-Munn, and Torre, 2005).

The research was all the richer because it had deep local roots in particular youth research collectives tied and committed to real spaces—the streets of Paterson, the desegregated schools in New York and New Jersey, the community-based activist organization Mothers on the Move (MOM) in the South Bronx, and small schools in New York City—and because we facilitated cross-site theorizing and inquiry to deepen the cartography of inequity we were crafting. Thus, as if a friendly amendment, we took seriously Michael Apple's call for *thick, local democracy* and then added research and organizing that would enable *wide, cross-site analysis.* By blending deep local work with relatively homogeneous collectives, with critical, cross-site analysis, we were able to chart the uneven distribution of finances, cultural capital, opportunities, hope, despair, and resistance. Documenting inequity through youth research we were also nurturing the tools of critical resistance broadly and deeply in this next generation.

At our first session with close to 50 youth from six suburban high schools and three urban schools, the students immediately challenged/disarticulated the frame of the research:

> When you call it an achievement gap, that means it's our fault. The real problem is an opportunity gap—let's place the responsibility where it belongs—in society and in the schools.

With democratic challenge stirring, we—including the embarrassed adults—quickly changed the name to the Opportunity Gap Project and reframed our investigation, sheepishly remembering Friere's words:

> the silenced are not just incidental to the curiosity of the researcher but are the masters of inquiry into the underlying causes of the events in their world. In this context research becomes a means of moving them beyond silence into a quest to proclaim the world.
>
> **(Freire, 1982)**

Students met as research collectives within their local spaces, and they also participated in a series of cross-site "research camps," each held for two days at a time in community and/or university settings.[2] In our early sessions, the agenda and questions were set—in pencil—by the adults. At the first retreat, we brought in a "wrong draft" of the survey, which the young people quickly trashed, revised, and radically transformed, and we set much of the skills-building agenda. Over the course of that first weekend, we redesigned the survey to assess high school students' views of race and class (in)justice in schools and the nation. Over the next few months, we translated the survey into Spanish, French-Creole and Braille, and distributed it to 9th and 12th graders in 13 urban and suburban districts. At the second and third camp, another group of youth researchers from the same schools (with some overlap) analyzed the qualitative and quantitative data from 9,174 surveys, 24 focus groups, and 32 individual interviews with youth.

After that first session, the local research collectives began to take up their local work. Within individual schools, community-based organizations, and neighborhoods, the youth research teams determined, with adults, the questions they would study, what they would read, who they would interview, the music they would listen to, and the methods they would deploy to investigate questions of justice and consciousness. (For more information about these local research projects, see the Participatory Action Research Collective at the CUNY Graduate Center: http://web.gc.cuny.edu/che/start.htm.)

Across the three years and these varied settings, we studied up on the history of *Brown*, Emmett Till, Ella Baker, Bayard Rustin, finance inequity, tracking, battles over buses and bilingualism, the unprecedented academic success of the small schools movement, new schools for lesbian/gay/bisexual/transgender students, and the joys, dangers, and "not-yets" of integration. We read on the growth of the prison industrial complex at the expense of public education, and we reviewed how, systematically, federal policy has left behind so many poor and working-class children.

We collected and analyzed data from the large-scale, broad-based survey moving across suburban and urban schools, and also rich, local material from the site-specific research projects. Designed to dig deep, these local projects included an in-depth study of the causes and consequences of finance inequity; an oral history of a South Bronx activist educational organization (MOM), in which founding members were interviewed by their children and grandchildren; a systematic investigation of the racialized tracking of students in middle school mathematics; cross-school visits, interviews, and senior transcript analysis to document differential access to AP courses and suspension rates by race/ethnicity and track in suburban schools (e.g. the extent to which "test scores" differentially predict enrollment in AP classes by race/ethnicity).

Together we created a topographical map of the racial, ethnic, and class (in)justices in secondary public schools. We documented structures and policies that produce inequity, the ideologies and youth beliefs that justify the gap, and those spaces within schools and communities in which educators and youth have joined to create extraordinary collaborations to contest the "gap." We wrote scholarly and popular articles, delivered professional and neighborhood talks. We traveled the nation to gather insights, listen to young people, and to provoke policy, practice, and change with our research.

Our research, conducted across some of the wealthiest and poorest schools in the nation, confirms what others have found: a series of well-established policies and practices assure and deepen the gap. The more separate America's schools are racially and economically, the more stratified they become in achievement. In our empirical reports on these data, we refer to these ongoing sites of policy struggle as *Six Degrees of Segregation*:

- urban/suburban finance inequity;
- the systematic dismantling of desegregation;

- the racially coded academic tracking that organizes most desegregated schools;
- students' differential experiences of respect and supports in schools;
- the class, race and ethnicity based consequences of high-stakes testing; and
- the remarkably disparate patterns of suspensions and disciplinary actions (see Fine, Roberts, and Torre, 2004 for details).

Buoyed by our research findings and participatory process, during 2003 we conducted many feedback sessions in schools and communities throughout the suburban communities circling New York City, and we presented our material to groups of educators and policy makers throughout the country. As we traveled with the stories of our findings, we worried, however, about the limits of talk. We saw most audiences nod in solidarity, but met far too many adults who refused to listen to young people's complex renderings of *Brown*'s victories and continuing struggles. We sat inside schools where it was clear that the "achievement" gap—the latest face of segregation—was built fundamentally into the structures, ideologies, and practices of these schools; too heavy to move; too thick to interrupt. The state apparatus was well oiled and justified. We were caught in the waves of what Gramsci and Mouffe have called the passive revolution:

> The category of "passive revolution" . . . qualif[ies] the most usual form of hegemony of the bourgeoisie involving a model of articulation whose aim is to neutralize the other social forces . . . enlarging the state whereby the interests of the dominant class are articulated with the needs, desires, interests of subordinated groups.
>
> **(Mouffe, 1979: 192)**

We found ourselves trapped by obsessive questions pointing to poor youth and youth of color—What is wrong with them? Even in the same school building, we have a gap? But if we stop tracking how else can we teach students at their "natural" levels? We grew weary of the volley of youth interruption followed by adult denial; critical research presented and refused.

To illustrate we take you to a scene inside a feedback session in one of the participating high schools:

> "Now I'd like you to look at the suspension data, and notice that Black males in high schools were twice as likely as White males to be suspended, and there are almost no differences between Black males and Black females. But for Whites, males are three times more likely to be suspended than females: 22 percent of Black males, 19 percent

> of Black females, 11 percent of White males and 4 percent of White females." Kareem, an African-American student attending a desegregated high school, detailed the racialized patterns of school suspensions to his largely White teaching faculty. Despite the arms crossed in the audience, he continued: "You know me, I spend a lot of time in the discipline room. It's really almost all Black males." Hesitant nods were followed by immediate explanations about how in June "it gets Whiter," and "sometimes there are White kids, maybe when you're not there." Kareem turned to the charts projected on the screen, "You don't have to believe me, but I speak for the hundreds of Black males who filled out this survey. We have to do something about it."

Kareem tried to rearticulate the "problem'" of suspensions to his teachers as relational and indeed racial. He invited the faculty to collaborate with him on research to investigate these patterns. Once it was clear that the faculty was not likely to take him up on his offer, Kareem took up the persona of the social researcher, reporting the aggregate evidence as a call for action. He explained, calmly, that while the educators might choose to ignore his particular case, they would nevertheless have to contend with hundreds of African-American boys who completed the survey and reported the same. He tried to articulate that this is not an individual problem, not race neutral and not separable from the larger school culture. Kareem provided clear evidence that tore at the ideological representation of the school as integrated and fair. And yet, before our eyes, the school in their adamant refusal to hear, threatened to become ossified, in the words of Franz Fanon: "[a] society that ossifies itself in determined form . . . a closed society where it is not good to be alive, where the air is rotten, where ideas and people are corrupt" (Fanon, 1967: 182, 224–5).

Resisting this toxic atmosphere, Kareem was asking his faculty for nothing less than educational justice. As a youth researcher on our large-scale PAR project interrogating youth perspectives on racial and class (in)justice in public schools, Kareem developed, and then taught other youth, the skills of research, collaboration, and organizing.

And so, in spring 2003, with the anniversary of *Brown* approaching, we decided to move our critical scholarship to performance. We knew well from learning at the feet of Maxine Greene about performance, aesthetics, provocation, and that "A world may come into being in the course of a continuing dialogue" (Greene, 1995: 196). We extended our social justice and social research camps into a Social Justice and the Arts Institute. We brought together a diverse group of young people aged 13–21, recruited from the same schools and beyond, with community elders, social scientists, spoken word artists, dancers, choreographers, and a video crew to collectively pore through data from the Educational Opportunity Gap Project (Fine et al., 2004); to learn about the legal, social, and political history of segregation and integration of public schools; and to create *Echoes*, a performance of poetry and movement to contribute to the commemoratory conversation of the 50th anniversary of *Brown v. Board of Education* of Topeka, Kansas.[3]

We created a performance that brought together political history, personal experience, research, and knowledge gathered from generations living in the immediate and the long shadow of *Brown*. On May 17, 2004, an audience of more than 800 sat in awe of these youth and elders bearing witness to the unfulfilled promise of *Brown*. We also published a DVD/book of the work, including all the elder interviews, a video of the Social Justice and the Arts Institute, youth spoken word, detailed commentary by the adult and youth researchers and educators working on educational justice in desegregated schools, speaking on high-stakes testing, tracking, and the everyday politics of racism—*Echoes: The Legacy of* Brown v. Board of Education, *Fifty Years Later* (Fine, Roberts, and Torre, 2004).

Educating, Writing, and Performing through Critical Histories

We turn now to think about how PAR in the contact zone affects the consciousness and political work of very distinct kinds of youth by educating critically, writing personal troubles into political struggles, and performing for social justice.

To connect "personal struggles" with historic struggles for justice

One afternoon session during the summer institute, feminist lawyer Carol Tracy was helping the youth researchers/performers historicize the impact of the *Brown* decision on civil rights, feminism, disability rights, and the gay/lesbian movement. Tracy explicated how the *Brown* decision opened doors for girls across racial/ethnic groups, students with disabilities, and gay/lesbian/bi/trans students. The room filled with the now familiar sense of unease and debate. "So, can we talk about the Harvey Milk School?" A small school in New York City designed to support gay/lesbian/bisexual and transgender students had been in the news. "Is this progress . . . a school for lesbian and gay students? Or is this a step backward into segregation again?" The debate was lively, many arguing that all schools should be working on issues of homophobia and that segregating gay and lesbian students would simply be a throwback to the days of segregation.

But then Amir spoke. An African-American youth researcher who at the time attended a desegregated suburban school, Amir shared his deep disappointment with the unmet promises of his desegregated high school.

> When we were talking about the dancer [Kathryn Dunham] and how she walked off the stage in the South during the 1940s because Blacks were in the balcony, I realized that happens today, with me and my friends—at my high school they put the special education kids in the balcony, away from the "normal kids." They [meaning gay/lesbian students] may need a separate school just to be free of the taunting. Putting people in the same building doesn't automatically take care of the problem.

Only after hearing about Kathryn Dunham standing up for justice was Amir compelled to stand up against the injustices enacted in the name of "special education." Amir's poem, "Classification," reveals the connections he made from history, and with the lesbian/gay/trans students at the Harvey Milk School:

> Possessing this label they gave me,
> I swallowed the stigma and felt the pain of being seen in a room with six people.
> Yeah, it fell upon me and the pain was like stones raining down on me.
> From the day where school assemblies seemed segregated
> and I had to watch my girl Krystal from balconies . . .
> Away from the "normal" kids
> to the days where I found myself fulfilling self-fulfilled prophecies.
>
> See I received the label of "special education"
> and it sat on my back like a mountain being lifted by an ant—it just can't happen.
> It was my mind's master.
> It told me I was dumb, I didn't know how to act in a normal class.
>
> I needed two teachers to fully grasp the concepts touched upon in class,
> and my classification will never allow me to exceed track two.
> So what is it that I do—
> so many occasions when the classification caused me to break into tears?
> It was my frustration.
> My reaction to teachers speaking down to me saying I was classified
> and it was all my fault.

> Had me truly believing that inferiority was my classification.
> Cause I still didn't know, and the pain WAS DEEP. The pain—OH GOD! THE PAIN!
> The ridicule, the constant taunting, laughing when they passed me by.

Amir had been working with us for more than a year, as a youth researcher in his high school and then as a spoken-word artist and performer in the Institute. He had never told us about his special education status until that moment. In writing this piece, Amir drew on his experiences as an African-American student in a desegregated school, having spent too many years within special education classes. He pulled from three years of our cross-site research findings, the history of *Brown*, and what he had learned about the dancer Kathryn Dunham. With these strings in hand and mind, Amir argued for a separate school for gay/lesbian/bisexual and transgendered youth in a climate where the price of integration is paid in taunting and physical abuse. In this context of thick critical inquiry, Amir's voice, experience, and rage were embroidered into historic patterns of domination and exclusion, contemporary evidence of youth of color yearning for rigor, respect, and belonging.

> I was thinking on the way over [to the Institute] one day, this project is dedicated to exposing injustice . . . And I thought about how much it hurt me one day when I [realized] how they were—they were honestly segregating special education kids from the rest of the school. Like there was a constant effort to do so . . . And the pain I felt that day . . . [my friend] Anthony had to calm me down, because I was really angry. It actually brought me to tears. So I'm like, why wouldn't I bring something like that, to the [*Echoes*] group? I felt that I grew close enough to them to tell everyone . . . Because it's a really dangerous thing. That's why I said [in my poem] that the silence is just as painful, because like no one, honestly, *no one's* speaking about it. And that's what's killing us. And so I wasn't just talking on behalf of me; I was talking on behalf of everybody in it . . . I just saw it as an opportunity, you know? . . . [I]f I get it out here [at the Institute], it'll go directly where I want it to go. To the people who are doing it . . . and if I didn't use this [opportunity], it would be foolish of me, it would be stupid, and I couldn't call myself any type of activist.
>
> **(Amir Bilal Billups)**

Amir committed himself to bearing witness—for himself and the millions of students in special education who "can't speak." Amir's performance has been shown to audiences throughout the United States, in England, New

Zealand, Israel/Palestine, and Iceland, and in each session, amidst the tears, there are confessionals from youth, parents, community members, and educators about the scars of education and about that one teacher who "changed my life."

To convert individual experiences of pain and oppression into structural analyses and demands for justice

As if walking with the words of French social theorist Erica Apfelbaum whispering in his ears, Amir was driven by the "imperative to tell—the vital urge not to forget—. . . driven by the imperative to . . . awaken . . . others" (Apfelbaum, 2001: 30).

So too was Tahani Salah, a Palestinian-American young woman and spoken-word artist of the *Echoes* project. Tahani used the *Echoes* Institute to write through her individual experiences of pain and oppression and move them into structural analyses and political demands for justice. In her poem "How do You Know?," a piece she developed from work she began during *Echoes* Institute, she forces audiences to face everyday life at the very center of oppressive histories, policies, and practices. In the spirit of Apfelbaum, Tahani insists on remembering stories of Palestinian-Americans. Interrupting post-9/11 narratives, she speaks aloud of experiences that others wish to erase with fear and ignorance.

> The woman across from me thinks
> that I might not let her get home to her children tonight
> or ever again.
> The woman next to me feels bad for me.
> She wishes I had just as much freedom as she does.
> At the end of every day when stepping on to the subway car more then half of the people think that I am on some militant mission to kill them.
>
> This is not the cliché black man walks on to elevator white women cliché bag.
> This is I'm going to kill you for a political statement.
> I have nothing to live for but destruction.
>
> How do you know?
> All because you couldn't understand my faith.
> So then you created this idea of a savage.
> This inhuman beast.
> With empty eyes to match the empty heart.

If you only knew how I fill trusted eyes with revolutions.
How spoken word has freed me from literal shackles
How words light signal fires within me.

As I stood at the end of the subway car
train swerving back and forth
I could hear the heartbeat of the people
Getting faster and faster.
They were finally going to face their truth

I will no longer be the guinea pig of America's idea of
what a Muslim American woman should be.
I am a student of an Ivy League school
three jobs and two that I don't even get pay for.
I have more than enough to live for.
But most of all I have god I have my faith.
Every morning and every night that I've been blessed with
Everything that has been stolen from my parents
I have everything that's been ripped from their finger tips
Everything they couldn't fight.

My life, my voice, my freedom

So speak the unspoken
And the lord has given you a voice
And they have been given the power of defeat.
Don't you dare let them defeat you.

To interrogate the unfairness of privilege

Echoes was *not* designed as a safe space for demographically similar peers to challenge injustice nor to learn about how "others" suffer. It was not a precious, protected corner to critique stereotypes and the micro-aggressions of everyday life. While we have great respect for the need and life of "safe spaces" in which historically oppressed groups gather to be free of, safe from, and challenging of dominant policies and practices (Fine and Weis, 2000), that was not our project, not this time. We set as a goal, instead, to bring very diverse young and older people into a space, strewn with dynamics of privilege and power, and take up just those questions in our search for a project of collective struggle.

A number of the youth performers, particularly White students from the suburbs, used the *Echoes* space to work through their own questions about privilege in "desegregated schools" where they benefit enormously, if ambivalently (Burns, 2004), from the well-known and equally well-silenced racialized stratifications in their schools. One such youth performer was Elinor Marboe, a White young woman who wrote with wonder and rage about the racialized practices newly visible to her within her desegregated suburban high school:

Self segregation in my public high school
Different colored threads, on separate rolled spools.
Is this a topic on which I can speak?
Because my skin isn't brown
versus Board.

The Hispanic kids who sit in the Post Cafeteria—do I sit with them?
Well, no.
We get along. We get along well. One hand.
One hand of the solution.
But few kids have friends of other races.
Where is that other hand?

There was one black girl in my AP American class.
One day we read a poem comparing Booker T. to W. E. B.
And we all stared at Alana
waiting for her response.
Then we realized we were staring,
and slowly turned our heads, real casual,
like nothing had happened.

But it had.

Kids are taught at my school that communities are divided by race—
This is the norm. This is acceptable.
This blister of a problem, turning purply red and filling with fluid as we speak:
My education, my school is shaped like a barbell,
And I'm only at one end.

(From *One Hand Clapping* by Elinor Marboe)

In the beginning of the week, Elinor was asking herself and others about whether or not remaining silent in the face of injustice is problematic. By Thursday, she was clear that *not* speaking up against racially inequitable settings could not be justified as neutrality. In her performance, after speaking the words, "slowly [we] turned our heads, real casual, like nothing happened," she wrote the following stage directions: LONG PAUSE, TURN OF THE HEAD, and then, LOOKING STRAIGHT AT THE AUDIENCE, and then, said "But it had." Elinor narrated, for fellow White students and audience, the damage wrought by refusing to speak out and turning away.

The *Echoes* collaborative provided an opportunity for youth performers to reach in and meet parts of their identities not often felt or exposed. For Elinor this meant a chance to think through her relationship to power, the silence of privilege and the vulnerability of participation. This process was facilitated by regular group conversations, check-ins, poetry read-arounds, and group feedback sessions, in all of which everyone (from youth participants to workshop presenters) had the opportunity to comment and contribute ideas. The layering of these activities across the writing, movement, and research components allowed youth to participate differently in different moments—highlighting alternate parts of their identities as they desired. Elinor described this as a "fresh start," a rare moment to try a new set of selves:

> Well being around a group of people that's like a completely fresh start, like there wasn't . . . I don't know, I didn't feel like I was the kind of quiet sarcastic girl, you know, which comes out more in school . . . [laughs] in the beginning [of the Institute] the things I wrote were kind of like humorous, or like they were [laughs] surrealist. I guess they were a little more like, safe, but they were also more prosy . . . And then as the week went on [I began] writing more in the style of poetry and then writing about choosing to be silent, which was so personal and which is like something that I know a lot of my friends say about me and I've never been able to defend that much to them. Well, because we don't really talk about it. But I know they think of me as quiet or as, not necessarily quiet, but not really sharing like really intimate things with them. And to be able to talk about that and then, think about my own school and tracking was really personal too. And I don't have too many spaces where I'm really honest about things that are difficult or painful.
>
> **(Elinor Marboe)**

Her experience of the contact zone challenged her to think deeply about her ideas and experiences, incorporating some and resisting others; opened her to new levels of intimacy and vulnerability; and introduced her to the power of collaborative creativity and action. We have found this work—the deconstruction of privilege—to be critical to PAR in the contact zone. If privilege is allowed to sit unchallenged, then seemingly integrated spaces will dangerously reproduce the damage of social stratification and injustice.

To migrate activist research into youth organizing movements for social justice: Igniting the fire for future revolutions

Within the *Echoes* contact zone, bodies and standpoints of privilege sat side by side with bodies and standpoints of historic oppression. Both brought into this space a set of perspectives that would be voiced, reworked, and blended, gently, deliberately, and intimately. Our differences, discordances, and rough edges were on display. While no one person stood as the embodiment of either privilege or oppression, together we could disarticulate the embodied workings, perversions, benefits, and assaults of social injustice. And only together could we rearticulate a vision of what could be.

> Writing "Rap Star" was a very interesting experience for me. My inspiration for the poem came from seeing a kid get arrested. This cop grabbed this African-American kid saying to him "get in the car rap star." It hit me like a ton of bricks. Hearing the cop say that to this kid made me think, damn is that all he really is to you—just a rap star? And then I thought to myself "you know what, that's probably what that kid thinks about himself too." So I wrote about it.
>
> **(Natasha Alexander)**

Simply being gifted
Was your limitation
Not encouraged to be a doctor or teacher
Made to believe that
Your only true place of success
Is in being some sort of entertainer or athlete

Talk in the staff meeting
Not about your B+ paper
But about how many yards you can throw a football
Or your three point shot
Or your beautiful tenor voice

You're behind bars now
Upon you those teachers look down
Because they say they put all their time into you
Your path is what you choose, right?
I guess they were never taught that teachers have a high calling

Oh Rap Star, the basement is just cold
No stage lights, hoes and cars
No buying rounds of drinks at bars
Just the silent memories of young men in this cell before you
Echo from window to door
You can feel it from ceiling to floor
You're dead to the core
You felt this before

About to be shipped off
Too far from the freedom
You were once used to
The liberty God gave you
The only real privilege you were born into

Gone, gone with the bang of a gavel
In a court room
Where Justice, who can't see
Points arms outstretched to sentence you
To life, to real life, to the rest of your life
To the life of so many other young men like you
Who share this same fate too.

(From *Rap Star* by Natasha Alexander)

After writing and performing this poem, it was published in a newspaper in Manila. A reporter from a newspaper there asked me to send him a copy of "Rap Star" because he thought the issues were relevant to young men in the Philippines—which made me think about young men of color all over the world and about the similarities of their experiences, the injustices they face. I also performed it for a youth-produced documentary called "Pipeline" about the youth to prison pipeline. People have had very strong reactions to my poem—they have told me it's "so beautiful," "so moving," "so powerful" which makes me wonder, how can I take this power and emotion and turn it into action?

(Natasha Alexander)

Since the performance, these youth researchers have published, lectured, and brought their skills to other social movements for educational justice. Some have gone on to participate in the Campaign for Fiscal Equity, researching and organizing for finance equity in public schools in New York State. Others have testified in State Legislature for the Performance Assessment Consortium, arguing for multiple forms of assessment in New York State, rather than the single, high-stakes testing regime that has spiked the dropout rates for poor and working-class African-American and Latino students. Those still in high school have brought their concerns about lack of respect, computers, gym, and college-application support back to their schools, communities, peers, and organizations of educational professionals and organizers. White suburban students have launched campaigns for detracking and a serious look at racial inequities in their schools. Together, the collective has presented its research and spoken word pieces at the National Coalition for Educational Activists, the Public Education Network, and the Cross Cultural Roundtable. These youth have learned the skills of critical research—to reveal and provoke. And they understand that their fame and performance means nothing if they stand alone. For in the end, all came to Amir's conclusion, "I had to speak for the others because the silence, oh the silence, is just as bad."

We leave you with reflections from Yasmine Blanding, a young African-American woman and *Echoes* performer. Two years after the performance at John Jay College, we gathered a collection of "letters to *Echoes*" on the impact of the project on their lives since.

> *Echoes* . . .?
>
> More like shadows . . . I can't shake it.
>
> The feeling, the voices. I WON'T let it leave me . . . It JUST will not leave me.
>
> You know what? I don't want it to leave me either. It keeps me grounded. It keeps me running, keeps me wanting. Grounded—grounded enough to keep my head up, and to walk with authority, to keep my eyes bright, and to speak up when necessary and certainly when spoken to. It keeps me running, when I think of *Echoes* I think of so much work that has been done, and yet so much work that needs to be done . . . it's funny. It's almost like I don't run out of energy. I get tired only when I run out of thoughts. It keeps me wanting, wanting to be alive, wanting to continue to speak, to share, to change, wanting a world. Wanting a world, with hope of perfection . . . I guess *Echoes* provided vision and voices for me. *Echoes* gave me muscles.
>
> What's so chilly most lol [translation: nice, fly, great] about *Echoes* is, there were so many voices and hands involved . . . how could you forget your mission; your journey? Sometimes things happen, things are said and we get mob mentality. We get all hype/excited for that moment . . . and then the moment's over . . . and so are we (that feeling we had . . . gets lost or subsided). I don't feel like that about *Echoes*. I feel like my mentality is still there, my light isn't even dim. My mob . . . I don't even feel like, I need one anymore. I know that

EVERYONE, needs, SOMEONE. But somehow I don't feel like I have to prove anything anymore. So I've removed my energy from the problem and have dedicated my energy to the solution. *Echoes* . . . the project was revolutionized. It was the battle.

The brain is the strongest muscle we have. I'm happy that I experience *Echoes* . . . and I'm happy to have left my footprints . . . and I excited to say . . . I'm still walking . . . MARCHING. So I feel privileged to say there will be more of MY FOOTPRINTS in the sand, and it makes my heart smile to now be able to say and so will my son's footprints . . .

(Yasmine Blanding)

Notes

1 Out of the 13 who applied, all but one were accepted. Three young women applied from the same school. In our attempt to create as diverse a group as possible, we decided not to have more than two students from the same school.

2 Many students received high school credits (when a course on participatory research was offered in their schools) and 42 received college credit for their research work.

3 The 13 youth were drawn from wealthy and economically depressed communities in the suburbs surrounding New York City and within the city; representing the kind of wisdom born in Advanced Placement classes and the kind born in Special Education classrooms. We joined Christians, Jews, Muslims, and youth with no religious affiliation; those of European, African, Caribbean, Palestinian, Latino and blended ancestries; young people headed for the Ivy League and some who have spent time in juvenile facilities; some who enjoy two homes, and some who have spent nights without a home. We recruited youth interested in writing, performing, and/or social justice from youth groups and public schools in the greater New York metropolitan area including northern New Jersey. We gathered together an intentionally diverse group of young people—by gender, race, ethnicity, class, sexuality, (dis)ability, "track"; by experiences with racism, sexism, homophobia, school administrators, social service agencies, "the law"; by (dis)comfort with their bodies, dance, poetry, groups; etc.

References

Anzaldúa, G. (1987). *Borderlands/La Frontera: The New Meztiza*. San Francisco: Aunte Lute Press.

Apfelbaum, E. (2001). The dread. An essay on communication across cultural boundaries. *International Journal of Critical Psychology* 4: 19–34.

Burns, A. (2004). The racing of capability and culpability in desegregated schools: Discourses of merit and responsibility. In *Off White: Readings in Race, Power, and Privilege*. New York: Routledge.

DuBois, W. E. B. (1990). *Souls of Black Folks*. New York: First Vintage Books.

Fanon, F. (1967). *Black Skin, White Masks*. New York: Grove Press.

Fine, M., J. Bloom, A. Burns, L. Chajet, M. Guishard, Y. A. Payne, T. Perkins-Munn, and M. E. Torre (2005). Dear Zora: A letter to Zora Neal Hurston fifty years after Brown. *Teachers College Record* 107(3): 496–529.

Fine, M., R. A. Roberts, M. E. Torre, with J. Bloom, A. Burns, L. Chajet, M. Guishard, and Y. A. Payne (2004). *Echoes of Brown: Youth Documenting and Performing the Legacy of* Brown v. Board of Education. New York: Teachers College Press.

Fine, M. and L. Weis (eds) (2000). *Construction Sites: Excavating Race, Class and Gender among Urban Youth*. New York: Teachers College Press.

Fraser, N. (1990). Rethinking the public sphere: A contribution to the critique of actually existing democracy. *Social Text* 25/26: 56–80.

Freire, P. (1982). Creating alternative research methods. Learning to do it by doing it. In *Creating Knowledge: A Monopoly*, ed. B. Hall, A. Gillette, and R. Tandon. New Delhi: Society for Participatory Research in Asia: 29–37.

Greene, M. (1995). *Releasing the Imagination: Essays on Education, the Arts, and Social Change*. San Francisco: Jossey-Bass.

Greene, M. (2003). Teaching as possibility: A light in dark times. In *The Jossey-Bass Reader on Teaching*. San Francisco: John Wiley & Sons.

Mills, C. W. (1959). *The Sociological Imagination*. London: Oxford University Press.

Mouffe, C. (1979). *Gramsci and Marxist Theory*. Boston: Routledge & Kegan Paul.

Pratt, M. L. (1991). Arts of the contact zone. *Profession* 91: 33–40.

Rahman, A. (1985). The theory and practice of participatory action research. In *The Challenge of Social Change*, ed. O. Fals-Borda. Beverly Hills, CA: Sage Publications.

Torre, M. E. (2006). Beyond the Flat: Intergroup contact, intercultural education and the potential of contact zones for research, growth and development. Unpublished manuscript. City University of New York.

Tuck, E. in conversation with M. Fine (2007). Inner angles: A range of ethical responses to/with indigenous and decolonizing theories. In *Ethical Futures in Qualitative Research: Decolonizing the Politics of Knowledge*, ed. N. Denzin and M. Giardina. Walnut Creek, CA: Left Coast Press: 145–68

Response to Chapter 3

MAXINE GREENE

I must write about my own perspective, passions, and limitations before attempting to offer a response to a chapter in some ways out of my field. I "do" educational philosophy, meaning that I work to engage students in thinking about their own thinking with regard to the surrounding culture and its symbol systems, centrally involving the arts. In the process, I am concerned about the connections between such concerns and various modes of praxis within and outside of classrooms. I do not consider myself a researcher, although some of my writing falls under a qualitative rubric; and, sympathetic as I am to action research, I cannot claim to have participated in it. Since high school days, however, I have thought of myself as an activist, beginning with work in support of the fated Spanish Republic in the 1930s, including much anti-war and anti-fascist activity, campaigns against capital punishment and censorship, and (obviously) as much intellectual and physical resistance as possible to this administration's and its allies' undermining of whatever remains of our democracy. I say all this in order to communicate my support of the principles guiding and underlying the action research described in the chapter to which I am responding. A research project lacking an action component always has seemed to me a more or less useless undertaking . . . Like Dewey, Freire, Sartre, Merleau-Ponty, Virginia Woolf, Toni Morrison, and many others, I think ideas are of little moment if they exist abstractly beyond the world of human experience; and this seems particularly the case when it comes to educational research and the actualities of teaching and the schools.

If education is thought to be an undertaking aimed at the awakening of every young person, no matter what the "local knowledge" of her/his background may happen to be, to the means of coming to gain a critical understanding of the multiple realities of the world, coming awake in this fashion as participant in ongoing dialogue or conversation, the learner may enter (hopefully in answer to her/his own questions) the diverse provinces of meaning: natural science, social science, the humanities, the arts—and the kinds of praxis each entails. Made to feel inferior, stigmatized, invisible as a living person, no one can feel worthy enough to pose her/his own questions or act to initiate her/his own learning. Racism and the other ways of demeaning human beings are clearly anti-educative . . . because they erode the sense of agency that might allow them to embark on new beginnings—and to begin is to open up spaces of untapped possibility.

When I speak of the provinces of meaning or the range of subject matters that may make accessible diverse perspectives, I am not necessarily arguing for discussions (in the contact zone, the research camps, the range of spaces where young people gather) founded in the liberal arts or any of the social or natural sciences. It does seem to me, however, that what is taken to be "knowledge" in the processes of "action research" is some kind of natural or spontaneous response, for instance, to what may be experienced as oppression. It may be a feeling of being pushed in an unwanted direction, of being powerless under someone else's domination, of being unfairly excluded. There is little sense of people reflecting on oppression in specifically described forms, as when Freire, for instance, speaks of "banking education," or Dewey, of the "miseducative." Nor is there much examination of the sources of oppression, the intentions of particular oppressors, the modes of resistance (found in history, for example). One tends to be left with a feeling of sympathy, but with little comprehension of why schools today are oppressive, whether the aim of public education is to track, separate, segregate, apply the kind of "sorting machine" that favors the privileged and treats the others as mere objects, mere "things." Or why so many classrooms are "silent," meaning that few students are released to find and use their own voices.

Impressed by a young researcher like Kareem and his careful work on suspension, by Natasha and her effort to understand higher and lower power groups, and by those who so significantly changed the phrase "achievement gap" to "opportunity gap," I could not but keep thinking about the discoveries these young people would make if enabled to go beyond naming or describing into serious inquiry with regard to the many meanings and manifestations of "power," for instance. I remember my own students' interest aroused by the idea that power is not only exercised from above through the orders, public gestures, and behaviors of those "on top" (presidents,

CEOs, generals, and the like) but disseminated in all sorts of ways: through grading systems, the use of the bell curve, tracking practices, special education, even by the seating arrangements in classrooms. Often these are techniques for neutralizing, instances of "passive revolution." To point to and study such phenomena in their concreteness is to carry researchers beyond mere abstraction where notions such as "power" are concerned.

Given the culmination in the composition and performance of *Echoes*, it is difficult not to hold in mind that the 1954 decision was made about a half-century ago. Even the striking presence of the "elders" could not eradicate the difference between memory and history. This, too, might be brought to the surface, especially when the differences among memories are recognized. This is a point at which novels might be used—fictions that embody the pain and the awarenesses of persons still personally seared by slavery and the glimpses of possibility that might now and then appear. (I think of *Beloved*, *Song of Solomon*, *The Known World*, *March*, and others.) For those who confront the contact zone as primarily a place where ethnic and other dissonances might be overcome, I recommend works coming out of the East and Middle East, as well as Africa, that make it clear that, for all the importance of cultural experience, identity is not wholly defined by cultural membership, that there remain unduplicable persons to be found in a contact zone.

This was a memorable adventure for me. The very idea of attending to the spoken and written experiences in contexts like those described fills a void in what we think of as educational research. I greatly appreciate as well the tapping of imagination made evident in *Echoes*. If nothing else, the ways in which the making of it contributed to the participants' sense of mutuality and understanding must be emphasized.

My suggestions are that questioning becomes deliberately encouraged; since it seems so obvious that authentic learning begins with the framing of those Freire called "worthwhile" questions. It is the case that "social justice" must be sought, but how are those terms understood? What of the "sense of injustice"? How does freedom relate to justice? What is the "public space," and why is it referred to here as a "bourgeois sphere"? Can particular instances of action be identified here? How can a young person's feeling of being personally and unjustly injured lead to or be related to common or collaborative action? To what degree can a common cause (anti-war work, for example) overcome some of the profound differences in the contact zone?

CHAPTER **4**

PAR Praxes for Now and Future Change

The Collective of Researchers on Educational Disappointment and Desire

EVE TUCK, JOVANNE ALLEN, MARIA BACHA, ALEXIS MORALES, SARAH QUINTER, JAMILA THOMPSON, AND MELODY TUCK

"CREDD is the place to interrogate the education system that turned its back on me."

(Alexis)

"CREDD makes me know that I was sitting down when I should have been standing."

(Jodi-Ann)

Our Collective

The Collective of Researchers on Educational Disappointment and Desire (CREDD) came together in early 2006 to be a space for youth participatory action research (YPAR) on education in New York City. We are united by our disappointment in the New York City public school system and our desire to effect political and educational change in school policies and practices. A group of 12 youth aged 16 to 22, CREDD researchers are lower and working class, ethnically diverse, live all over the city, and represent a wide range of educational experiences, although many identify as being *pushed out* from our former schools, and all of us have felt unwelcome at school.

Figure 4.1 The CREDD seal. Created by Sarah Quinter.

We have developed a critique of a school system that was never intended for us in the first place. Our group defines itself against racism, sexism, homophobia, ageism, the criminalization of poor people, and push-out practices in New York City public high schools. We are in favor of schooling that is rigorous, accessible, and free.

"CREDD is exactly what it sounds like. Unique, questioning, and a word that makes you ask *what?*" (Melody). CREDD is different from other research spaces because we are not an academic or government space; usually the academy or government has a monopoly on research. We fill different roles based on our interests and talents, where in other research spaces, power is usually only held by those with the most research experience. Finally, we engage in our own process of decision making, whereas other participatory spaces may rely on a one-person, one-vote decision making model that will always muffle the voices of those in numeric minority (Smith, 2000).

CREDD's approach to PAR holds that those whose backs research has historically been carried *on* are instead researched *alongside*. In our work, PAR has been a way for young men and women who are marginalized by race and ethnicity, class, gender, and sexuality to not only demand access to the conversations, policies, theories, and spaces which we/they have been systematically denied, but better yet, demand that our research informs and inspires these efforts. CREDD's approach to PAR is concerned with what knowing is and where knowing comes from, believing that it is often those at the bottom of social hierarchies who know the most both about social oppression and also about the radical possibilities toward redressing domination (Anyon, 2005; Fine et al., 2007).

Further, CREDD understands PAR as *politic*—an embedded and outloud critique of colonization, racism, misogyny, homophobia and heterosexism, classism, and xenophobia in our society, in our research sites, amongst our research collective, and within the larger and historical research community—rather than a fixed set of methods. At the same time, CREDD takes method seriously, crafting each instrument to be interactive and pedagogical, drawing from qualitative and quantitative traditions, and growing our own legacy of hybridized methods utilizing visual arts, theater, and schoolyard games.

For us, PAR means that:

- There is transparency on all matters of the research;
- The research questions are co-constructed;
- The project design and design of research methods are collaboratively negotiated and co-constructed;
- Analysis is co-constructed; and
- The products of the research are dynamic, interactive, and are prepared and disseminated in collaboration.

Our work stands in opposition to the kinds of research that have been and continue to be used for domination. Everyone is involved in developing research questions, project design, data collection, data analysis, and product development. Everyone is responsible for making our space a participatory space. We do not erase ourselves from our work, and our whole selves are involved because lots of kinds of skills and thinking are needed, not just one. By action, CREDD means demanding justice, starting a conversation, taking a stand in order to build power, and redefining reality. Action happens all throughout the research, not just at the end. By research, we mean looking again in order to make our own interpretations, breaking silences, and reclaiming spaces that have been used against us. Finally, research means refusing to accept analyses that paint us as lazy, crazy, or stupid.

> I've learned that it can be more helpful for me to look for people asking similar questions than to count on those offering answers. I came across CREDD and saw a group of people who were also searching for answers about education and youth achieving self-determination. I'd never done research before and had never even heard of PAR. I ended up joining a diverse group of young researchers who are trying something that hadn't been done before.
>
> **(Sarah Quinter)**

The Long-Short Herstory of CREDD

We co-founded CREDD in February 2006, though the events in our individual lives were bringing us together long before then. For instance, Alexis, Jovanne, Sarah, and Maria (aka Bacha) were suffocating in their former schools; Eve was working with brilliant youth organizers who were desperately dissatisfied with school; Melody and Jamila were seeing loved ones struggle to keep their heads above school waters.

We came together at first to do a research project that attended to the overuse and abuse of the General Educational Development (GED) credential as a disguise for pushing out unwanted students in New York City high schools; this project became our Gate-ways and Get-aways Project. Some of us had met over the years; others we met when we put out a CREDD call for youth researchers throughout various New York City-based listservs. In some ways, it was Eve's idea to come together, but as we worked in our twice-a-week meetings to create our research questions, develop our project design, design our research tools, and to learn together how to do research, any feelings of her ownership of our group and our process disappeared, and we all became co-founders. We collected most of our data over summer 2006, but our data collection spread over nine months and concluded in December.

Also toward the end of 2006, we began consulting on other youth PAR projects, and began our involvement with a larger citywide initiative to replace mayoral-controlled schooling with human rights-based schooling. In early 2007, we facilitated a participatory action research project with another group of local youth, the newly formed Youth Researchers for a New Education System (YRNES). This project seeks to document students' visions for school governance, schooling based on collaboration rather than competition and control, and the purpose(s) of schooling. Concluding in the summer of 2007, YRNES' project will involve over 1,000 surveys and three focus groups.

We're not sure what the future holds for CREDD. We know that it has become an important space for us, and that a space for participatory action research with youth on education is a valuable space for our city and our public school system.

The Gate-ways and Get-aways Project

We call our first research project the Gate-ways and Get-aways Project because we are interested in the GED both as a gateway to higher education and employment, and as a get away from dehumanizing high schools. The GED is a credential of General Educational Development that was never intended for widespread use as an alternative to a high school diploma. In the United States and especially in New York City, both numbers of GED earners and the numbers of youth GED earners have increased in the past decade. The pre-existing research on the GED often questioned the value of the GED credential in higher education and employment—but never asked youth why they continue to flock to "a depleted credential."

We believe that the increase in numbers of youth GED earners in New York City, even in the face of a possibly diminished value of the GED, can be linked to what it feels like to be in high school. To really understand this link, we needed to do participatory action research. Our collective, which includes youth GED earners, designed the Gate-ways and Get-aways Project to privilege the experiences of youth GED earners and seekers in order to challenge mainstream attitudes toward the GED as being an empty credential, and to understand the lived rather than perceived value of the GED. Seeking out the lived value helped us see how federal mandates (such as No Child Left Behind) and state-mandated exit exams (like the NY Regents) put pressure on schools to push out students who would not do well on standardized tests. Youth of color and poor youth (many who do not feel like school was made for them anyway) are explicitly and implicitly pushed out and pushed toward the GED. Many youth are misinformed about the GED process and mistakenly think that they will be swapping one set of tests for another without having to attend four years of high school. Our participatory action research has taught us that the value of the GED lies less in it being a gateway to higher education and employment and more in being a get-away from inhospitable high schools.

Research Questions, Areas of Inquiry

Rather than specifically worded research questions, we have designed this project around four interconnected areas of inquiry, so that each one of us can use our own words to describe our work, depending on our audience or the situation. The areas of inquiry in the Gate-ways and Get-aways Project are: the perceived and lived values of the GED; push-out practices in New York City public high schools; educational alternatives to state exit exam based curricula; and meritocracy and the myth of the American Dream. Each one of these four areas of inquiry is full enough to be the source of many years of research. However, our commitment to interconnectivity, our urgency of critique of the pre-existing literature on the GED, and our genuine curiosity compelled us to craft our research to ask questions in the territories of each of these areas, and in the intersections between them.

Research Methods

We have recently begun using the metaphor of a watercolor box to talk about our methods. We try to use the best color to paint the picture we

Figure 4.2 Educational map created by focus group participant and GED seeker Dominick Sepulveda.

are trying to see, and use the colors in harmony, rather than muddying the image or weakening the paper by using too many colors at once. In this paint box, our primary colors are individual interviews and group interviews and focus groups. These are the foundations of our research, and our painting would be incomplete without them.

Our secondary colors have been surveys, opinion polls, cold calls, memoirs, archival research, and mapping. These colors can be blended with one another, but especially the primary colors to create light and shadow, depth and complexity in our work.

We have also mixed colors to create new colors, or new methods such as borrowing activities from Augusto Boal's Theater of the Oppressed, popular education's problem tree, and schoolyard games such as the slambook and board games. These hybrid colors come alive in participatory action research and are indeed some of the most radical and compelling examples of the possibilities of participatory action research.

A final extension to the metaphor: water, participation, is the stuff that moves the pigment from box to brush to page, that makes the stroke translucent or opaque.

In the Gate-ways and Get-aways Project, we carefully designed each of our methods to be deeply participatory, interactive, and pedagogical. We approached the project with genuine questions (our areas of inquiry) and with a feeling of genuine urgency. Our counterparts are being pushed out from school, and in many cases the GED is being abused as a cover for it, right now, this minute. In some of our encounters with research participants, especially youth,[1] such as the interviews, survey, and focus groups, we made sure that they would feel like experts and collaborators in our analysis and theorizing on the GED and push-out experiences. In our over 40 hour-long interviews with youth GED earners and seekers, and with adults who earned GEDs in their youths but are now in their thirties, we began each discussion by asking the interviewee to tell us what they wanted us to be sure to carry with us. The interviews invited participants to recollect and rethink, to try ideas on and set forth new ideas, to imagine, and to advise.

In one of our three distinct focus groups (which we did three times each with youth GED earners and seekers), we used an individual educational journey mapping exercise as a platform for participants to discuss the crossroads of the lived and perceived value of the GED. In another focus group on push-out practices in NYC public high schools, we used a problem tree exercise (Ferreira and Ferreira, 1996) and an exercise from Boal's (2002) Theater of the Oppressed in order to co-theorize with our participants the connections between being and feeling unwelcome in school and attitudes and beliefs about young people and schooling and systematic and ideological supports of pushing out unwanted students.

Figure 4.3 Educational map created by focus group participant and GED seeker Zhi Huang.

Our third focus group utilized group mapping of now and future life satisfaction, and a conversation-starting a CREDD-revamped version of pop-o-matic trouble in order to together think through the limits of the meritocracy and American Dream narratives.

Even our survey was designed to be interactive and made use of a range of survey instruments that were decidedly unlike school tests. We created two versions, a full-length 45-minute version that included many short answer questions, which was completed by 100 youth, mostly GED earners and seekers; and an abridged 10-minute version that contained fewer short answer questions, completed by 400 youth, in-school and out-of-school alike.

Some of our methods, such as the cold calls to college admissions officers and employers, our archival research, and our slambooks, were created in order to expose biases against the GED. We have completed over 200 cold calls to representatives of higher education and employers to interrogate the equivalency of the GED to a high school diploma, but more, to call attention in these offices to their unequal treatment of GED earners, despite professed equal regard.

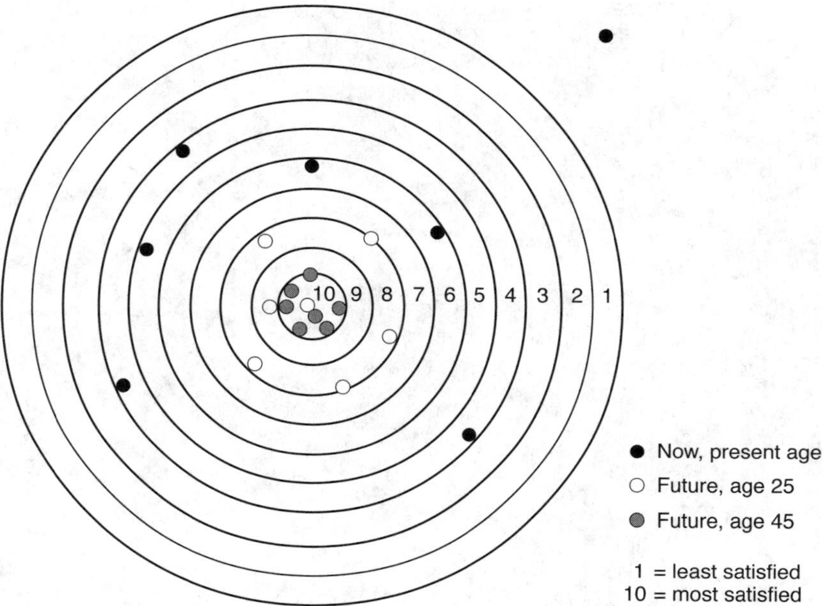

Figure 4.4 Reproduction of one of our "Satisfaction in Your Life" group maps. Focus group participants place green stickers (shown here in black) to mark their current experiences of satisfaction in their lives. As the participants place the stickers, they explain why they chose the location. In the next round, participants place yellow stickers (shown here in white) to mark their anticipated satisfaction in life at the age of 25. Again, participants share their reasoning with the group. In the final round, participants use orange stickers (shown here in gray) to mark their anticipated satisfaction in life at the age of 45, sharing their logic for why with the group. The mapping exercise is completed after the CREDD researchers facilitate a group discussion to answer the question, "What is a satisfied life?" in order for the group to theorize together what the scale of 1–10 on the map means.

Our archival research meant reading everything we could get our hands on, including legal documents, policy documents, academic articles, newspaper clippings, theory, and fiction, in order to make an informed critique of the current framing of the value of the GED and the invisibility of the push-out experience, slipping in and out of power discourses to fulfill our own needs.

We produced and slid 30 slambooks into asking questions about young people's views and their schools and politics schools and youth circles. These notebooks covered in youth ideas were meant to be found and read, to be inviting to youth and provocative to adults. As we anticipated, many of the slambooks were confiscated, but we received 15 of them back.

Finally, some of our methods we created for ourselves. Over six months, all of us created educational memoirs, and as a closing to our data collection period, we shared them with one another in an evening of food and

Figure 4.5 CREDD's meritocracy board game. Players are divided into four differently resourced teams represented by game board colors. Red (left) = large one-family home on Long Island, owned for generations; Yellow (bottom) = rented apartment in a two-family home in Jamaica, Queens; Green (right) = new urban-feeling suburb outside of Newark, NJ; Blue (top) = a project in the South Bronx. Players try to reach all the way around the board to their "American Dreams" without getting tripped up by health, housing, education, policing, or social issues or without getting squeezed out or gentrified by opponents. This game is followed by a facilitated discussion on the fantasies of meritocracy and implications on schooling. Artwork by Sarah Quinter.

sharing. One of our researchers has developed a spin-off q-sort project which she describes as a q-sorta. We have also engaged in a self-reflection process in order to research our own dynamics in working together.

Communicating Our Findings

The products of this research will include a youth-to-youth guide to the GED, a youth-geared website that shares our work, and an extensive community talking tour. We have appeared on radio shows, on numerous panels,

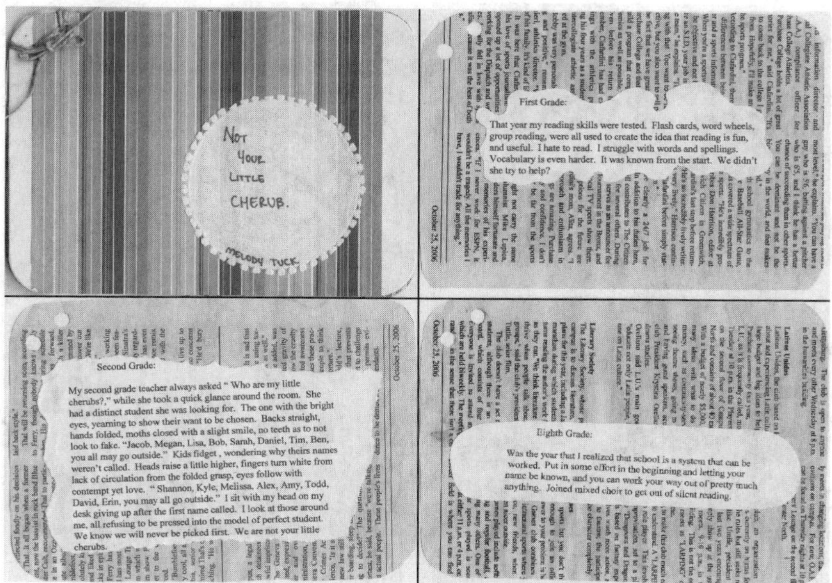

Figure 4.6 Excerpts of an educational memoir by Melody Tuck. Handmade book (4″ x 6″) using decorative paper, newsprint, text, and twine.

and have joined a coalition with other organizations on issues pertaining to out-of-school youth, a coalition whose work is informed by our findings.[2]

Common threads

Gate-ways and Get-aways was an ambitious research project, and knowing that our own experiences of disenchantment with schooling are felt exponentially by many other youth in New York City, we sometimes think of it as com/passionate ambition. Our process matters. Sondra Perl writes about the "felt sense" in writing as being, "the feelings or non-verbalized perceptions that surround the words, or what the words already present evoke" (Perl, 1980: 367). The notion of the felt sense really resonates with us, not only in writing, but especially in our research design, and now in our data analysis. "The felt sense is always there, within us. It is unifying, and yet, when we bring words to it, it can break apart, shift, unravel, and become something else . . . What is elicited then is not solely the product of a mind, but of a mind alive in a living, sensing body" (Perl, 1980: 367).

Through everything, whether we are getting surveys done, doing a focus group, or interviewing youth, our felt senses come into play. My

Figure 4.7 Educational memoir by Sarah Quinter. Handmade map (2 x 1.5) using a map, paint, chalk, pencil, text, found objects, journal cuttings, childhood drawings, and school assignments, and other bits of life collected over many years.

> felt sense is very important in my work, and I am aware of it when doing interviews with other youth who have been pushed out. I can relate: When I was in school I don't remember actually meeting with my counselor but I remember the late letters coming home. My counselors and teachers couldn't care less about what was going on for me at home and the reasons why I was late or absent, and that is a memory that is alive in me while I am doing research. The emotion, the frustration, and anger that came out in my interviews were electric.
>
> **(Alexis Morales)**

We have come to our project by attending to our felt senses, by listening to our hunches, by being unafraid to ask each other to say more at the point where our felt senses may be just about to break apart, to care about words and ideas, to try things on, to say what feel like small things out loud and listen to the echoes. In this way, we engage collectively in reconstructing our own realities. We engage together in/toward self-determination and re-cognition. We are constantly switching between inhabiting this current world and the world we want to inhabit, struggling to clarify our vision, like shaking a TV antenna to get a clear picture.

As CREDD researchers, each of us has an intimate, nuanced understanding of what it means to work for social justice, and what each of us means by social change. Broadly, CREDD operates on the premise that our educational system is set up to maintain the status quo, including race, class, and gender divisions. We realize that reforming the school system and challenging these various forms of oppression are linked struggles, so our approach to social justice focuses on challenging the status quo through PAR, and at the same time modeling the kinds of interactions we want to have.

Many times throughout this work, each of us has said that *we have been waiting our whole lives be a part of a space like this*. We have wondered aloud what an amazing difference it would have made for our schools to be sites of collective inquiry and meaning making, as CREDD has become for us. Our schooling has marked us, but this experience as CREDD has marked us too.

The Roles of Theory

The Gate-ways and Get-aways Project and all of our works are influenced by indigenous theories of sovereignty and interconnectivity (Deloria, 1988; Grande, 2004), by critical theories (Anzaldúa, 2002; Crenshaw, 2000; Matsuda, 2002; Moraga, 1993; Morrison, 1970), and by theories of the rhizome (Deleuze and Guattari, 1987) and third-space (Soja, 1996). We think of CREDD itself as a third-space to graduation and the streets. These theories help us understand how our work negotiates pre-existing systems of domination and exclusion and also experiences of disillusionment and degradation at the behest of hegemonic schooling. These experiences of educational disappointment and desire become our data along with the data our methods have yielded. Most importantly, we use these theories as a jump-off point to do our own theorizing, to research and theorize back (Tuck, in preparation).

PAR Praxes for Now and Future Change

Though throughout our work we have been writing our own feature articles and memoirs, this chapter, written over four months, is the first piece we have written collaboratively. We began by deciding that we would use the space of this chapter to collaboratively explore (by writing together, by employing writing as a method) some of the important moments in our work together; this chapter focuses on our collective rather than our work with those who participated in our data gathering. We identified teaching moments that shifted our understanding of our work. Each author wrote about one or two of these moments from her perspective. Next, one or two of us wrote back to the author and our readers in order to contextualize these moments in CREDD's work.

Then, together, we decided to organize the moments and the chapter around three discussions, three praxes: (1) tailoring research to be ours; (2) reclaiming, recovering, carving out personal/political space; and (3) cultivating and sustaining our commitments to our research. We understand praxis as the clasped hands of reflection/theory and action/practice "directed at the structures to be transformed" (Freire, 1997: 107). The three praxes we describe in this chapter reveal some of the difficult, inspiring, and teaching inner workings of our group, how we thought together and apart about them, how we continue to think about them, and how they have shaped our continued work together.

The three praxes can also be described as praxes toward sovereignty (see also Tuck, 2007). Still too new an idea for us to fully explicate here, we are challenged and inspired by Sandy Grande's (2004) charge of indigenous sovereignty as a prerequisite to democracy. Recognizing that democratic practice is widely understood as a tenant in/of PAR, but also aware of the ways in which "democracy" has been wielded in the United States and across the globe as a weapon of mass occupation and assimilation (see also Fine et al., 2007), we have strived to use our collective space as a space to engage in what exactly we mean by democratic practice, and what a democratic practice that honors and supports self-determination might look like. This work is in service to larger theoretical conversations concerning sovereignty and US foreign and domestic policy, sovereignty and federal and state educational mandates, and sovereignty and school and social control (Tuck, 2007).

There are parts of this chapter that are in a "we" voice—parts that one person had to be brave enough to write in a we voice and submit to the group to use as a jump-off point, truly a first draft. There are also parts written in an "I" voice—parts in which each of us tells the story of CREDD from our own viewpoint with the encouragement of our co-researchers behind us. We have listed the names of the authors of the first-person pieces to honor their point of view, but also want to recognize that these pieces were written and workshopped in our group, that we have supported each other in arriving at these voices.

We know that when we or any group writes in a we voice it can make the words seems smoother, easier than they really are. Writing as "we" linguistically stubs the toe on the process it has taken for us to speak of ourselves as a we. Further, if you would map any "we" in this chapter, where each of us is in relationship to the we voice—curled up in the lap, emptying the dishwasher, unhappy upstairs under the bed—would make the we more feather-shaped than brick-wall-shaped.

But finally, we also know that our work is vulnerable. So as a group of youth (except for Eve), as mostly young women of color, as PAR researchers, as big-mouths, as "trouble makers," we are not always entirely sure how much of ourselves we want to reveal in our writing, how much of ourselves we are willing to serve up.

This can compound the we voice's likelihood to come across as peachy-keen and even sappy: all of those things that are lobbed at women and youth to undermine their ideas and realities. We are a hopeful bunch, a committed-to-each-other bunch, a strong and sometimes sappy bunch. We are a proud bunch, an intentional bunch, a watchful bunch.

Some of us identify as writers and have for many years, while others of us are just beginning to come into our identities as writers. Others of us hate writing; have been taught to hate our own writing and to be quiet. All of us have taken on this chapter anyway, knowing that it would be a loss to leave out the voices of those who are ambivalent about what a book chapter can do.

We have a similar relationship to research, and at some or many points throughout our work have turned to each other and asked, "What can this do anyway?" For many of us, what we have known about research through the experiences of our families and communities has taught us that research can too easily be employed as a tool of colonization and domination, used, as in the eugenics movement, to forward racist agendas and to reaffirm the status quo. We would not be researchers without an inherent commitment to action toward the relief of social injustice, especially in education. We would not be researchers without an inherent commitment to participation, dissolving the traditional researcher–subject hierarchy toward the refusal to use the power of the language of research to speak against our people and ourselves.

Our relationship to writing and research is important to us as expatriate and exiled students. Michelle Fine and Pearl Rosenberg write, "Critical perspectives on social institutions are often best obtained from exiles, that is, persons who leave those institutions. This is perhaps why exiles' views are frequently disparaged as deviant and in some cases, conspicuously silenced" (Fine and Rosenberg, 1983: 257). Many of us exiled students, others of us marooned, we in creating CREDD but also in creating our Gate-ways and Get-aways Project, make ourselves *present exiles.* As present exiles, our still-here bodies prove the disarray of the dumping grounds, our still-here voices prove the illogic of the erasure, and our still-here drives for justice prove the betrayal of a school system that aims to stamp and sort us according to our race and ethnicity, our gender, our class, our ability, and our language in order to contribute to a wider disparity of wealth, the further disenfranchisement and political isolation of poor communities and communities of color, and the consolidation of white supremacy. Further, our approach to participatory action research, which aims to document the presence and experiences of the

NYC public school system's present exiles, amplifies the disarray, illogic, and betrayal in order to demand change in policy and practice.

> I locate research in the realm of education and learner. At this moment, I feel like the skins of researcher and learner are synonymous for me.
>
> There is some dominant thought in the US that in order to create change, one must launch a campaign around a specific issue, target, demand, or winnable victory. Furthermore, it is assumed that we should demand our victory from the state, corporation, or someone with power (cause we don't have any, except that power that we gain through following this method). Who came up with this and how does it get continually imposed?
>
> Knowledge is power. Our identities, the options available to us and our education are extremely powerful. Education can determine our lives. Education can create change.
>
> We need a diversity of research, strategies, tactics, options, and types of power.
>
> **(Maria Bacha)**

In this vein, and before we turn to the three discussions below, we want to say something about the how-to-ness of this chapter. At our presentations, many people come up to us and ask us about the steps involved in making a research collective, or somewhat creepily, how to get "buy-in" from young people. What we know is this: a big part of "how to" do this work depends on how the group has constructed themselves and the work—thus, we will offer how *we* have constructed ourselves and the work. For us, how we do this work has in its sights big, full, round goals of social justice, not only as a lofty end-of-the-road goal, but also in everyday practice. It is really hard, and we have messed up lots of times. We trust each other and the validity and importance of our work enough to not be deterred by messing up and continue working for now and future change.

Praxis One: How We Have Tailored Research to Be Ours

This section involves the telling of CREDD's first retreat/training weekend and the process that yielded CREDD's research design and a telling of how we approach sharing the work of our research in order to describe how we have made research, an activity we would have never anticipated for ourselves, our own. How did we get the guts to call ourselves researchers and call the work we do research?

One part of the answer lies in our critique of how research has historically, in the United States and abroad, been waged on oppressed people.

Informed by indigenous critiques of this (ongoing) history and buttressed by our own experiences in communities where outsider, often white, research types come in for a hot minute and then, having extracted whatever they need, take off for the next community "in need," we are wary of the practices of research and of researchers.

> It appalls us that the West can desire, extract and claim ownership of our ways of knowing, our imagery, the things we create and produce, and then simultaneously reject the people who created and developed those ideas and seek to deny them further opportunities to be creators of their own culture and own nations.
>
> **(Smith, 1999: 1)**

The other part of the answer has to do with our own desires for "no action without research; no research without action" (K. Lewin, as quoted by Adelman, 1997). From our own experiences under the treads of the uninformed policies that have rolled through our schools, it only makes sense for us to take the matters of informing ourselves and others into our own hands. There is a lot of valuable knowledge in those treads.

From time to time over the course of this project we have looked at one another with a twinkle in our eyes and asked, "Does it feel like *science* yet?" Elbow-deep in slightly damp surveys (see below); hung up on for the fortieth time; dragging a big pad of paper on the subway to a focus group; balancing a stack of slambooks; searching on our hands and knees for the missing yellow piece of our nothing-but-trouble game; we have to look at each other with a laugh and say "yes."

Deciding upon and developing our methods—Eve Tuck

I remember that I was really nervous the day that we were going to begin selecting our research methods. I had a full itinerary of research methods to present to our group, and being practically famous for my absentmindedness on time when in the heat of discussion, I was worried that I had planned to talk about way too much in way too little time. Also, even though I had known many in the group for years, I felt shy about talking with them about research methods—while used to talking with them about writing or organizing or scary movies (hate them) or reality TV shows (love them), talking about research methods felt like pulling on my Dad's shoes over my own when I was a girl: clunky, awkward, pretend-like.

Also, I had a lot of nagging worries about how all of this was supposed to happen . . . How was I supposed to smoosh all of the methods that it had taken me four years to learn into a two-day retreat? How was I supposed to really support the group in choosing which methods to use when all I could offer was what I knew? There were a lot of methods that I didn't plan to share with the group—was I being too limiting? There were also a lot of methods that I was really curious about but had no experience in; was it okay that I planned to offer up research methods that I couldn't personally vouch for? There were also a few ideas I had about some "new" research methods, five-finger discounted from popular education and organizing, and others modified from school games. How was I to present these methods alongside the tried and true pillars of qualitative research such as the interview and the focus group?

I was encouraged by friends' reminders that it hadn't taken me all that long to get the gist of these methods; that we can only offer what we know; that I could be open about what I did and didn't know, but also what I was tempted to try out; that I could share my own hunches around "new" research methods, as long as we made room for ourselves to be critical and curious about all of the research methods. I entered CREDD's methods retreat armed with an agenda detailed to the minute, and a gift from my partner: the biggest, loudest kitchen timer he could buy.

I developed a series of activities or encounters for the whole group, with strict time limits on my own talking. Each method got ten minutes, of which I was only allowed to present for two minutes. The gigantic kitchen timer was very helpful in keeping me from going over two minutes of presentation on each method, and I had photos, copies, film footage and mock up examples for the group to see and explore. The remaining eight minutes consisted of almost rapid-fire questions and clarifications, and importantly, the group shared what they already knew of each method. After the ten minutes, we took five minutes to write in our researcher journals, listing notes and first impressions of the method, further questions, and ideas for implementation in our design.

We spent much of this day in this way—intense bouillon cube discussions around possible methods broken up by quiet moments of reflection through writing—fueled by pizza and salad, curious about what was going on in one another's notebooks.

Taking a deep collective breath and diving in to choosing our methods proved to be a great way to try out our newly established decision-making process (see Praxis Two, this chapter). There was no magical moment where our methods became evident: we just felt our way through, sharing with each other which methods seemed compelling, which seemed to speak to one of our four areas of inquiry, which methods would generate some intrigue from the youth we wanted to talk to. At one point in the conversation, we wanted to do all of the methods! At another point, we wanted to do all of the methods and also seek out more!

We used this conversation to decide for ourselves what methods actually are, that is, what role they would have in our research. Rather than choosing methods that would corroborate our data, we were interested in selecting a range of methods that would yield data from multiple perspectives and positions. Being familiar with the ways in which research on the GED had been conducted in the past, we also wanted to select methods that attend to the gaps in existing research, especially research that has excluded youth voices.

In the end, we chose to use over 18 different tools (see our list at the beginning of this chapter) and did so knowing that it would be ambitious and nearly impossible to accomplish on our timeframe and our budget. Our big dreams were in part due to being big dreamers, but also in part as a response to the complexity of our research interests, a killer combination.

Sharing the work—Alexis Morales

When I took a step back and saw all of the work that CREDD decided to take on, I admit I felt confused. I thought the workload ahead was going to be overwhelming because we had so much to do and so little time in which to do it. I thought the goal was unrealistic, but as time went on and I saw the methods and division of work within the group, I began to feel relieved.

Over time, when something has felt heavy and overwhelming, I have had the support of my group members, and the feeling of being flustered seemed to fade away. CREDD began to feel like a safety net.

The roles of CREDD are not exactly assigned to each individual because we have our own way of getting things done. When we have certain tasks to do or deadlines to meet, we use our meeting times to generate and go through a to-do list and everyone speaks up on what task they would like to take on.

Dividing the roles is usually pretty easy. When someone feels strongly about an assignment they volunteer to take that particular task on. Then we go from there. With all the different interests and talents in the group, things can at times get lopsided for a week or two, but we all have the CREDD agenda in mind so we try to divide things as evenly as possible.

We try our best to balance things so that no one's worth, dedication, or desire goes unnoticed, there is always a way for someone to bring their talent to the table. For example, for one of our focus groups, we created a board game that portrays the unfairness of meritocracy, and it was a perfect opportunity for Sarah to express her artistic talents.

It's important in my collective that everyone is satisfied with the work. We don't like to assign tasks that seem like a chore. We all make decisions together as a team, no researcher knows more than another, and no one is any more or less valuable than another. We are a unit that works together. As the saying goes, "there is no I in team" and there certainly isn't an "I" in CREDD.

One of the fantasies that people might have about PAR, especially among youth, is that we all have to be the same and do everything the same way. PAR isn't synchronized swimming! CREDD has become a space for us to put into practice our theories and politics that are committed to addressing one another as a whole person. We appreciate and *go there* with each other as thinkers, as people with souls and histories, as people who are conflicted and complicated, and brimming with desire to be seen in this way. We often take the time to write together and read our words to each other as a way to ensure that the time for really hearing and seeing one another is built into our everyday work.

Hearing and seeing one another as whole people also often happens in unplanned ways when we are trying to do something else. A decision to use a "female, male, or other" multiple choice question, or blank answer question to capture gender on our survey gave way to a revealing, unforgettable discussion on the politics of gender and race and sexuality, a discussion that we return to frequently. In another example, when during a major summer heatwave we anticipated that like us, many other youth in the city would need to have some fun in the Astoria pool to beat the heat, we went on a CREDD family outing and brought a stack of our surveys to conduct with the hundreds of youth waiting in line to get in. Working alongside one another, seeing each other in action, and then a celebratory dip in the pool helped us meet many of our needs at once.

Praxis Two: Reclaiming, Recovering, Carving Out Personal/Political Space

This section is crafted around two moments, the first depicting the session in which CREDD solidified our decision-making process, the second depicting what will go down in the CREDD history books as "our first fight," told from the perspectives of the women at the center of the argument. We have identified both of these moments as pivotal crossroads in our attempts to carve out a political and personal space for our collective. Much of the carving work has actually been work of reclaiming and recovering. Our understanding of this has been informed by the work of Maori scholar Linda Tuhiwai Smith. Her concept of "researching back," in the legacies of "writing back" and "talking back," involves, "a 'knowingness of the colonizer' and a recovery of ourselves, an analysis of colonialism, and a struggle for self-determination" (Smith, 1999: 7).

Part of the reclaiming has to do with taking back words and languages that have been used against us, for example, (un)intelligence, (limited) capacity, and discourses of (trickle down) power and democracy. Part of the recovery has to do with tapping into parts of us that have been discouraged in our schooling, such as asking questions, being curious about the underbelly or behind-the-scenes dynamics of everyday life, writing in order to discover what we really believe about something, relying on someone else when overwhelmed or unsure, allowing ourselves to be vulnerable, and being motivated by a shared goal rather than competition. These thoughtful, reflective parts of ourselves, often otherwise silenced or swept away by the hustle and bustle of city life, are nurtured in our collective work.

In addition, indeed because we have created CREDD as a space and practice of reclamation and recovery, CREDD operates as a thirdspace (Lefebvre, 1991; Soja, 1996) to many of the binaries in our own lives such as work/home, teaching/learning, talking/listening, but also as a thirdspace to ideas such as reproduction/resistance, success/failure, and reality/hope. The verb or activity of thirding "is the first and most important step in transforming the categorical and closed logic of either/or to the dialectically open of both/and also . . ." (Soja, 1996: 60). Linked to our always circling back wistfulness for our schooling to have looked, or more importantly felt, like CREDD, it is our very work together that underlines our critique of schooling, while simultaneously showing that such an educational space is possible. "*Everything* comes together in Thirdspace: subjectivity and objectivity, the abstract and the concrete, the real and the imagined, the knowable and the unimaginable, the repetitive and the differential, structure and agency, mind and body, consciousness and the unconscious, the disciplined and the transdisciplinary, everyday life and unending history" (Soja, 1996: 56).

The work of reclaiming and recovering and thirding is difficult, messy. It is especially so when it becomes the work itself, detached from the project of researching back. There have been moments when our confidence has been shaken by someone outside our collective who devalues our work or underestimates the validity of research by urban youth. By our very naming of ourselves as researchers, we sometimes cause a stir. "Trialectical thinking is difficult, for it challenges all conventional modes of thought and taken for granted epistemologies. It is disorderly, unruly, constantly evolving, unfixed, never presentable in permanent constructions" (Soja, 1996: 70). It is because we are engaging in research that has grown from our own experiences that we can speak to the everyday meaning of these ideas and have been able to resist spiraling off too far into the abstract: we always remind ourselves that there is work to do.

> This is an intervention. A message from that space in the margin that is a site of creativity and power, that inclusive space where we forever

> recover ourselves, where we move in solidarity to erase the category colonizer/colonized. Marginality is the space of resistance. Enter that space. Let us meet there. Enter that space. We greet you as liberators.
> **(hooks, 1990: 152 as quoted in Soja, 1996: 98)**

Deciding how we would decide—Melody Tuck

One of the things we noticed early on in CREDD was that everyone in the group had a different take on democracy and how it is put into practice. Some of us who are indigenous or immigrant to the United States see democracy as a code word for something that has been used against us and our families to limit access to power, land, resources, and sustainability. Others of us who are readers of critical theory or critical pedagogy employ those discourses' use of "democracy" to signal a "for the people, by the people" approach to knowledge building and learning. Still others had little time to think about democracy (these groups are not mutually exclusive). The most prevalent experience with democratic process for all of us has followed a scenario where at a given time in a group everyone stops and votes, with or without a prior discussion and with or without a discussion after, the votes are counted, and the results lived with.

When during one of our first CREDD meetings Eve urged us to spend some time together "deciding how we want to make decisions," it's probable that all of us felt under-prepared for such a discussion. All of us had been burned by the one-person, one-vote model, from family decisions to classroom voting to the presidential election. Some of us had been in situations where voting had been redone and redone until finally the facilitator's wishes had been granted. This is an abuse of power that CREDD would not tolerate in our group.

Eve's friend Kym took notes as we listed ideal elements of decision making: Having a time limit; dealing with a real issue not an abstracted issue; working as a group from proposals or first drafts rather than starting from scratch; being able to decide something without coercing everyone to agree; getting to a place in decisions where everyone feels okay, even if it's not their first choice.

We then used these elements to both be the basis of our decision-making process and as a guide to our process in deciding our decision-making process. We set a 45-minute time limit and used the list we had brainstormed as our first draft. We paid attention to people's disagreements and prodded silences and used these views to modify the first draft. Knowing that we had a limited amount of time to complete the discussion meant people didn't talk too much or too little.

This is the document that all of CREDD has signed . . .

Our decision-making process works because we believe in sharing responsibility for this space and work.

- We begin by opening the floor and setting a time limit for discussion.
- We bring forth issues, collectively brainstorming—each of us taking notes and reflecting on how strongly we agree or object to ideas.
- Then, people take on the responsibility of making suggestions/proposals/first drafts which synthesize multiple ideas from the brainstorm.
- After questions and modifications, the facilitator can check in with the group using red, yellow, green or throwing Cs.[3]
- We strive to get a place where all of CREDD is okay with moving forward with all of our decisions, even if the final choice is not their first choice.

It certainly was not an easy process. If we did not all trust that it was worth it then it could have fallen apart into a frustrating mess. To decide how to decide, everyone in the room must believe that it is worth figuring out how to listen to each other, how to treat each other and our ideas fairly, and put a critique of society into practice.

It's hard to step away from a method that has "seemed" to work in the past. The one-person, one-vote model, or single-voiced model of democracy is the way our government works, how workplaces are run. One voice is elected/heard and that is the only voice that is followed. We didn't want that. We wanted a method that let everyone be heard, and that allows an open space for people to express their thoughts and concerns without someone being stepped on. We wanted even the smallest voice heard, both because we have a critique of how voices are steamrollered over in society, but also because it is these small voices, outliers, counter-stories, that help ensure the fullest design and analysis.

Creating a decision-making process is hard to do when you are just meeting people for the first time, because you don't know how others think, work, how they will respond to your ideas, how you will respond to their ideas. The brainstorming process allowed us the opportunity to open ourselves up, granted everyone a chance to see who we are as people, working together to build the foundation of CREDD.

CREDD's first argument—Jovanne Allen

CREDD has had its first argument; it sure won't be the last. With a mix of ethnic identities, including African-American, Latina, Jewish, Native American, White and biracial, a range of gender identities, and a variety of identities of sexuality, bringing together such a diverse group of opinionated youth almost guarantees disputes. However, just because we have had a fight doesn't mean that we don't all have an overall respect for one another.

I worked with Sarah and Jamila on the design of a focus group that would try to understand the lived value of the GED from the point of view of GED earners and GED seekers aged 16–22. At the previous meeting, Jamila had promised to revise the questions we had drafted in time for us to pilot the focus group with the rest of CREDD.

When the day of our pilot came, I came to the meeting to find that neither of my group members had arrived early as we planned in order to index cards for our questions. Soon after, Sarah arrived and apologized, but Jamila didn't arrive until moments before we were set to begin. I was hurt. Jamila hadn't called to say she would be late and I took it personally, because I have a GED, and I felt that I was taking our project more seriously than she, a person with a high school diploma and not a GED.

Though I was aggravated, we tried to go forward with the focus group anyway, when I soon became even more frustrated with Jamila for asking what felt like too many follow-up questions and not paying attention to our time limit. I felt disrespected by her disregard for the plan we had made, and decided to speak up.

We ended up totally abandoning the pilot and had it out in front of the whole group. It was a very heated argument, and at one point I told her and the group that I felt that I would never be able to work with her.

For a few minutes the entire group tried to see if there was a way that Jamila or I could work on another focus group planning team, but the other teams had already done a lot of work too and were happy with the way things were. Seeing that, I announced that I did not have to like her as a person to work with her as a partner in our project, but that still wasn't a satisfying situation for anyone.

The group was quiet for a long time. Actually, Eve made us take a ten-minute quiet together break, and afterwards asked everyone if they had "arrived at anything." Everyone else shared that they cared for and respected both of us, and that it was hurtful to see us disrespect one another. In the moment, I took it in, but still shared that I was angry.

Eve next said that we should maybe use one of Augusto Boal's games in which we had to attack one another with imaginary swords. Everyone played, but it ended up being that when it was my turn, I had to attack Jamila with my sword, making her jump up and crouch down and leap from side to side. (At the time I was still so mad it would have been heaven if I really could have attacked her with a sword—smile.) She got to make me jump around too, and we both were cracking up. The whole group was laughing.

It has been several months since the "fight," and though I couldn't guess that I would then, I have fully gotten over it. I know now that it was really unrealistic to think that we all work so close together and not fight. However, it also was unrealistic for me to think that I would not work with her ever again. It's not about the fight, it's about what happens after—.

Communities of resistance—Jamila Thompson

> Communities of resistance should be places where people can return to themselves more easily, where the conditions are such that they can heal themselves and recover their wholeness.
>
> **(Thich Nhat Hanh)**

My best friend's mother is a woman of color and has a prestigious position at a Fortune 500 company and she revealed to me her regret of once complaining to her boss about the "work ethic" of her former colleague who is also a woman of color, especially since she understood the difficulties that her former friend was having outside of the office. My best friend's mother understood the implications of such a complaint in the corporate world, but she explained to me that she also learned from that incident her obligation to a fellow Black woman in a work environment that was potentially treacherous to them both.

My first conflict in CREDD was with Jovanne, the only other biracial/part Black woman in our group, though I was only able to appreciate the significance of this later. For the past two years I have been attempting to help build community with sisters because there are many obstacles in the way of us loving, caring for and respecting one another. This is especially the case in workspaces. But CREDD is not corporate America; it is not of the mainstream. We are a collective whose purpose is to transform and remold our society, but after my conflict with Jovanne I feared that we were adopting the individualistic values of the very institutions we are struggling against.

My lateness and incompletion of my part of the pilot preparations sparked Jovanne's annoyance with me, but when Jovanne asked me, "Do you need to ask so many follow-up questions?" I was insulted. I retorted that the key to rich data was follow-up questions and that I did not appreciate her attitude. We went off. When Jovanne questioned my dedication to CREDD I was infuriated. In any other situation I would probably have explained my situation, apologized, and kept it moving, but the stress of my outside life in conjunction with my self-righteousness—I just knew that I was giving everything I possibly could and this was challenged and not acknowledged—amplified things.

At that moment, I had been taking three summer courses and CREDD was one of my two jobs. My rent had been increased and, struggling financially, I had walked to CREDD from my job that day to save enough train fare to get back to Brooklyn after the meeting, and so arrived late for the pilot. Still, I was hurt and disappointed with myself for allowing the situation to escalate. What I needed at that moment was understanding and what Jovanne needed, I think, was context.

> We looked both from the outside in and from the inside out. We focused our attention on the center as well as on the margin. We understood both.
>
> **(hooks, 1984: ix, as quoted in Soja, 1996: 100)**

Jovanne: We overcame our argument because we realized that CREDD's work is made better by our continued collaboration, and because we know that disagreements do important work in collectives to share, negotiate, and solidify ideas. All of us have come to see that people do have other things going on in their lives, and there needs to be a balance between our lives and CREDD.

Alexis: One thing that is important to say is that this argument is different than what would be expected from young women of color. Many people would expect us to always be involved in "cat fights," all crying and emotions. I can assure you we are all very professional women, and for us that means that we take the work personally. We love, care for and have a deep respect for this project and so we do show emotion. We are not robots who come to work every day with the same expressions on our faces: sometimes we are happy and excited and sometimes we can be a little frustrated.

Jovanne: When you work in a collective where there is no one in the "boss" role, and no one in the "employee" role, the only thing that keeps the work going is that each of us follows through on our promises. Trying to do PAR without everyone following through is like trying to build a room with four walls but no floor. Ideally, all the researchers in the collective would need to bring 100 percent to the table, but in our society we can't. The New York life is fast and expensive. Sometimes you have to let go of your promises, even if they are your dreams and life-love, just to make sure ends meet.

Jamila: Viewing ourselves and each other as inhuman objects whose purpose and meaning is to achieve an end result or a product (research data and findings), is not acceptable in PAR/social activist groups. First, this disables us from creating the group dynamics that are vital to PAR research. Second, if our goal is to radically restructure our society then we cannot reproduce the detrimental attitudes of mainstream institutions. If we are to stand in opposition to disregard for human worth we must be conscious of our attitudes and perceptions of one another.

Jovanne: It feels like a long time since CREDD's first fight, and other arguments have happened along the way. We know that these haven't been damaging, but part of our process and growth.

Jamila: I am a complex individual who strives to contribute to the communities that I inhabit as best as I can. I have learned to remember that about all of CREDD's researchers. We try to be conscious of each other and what is going on in our lives. We have had conversations where we've expressed and explored the experiences and ideas that make us who we are individually and collectively. We appreciate differences and we consciously nurture one another. Recently, Jovanne and I led a CREDD meeting together. We had two hours between the two of us as facilitators to complete a number of tasks, and ended up finishing early. After we finished, Jovanne said "Now do you see how fast Jamila and I can get our work done and get you all out of here at a decent time." I blushed. To me, that statement was a demonstration of how far we have come.

Praxis Three: Cultivating and Sustaining Our Commitments to Our Research

In this section, we describe two events: one an impromptu ceremony created by CREDD that solidified our commitment to our project and social justice, the other, an exercise that helped establish CREDD's commitments to one another as researchers, and to our larger community. In our experience, commitment is the element of PAR that most determines a collective's possibilities and challenges. We are asked about it all the time and talk about it among ourselves all the time: what we can say is that it is really difficult to keep in balance.

To be painfully obvious, commitment cannot be forced or faked, it has to be grown. Further, it can feel illusive and it always feels like you need it before it's really able to be there. In many ways, our commitment to this project springs from our own experiences and linking our work on this issue to our own personal well-being. However, this has also been true for others of our researchers who have fallen out—so we know that this, in the face of financial, emotional, and family hardships, is not enough to sustain a researcher's participation.

Further, linking the success of a research project to our own personal projects of justice and well-being can generate a lot of pressure on us. Internally, we also know that commitment is something that youth "drop-outs" are thought to be void of, so proving this attitude wrong with our own staying power ups the stakes for us. It's difficult to be thoughtful and creative and curious when under so much self-pressure.

All we can do is remind ourselves that in PAR, doing the work *is* doing the work.

The two moments in this section both happened during a sleep-away retreat in June 2006. In the last hour of our retreat, Sarah facilitated a closing that has taught us a lot about CREDD as a (third) space of disappointment and desire.

It had been a full two days, crammed with workshops and writing and decision making, but also with swimming and volleyball and air hockey and quesadillas. We entered that closing with the electricity of our time together, with the new knowledge of who was afraid of ladybugs, who swims with his glasses over his goggles, who is suspicious of deer, who only eats with a spoon because "forks make food taste bad," and who knows all of the words to "Peanut Butter Jelly Time."

Eve had brought along a coconut wrapped in plastic wrap with the fantasy that someone would make good use of it, and it was present in all of our talks, in the corners of photos, passed around and shaken for the melody of its juice, made unofficial mascot of CREDD by the simple fact that it was there. Sarah made the connection more clear in her closing, leading us in an exercise that could be likened to Patricia Carini's (2001) method of close description: we passed around the coconut, freeing it from the plastic wrap, and described it, naming everything we ever knew about coconuts, claimed it. Coconuts can float, unlike other seeds. Coconuts can live for a long time after leaving the tree. Coconuts are thrives, are savory, are sustaining. The coconut has a rough, covered shell, protecting its water and air and flesh.

In our final go around, Sarah asked us to each hold the coconut again, and speak aloud our commitments to CREDD/the coconut. I will plant it to grow new knowledge, new understanding, new awareness; doing my share, doing my part in it; preserving this knowledge for years until I can find a nice place to plant it; love it, support it, baby it; break bread/break coconut with others over it because it is so good; live with it even when it is tough; know it for the long haul; not knowing what's inside, not knowing the immediate outcome, I'll trust it anyway; give it everything I know, all of my trust; protect it from what wants to eat it; being always down for its cause, never leaving it; making sure that I am its safety net (CREDD log 06.24.06).

CREDD and the coconut—Sarah Quinter

At the beginning of our data collection, we went on a retreat to plan our work and get to know each other. Eve had brought along a coconut that rolled around with us throughout the trip. A sort of spontaneous home-made ritual occurred during the closing I facilitated—we passed around the coconut, a symbol of CREDD's collective hopes, and each shared how we would be committed to it. We talked about how we would each do our part, preserving CREDD's knowledge like a rough shell protecting tender fruit. It seemed like a small historical moment.

At the same time that CREDD is coming up with our own symbols such as the coconut, and our own research methods such as the slambooks and the board game, I am trying to figure out my own ways of doing things in my life. I'm asking myself: What happens to people when they are forced to adapt to pre-made structures and conventions and expectations? Can someone become who he or she really is through this path? Are the structures of school and work scaffolding for our dreams or cages to contain us? Does that depend on your position in society? What if I can't grow up to be myself within these preexisting structures? What would it take to make my own? How can I build something strong and flexible enough to support and accommodate my needs? How do I avoid alienating others? When I tried to answer these questions honestly, I came to the conclusion that I couldn't be the person I wanted to be without rebuilding a lot of these structures from scratch with tools like art making, lists, charts, books, writing, the internet, intuition, advice from mentors, and solidarity with my peers.

There have been several times when CREDD has made its own ceremonies. This is a part of what makes our work special, beautiful, and unique. Making our own ceremonies is possible because we feel free to be creative and to not just have to do the usual. This is not because we do PAR, but through our PAR.

Someone took the coconut home, and a few days later, when we met again, we teased ourselves for having a magical moment with a coconut and letting it get away. Eve looked at several different stores for a replacement, and not finding one and in a pinch to make it in time for our next meeting, she bought some coconut milk in a can. The can took a place of honor at our meetings for a while, then, as the weeks passed, we began leaving it in the locker.

Still, when having a hard conversation in our meetings, someone usually goes to the locker and brings out the coconut in a can. It is a silent reminder of our overall goals, an inside joke on how we can be flexible and work under any conditions (in plastic wrap, in our shell, in a can) and a way to show our solidarity, even in the heat of frustration and disagreement.

Since the coconut ritual, we've made a lot of progress, but we've also had to deal with lateness, absence, missing deadlines, interpersonal conflicts, and everything else you'd expect when a group of people is struggling to attain ambitious goals together. But like a coconut that floats in the sea for

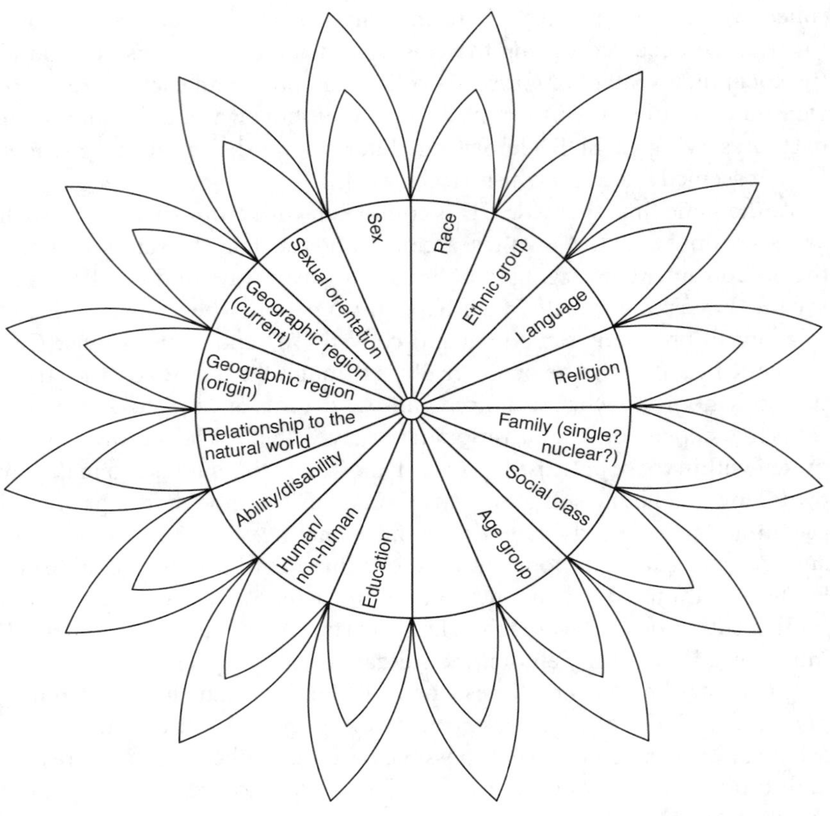

Figure 4.8 Source: Arnold et al., 1991: 88. This tool is used "for looking at who we are in relation to those who wield power in society" (Arnold et al., 1991: 13). In the authors' use, the inside petals represent categories of identity, the inner petals represent individual identifications within those identities, and the outer petals represent the dominant social identity.

years until it finds the perfect place to plant its roots, we are resilient and hold the potential to grow.

Commitment is a big deal in CREDD. Finding the reasons to get and be and stay committed can be difficult. Ultimately, committing to CREDD is committing to us. Investing in CREDD is an investment in us, not only because our research is dealing with our own experiences, but also because of the kind of space this is. It's rare to have the type of workspace where you're not piecing yourself off, but instead, you're nurturing your own self. CREDD fosters our individual growth, and our individual growth helps CREDD to grow.

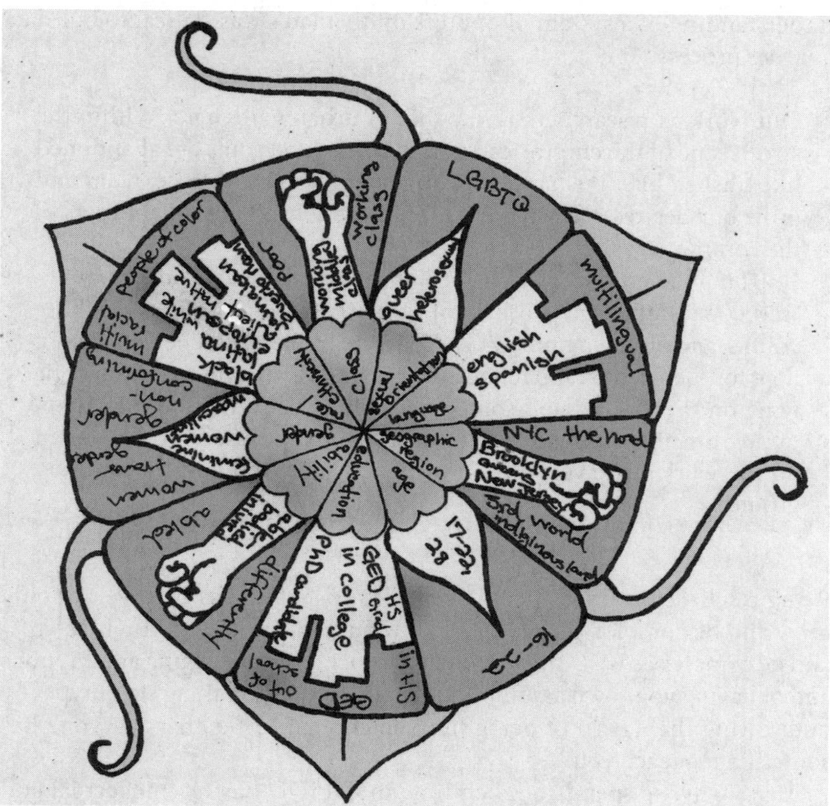

Figure 4.9 CREDD's version of the power flower, a departure from the original. The inner petals are similar to the original power flower, representing some of the facets of complex personhood. The middle petals represent our collectivity. The outer petals represent our people, our communities. Artwork by Sarah Quinter with help from Maria Bacha.

Crafting the power flower—Maria Bacha

It is through the creation of people-centered spaces that we challenge existing power structures. CREDD not only challenges oppressive power's business as usual, but also at the same time we build our own power, based on working with each other with love toward collective liberation.

On the first day of our retreat, Jamila, Q, and I facilitated the group in a power flower exercise (Arnold et al., 1991). We realized that we needed to break from the original power flower, which focuses on the individual and on power being outside of ourselves, to create something that represents both how we understand collectivity and how we understand power. The power flower exercise made explicit our collective power analysis and understanding of a system of oppression that later was critical to our data analysis process.

> Our work as researchers is like that of urban gardeners. Within the streetscape of the empire, our communities and souls are abandoned like trashed lots. We have come together to reclaim space, plant and grow our desires, and create a space for the health and happiness of the community.
>
> Doing the power flower helped us recognize that we didn't want to "serve" or "empower" youth. In my eyes, these terms undermine those youths' and our own humanities. To serve implies that a person cannot do it for themselves, and to me is represented by the image of someone lying on the ground and someone reaching over them to pick them up. We are not serving or empowering youth because as youth we can do this work ourselves. We can work with allies but only on common ground.
>
> **(Maria Bacha)**

Being a self-determined "people-centered space" means that we can only grow and be complex people if we allow our perceptions of others to grow and be complex as well. This is a lifelong process of challenging assumptions and of having your own assumptions challenged, of breaking stereotypes by outgrowing them, and of being humble enough to see that everyone has something to teach you.

That's why we spend so much time in CREDD having intellectual and political conversations around these issues. It's part of our work. Because CREDD is a "people-centered space," we need to stay conscious of how society's power structures play out in our interactions, so that we can challenge them and thus allow each other more room to grow. No matter how advanced CREDD gets in its work, we will always place a high priority on genuine, honest interpersonal relationships. Without these bonds and this striving to understand and respect one another, no strong foundation for change can exist.

> We have a lot of work to do. We need to keep a list inside our brains of all things we have left to finish, right beside where it says commitment.
>
> **(Jovanne)**

Concluding Statement

This chapter has described some of the powerful moments so far in our collective. It is our hope that by sharing these moments, the dynamics and praxes of PAR might be better understood, and that some of our readers might be encouraged to engage in participatory research.

We have been marked by our schooling—we have been told explicitly and implicitly that we are stupid, that we are wasted space, that we can't handle complex ideas. We have been oversimplified by small aspects of ourselves, caricatured as a bully, a troublemaker, as indecisive, scatterbrained. The moments we have described here all have been opportunities to remake our own names, to be seen in the ways we desire to be seen. The stumbles and scuffles that have happened along the way have stung like those old categories. In a heated debate, one of us might call another a bully, or intimate that another is scatterbrained. In the moment that old hurt comes back, and it makes it hard to see one another. It is sometimes what the rest of us do, or maybe a night to reflect and the apology that comes, that has taught us that the old hurts have less power here. We wouldn't take advantage of our intimate knowledge of one another. This too is a part of our work as researchers.

We think of PAR as being like Double Dutch, to do it you just have to jump right in, but we hope that by sharing some of the arcs of our ropes, those doing PAR might be comforted instead of bewildered when the rope makes a surprising turn.

We want to close this piece with an everyday moment because CREDD's work is both in the "ah hah!" moments and in the mundane: our nomadic workspace, our can of coconut milk, our jokes, our distractions, our photocopying, all to the hum of fluorescent lighting.

Deadline day—Melody Tuck

Today is a CREDD deadline for our survey and interview tapes and consent forms. It's not a meeting day, just a drop-off day and I am sitting here waiting for my sister to get out of her meeting, while one by one CREDD researchers are stopping off to turn in their surveys and interviews. Each one hands me a stack of papers, each filled with the stories of people on the streets who have gone through, broken away from, or are trying to survive the public school system. The researchers who hand me these fragments of life on ink-filled pages smile and wish me a good weekend.

I'm lucky to get to do this work because I get to research how education has failed its children, to reflect with my co-researchers, and to just think for once. Each chance I get to come be a part of CREDD makes my soul strong.

Dedication

This chapter is dedicated to students who have been pushed out and exiled, who are disappointed by schooling. We dedicate this chapter to all of those who have worked beside us to document the lived value of a "depleted credential," and the fantasies of the American Dream. Finally, we dedicate this chapter to our desires for public schools that are accessible, rigorous, honorable, and free.

Acknowledgments

Tyrone West, Shermel James, Rafael "Q" Quinde, Jodi-Ann Gayle, Crystal Orama, Luis Ravelo and Chris Alvarez. Sarah Zeller-Berkman, Maria Torre, Brett Stoudt, Beverly Tuck, John Tuck, Kevin Stasinski, Kym Libman, Rachel Castillo.

Notes

1 For the purposes of this project, youth participants lived in New York City and were current or former New York City public school students aged 16 to 22. The age cap coincided with those youth who were the oldest cohort (2003) affected by the New York state decision (2000) to make the Regent's exam the primary exit task in order to earn a high school diploma.

2 An additional product will be Eve's dissertation.

3 Red, yellow, green is a go-around tool that can be used in the middle or at the end of a discussion to check in with one another. Like a traffic light, each person says if they are green, or good to go, yellow, meaning they still have some questions or thinking to do, or red, meaning the conversation needs to stop and address a specific concern. By throwing Cs, we mean that to get a sense of the support of an idea, a researcher makes a "C" (for CREDD) symbol with her hands. Seeing this symbol, other researchers around the table show/throw their own Cs, or don't, signaling disagreement or confusion.

References

Adelman, C. (1997). Action research: The problem of participation. In *Participatory Action Research: International Contexts and Consequences*, ed. R. McTaggert. Albany: State University of New York Press.

Anyon, J. (2005). *Radical Possibilities.* New York: Routledge.

Anzaldúa, G. (2002). Speaking in tongues: a letter to 3rd world women writers. In *This Bridge Called My Back: Writings by Radical Women of Color*. Berkeley, CA: Third Woman Press.

Arnold, R., B. Burke, C. James, D. Martin, and B. Thomas (1991). *Educating for a Change.* Toronto, ON: Between the Lines Publishers.

Boal, A. (2002). *Games for Actors and Non-Actors*, 2nd edn. London: Routledge.

Carini, P. (2001). *Starting Strong: A Different Look at Children, School, and Standards.* New York: Teachers College Press.

Crenshaw, K. (2000). Playing race cards: Constructing a pro-active defense of affirmative action. *National Black Law Journal* 16: 196–214.

Deleuze, G., and F. Guattari (1987). *A Thousand Plateaus: Capitalism and Schizophrenia.* Minneapolis: University of Minnesota Press.

Deloria Jr., V. (1988). *Custer Died for Your Sins: An Indian Manifesto.* Norman: University of Oklahoma Press.

Ferreira, E., and J. Ferreira (1996). *Making Sense of the Media: A Handbook of Popular Education Techniques.* New York: Monthly Review Press.

Fine, M., and P. Rosenberg (1983). Dropping out of high school: The ideology of school and work. *Journal of Education* 165(3): 257.

Fine, M., E. Tuck, and S. Zeller-Berkman (2007). Do you believe in Geneva? Methods and ethics and the global/local nexus. In *Globalizing Cultural Studies: Ethnographic Interventions in*

Theory, Method, and Policy, ed. C. McCarthy, A. Durham, L. Engel, A. Filmer, M. Giardina, and M. Malagreca. New York: Peter Lang: 493–526.

Freire, P. (1997). *Pedagogy of the Oppressed*. New York: Continuum.

Grande, S. (2004). *Red Pedagogy: Native American Social and Political Thought*. Lanham, MD: Rowman and Littlefield.

Lefebvre, H. (1991). *The Production of Space*. Oxford: Blackwell.

Matsuda, M. (2002). Beyond and not beyond, Black and White: Deconstruction has a politics. In *Crossroads, Directions, and a New Critical Race Theory*, ed. F. Valdes, J. McCristal Culp and Al Harris. Philadelphia, PA: Temple University Press: 393–8.

Moraga, C. (1993). *The Last Generation: Prose and Poetry*. Boston: South End Press.

Morrison, T. (1970). *The Bluest Eye*. New York: Holt, Rinehart and Winston.

Perl, S. (1980). Understanding composing. *College Composition and Communication* 31(4): 363–9.

Smith, G. H. (2000). Protecting and respecting indigenous knowledge. In *Reclaiming Indigenous Voices and Vision*, ed. M. Battiste. Vancouver: University of British Columbia Press: 209–24.

Smith, L. T. (1999). *Decolonizing Methodologies: Research and Indigenous Peoples*. London: Zed Books.

Soja, E. W. (1996). *Thirdspace: Journeys to Los Angeles and Other Real-and-Imagined Places*. Malden, MA: Blackwell.

Tuck, E. in conversation with M. Fine (2007). Inner angles: A range of ethical responses to/with indigenous and decolonizing theories. In *Ethical Futures in Qualitative Research: Decolonizing the Politics of Knowledge*, ed. N. Denzin and M. Giardina. Walnut Creek, CA: Left Coast Press: 145–68.

Tuck, E. (in preparation). Trajectories for theory in the rhizome of researching back: Implications for educational policy. In *Using Theory in Empirical Research on Education*, ed. J. Anyon, M. Dumas, D. Linville, K. Nolan, M. Perez, E. Tuck, and J. Weis. New York: Routledge.

Response to Chapter 4

SANDY GRANDE

When I think of CREDD I imagine the loud and limber conversations I never had as a youth. I wasn't only "disappointed" in my education, I was angry. Even so, I didn't "desire" anything else—except dropping out—because I didn't know alternatives were possible. Instead, I remember an unfocused rage that sometimes traded places with apathy but was always aimed toward a school that wasn't as much "unwelcoming" as it was hostile in its profound banality and indifference. As such, I never thought about school or knowledge as being liberatory, and freedom was something unimaginable. I don't know that at the tender age of sixteen I could have made sense of transformation, knowledge, or empowerment in relationship to education—with or without participatory action research. Perhaps the only entryway—the one point of intersection between CREDD and my life—could have been the notion of collectivity. A collectivity makes me think of self-determination, of a group aligned in purpose but not necessarily means, and of the search for sovereignty. It makes me think of tribe.

Introduction

There are many strengths demonstrated in Tuck et al.'s chapter 4 of this volume, not the least of which is the young researchers themselves. The relatively mild metaphor of being "pushed" (as opposed to dropped or thrown out) belies their strength as well as the violence to which schools subject soul and psyche. It's worth noting that the women of CREDD have already defied the odds; it takes tremendous courage not to get lost in the cycle of cynicism and despair that accompanies the experience of being discarded. Though CREDD served as a life raft, the women clearly chose to climb aboard and take on the struggle of defining not only collective survival but also survivance.[1]

While CREDD's Gate-ways and Get-aways Project represents some of the best revolutionary praxis has to offer, I believe their most significant contribution to the field may come more from who they are and how they engage than from the research they conduct. Specifically, as a collectivity committed not only to their own self-determination but also to redefining the processes by which schools are governed, they engage a process by which they define the relationship between institutions—school, government, the state—and their own collectivity. Their struggle to define a collective identity brings to the fore important questions about group process, group formation, democracy, and governance as they intersect with issues of self-determination. In so doing, CREDD disrupts the fantasies of collectivity; shedding light on the struggle of building solidarity and complexities of defining self-determination as well as exposing the deep deficiencies of liberal democracy. While delineation of this tension may have been more of a by-product of their work, it is often within the unintended spaces of research that the most significant "findings" emerge.

Collectivity, Democracy, and Sovereignty

I have long advocated that the discourse of democracy must be fused with considerations of sovereignty, particularly indigenous sovereignty, if it is ever to realize its potential. Along these lines I have also argued that democracy must be rescued from the dictates of neo-liberalism and its attendant discourses, especially postmodernism. I maintain that these perilous relationships are what give rise to the fantasies of collectivity and not surprisingly, to tribe. Both are imagined as free and uniform spaces of cooperation, harmony, and docility or, in other words, as essentialized and exoticized spaces of domestication. While in the postmodern/postcolonial playing field of multiplicity, interconnectedness and interdependency, tribe and sovereignty are invited to sit alongside the state and democracy, within asymmetrical but always shifting relations of power, indigenous and other critical scholars have exposed the lies of the "postal" discourses, namely, the supposed disappearance of the hegemony of capital and the power of the nation-state, which despite the resounding death knoll, continues to rule the lives of native and other colonized peoples. For us, there is no postcolonial or postmodern, only the ongoing everyday struggle against colonization.[2] As such, sovereignty remains a struggle against empire—a political project that recognizes the danger inherent to any pedagogy that serves as a front for neoliberalism that equates equal access to the investor class with democracy.

As CREDD aptly illustrates, collectivities are complex and contradictory places, rooted in struggle, ground/land/locality, history, and shared knowledge. They are places where democracy is both contested and highly mediated, often serving as a homogenizing force. Indeed, one of the CREDD participants, Maria, interrogates, "... it is assumed that we should demand our victory from the state, corporation, or someone with power ... Who came up with this and how does it get continually imposed?" Though within a different context, indigenous peoples ask similar questions of the democratic process. Why must tribes petition the state for its "rights" and "recognition," legitimizing the conquests of colonialism? Shouldn't sovereignty call into question the legitimacy of the state itself and its formation upon stolen land and through policies such as the Doctrine of Discovery and genocide? Perhaps it is the state that should petition tribes for its recognition and right to exist. In a sense, both sets of questions beg a reconsideration of the relationship between democracy, self-determination, and sovereignty.

Therefore, my challenge to CREDD is to work beyond questions of (democratic) access—to education, to credentials, to employment—and toward issues of intellectual, spiritual, and political sovereignty. For example, in previous drafts, the authors of CREDD indicated that they began their process with "identifying themselves individually" and asking, "What is my experience? Where am I coming from? How have I been socialized?" Once reframed through the lens of sovereignty such questions become, Who are my people? What is their history? What knowledge/language do they bring to the table? What is the story of their land and the history of dispossession/colonization in their communities? What would it mean to build a pedagogical project around their story?

At the same time, I challenge CREDD to recognize the limitations of democratic structures, particularly the notions of shared responsibility and power. At times it seems that they struggle with equality (one of the root metaphors of democracy), running into tensions when someone is not taking their equal share of responsibility or assuming more of their share of power. In contrast, when framed through one of the root metaphors of sovereignty—balance—it becomes clear that power and responsibility can never be equally shared, nor should they. Elders have very different roles, responsibilities and levels of power in a community, as do men, women, and children, but when considered *as a whole*, they act in balance to each other.

Such understandings are inherent to *Red Pedagogy*—my own notion of pedagogical collectivity. Similar to CREDD, *Red Pedagogy* is an indigenous pedagogy that operates at the crossroads of Western theory and indigenous knowledge and asks that as we examine our own communities, policies, and practices, we take seriously the notion that to know ourselves as revolutionary agents is more than an act of understanding who we are. It is an act of reinventing ourselves, of validating our overlapping cultural identifications and relating them to the materiality of social life, power relations, and localities of place.

In the end, *Red Pedagogy* undertakes a deep examination of the colonialist project and its implications for *all* of us, understanding that at root is the quest for a reconciliation of the relationship between democracy (the rights of a nation) and sovereignty (the rights of a people). Specifically, it offers the following ways of thinking around and through the challenges facing American schools and education, in particular our need to define a pedagogy for decolonization:

- *Red Pedagogy* is primarily a pedagogical project wherein pedagogy is understood as inherently relational, political, cultural, spiritual, intellectual, and perhaps most importantly, place-based.
- *Red Pedagogy* is fundamentally rooted in indigenous knowledge and praxis. It is particularly interested in knowledge that furthers understanding and analyses of colonization.
- *Red Pedagogy* searches for ways it can both deepen and be deepened by engagement with critical and revolutionary theories and praxis.
- *Red Pedagogy* promotes an education for decolonization where the root metaphors of relationship, sovereignty, and balance provide the foundation.
- *Red Pedagogy* is a project that interrogates both democracy and indigenous sovereignty, working to define the relationship between them.
- *Red Pedagogy* actively cultivates a praxis of collective agency. That is, *Red Pedagogy* aims to build transcultural and transnational solidarities among indigenous peoples and others committed to reimagining a sovereign space free of imperialist, colonialist, and capitalist exploitation.
- *Red Pedagogy* is grounded in hope. This is, however, not the future-centered hope of the Western imagination, but rather a hope that lives in contingency with the past—one that trusts the beliefs and understandings of our ancestors, the power of traditional knowledge, and the possibilities of new understandings.

While the above principles serve as guides, it is important to understand that *Red Pedagogy* is not a methodology but rather a consciousness and way of being in/reading the world. As such, it is not something that can be "done" by teachers or "to" students, nor is it a technique that can be lifted, decontextualized, and applied to classrooms or any other setting. It is rather a way of thinking about knowledge and the processes of teaching and learning as it emerges within and through relationships—between and among students, teachers, communities, and places.

The participants of CREDD have already engaged the difficult work of building "genuine relationships" and of centering these "interpersonal relationships" as their foundation. But I believe their foundation(s) is much broader than the interpersonal and includes place, land, and community. Once framed in this way, interrogating the value of credentials toward survival may give way to questions of *survivance*—toward realizing their own sovereignty. That is, a restorative process that (re)asserts a people's "right to rebuild its demand to exist and present its gifts to the world . . . an adamant refusal to dissociate culture, identity, and power from the land" (Lyons, 2000).

Notes

1 Gerald Vizenor (1993) defines survivance as the power to live out "active presences and survivances rather than an illusionary democracy."

2 For the purposes of this chapter, colonization is defined as a multidimensional force underwritten by Christian fundamentalism, defined by white supremacy, and fueled by global capitalism (Grande, 2004).

References

Grande, Sandy (2004). *Red Pedagogy: Native American Social and Political Thought*. Lanham, MD: Rowman and Littlefield.

Lyons, S. R. (2000). Rhetorical sovereignty: What do American Indians want from writing? *College, Composition and Communication* 51(3) (February): 447–68.

Vizenor, Gerald (1993). The ruins and representation. *American Indian Quarterly* 17: 1–7.

CHAPTER 5

Different Eyes/Open Eyes

Community-Based Participatory Action Research

CAITLIN CAHILL, INDRA RIOS-MOORE, AND TIFFANY THREATTS

> Knowledge truly is power. Historically, the winner of the war has determined the telling of its own history and that of the loser. Those of us that have been living under the thumb of oppression have mainly suffered from a lack of information, a lack of access, and a lack of inspiration; we are not taught to ask "Why?"—we are not allowed to ask the questions that lead to a stronger mind. Participatory action research is one of the most potent weapons against oppression, it offers an opportunity to gain both skills and knowledge, to conduct an investigation that roots out both the questions and the answers that expose injustice. In the process of simply learning how to ask questions, a researcher is able to find themselves at the heart of those questions.
>
> **(Annissa, Fed Up Honey researcher)**

In this chapter, we detail a process that was profoundly personal, sometimes painful, and, in the end, definitively political. None of us knew quite what we were getting into when we signed on the dotted line and decided to be part of this project; we didn't know where our journey would take us. With the benefit of hindsight, we offer a retrospective reflection upon a community-based participatory action research (PAR) project in which we critically investigated our everyday lives in our neighborhood, the Lower East Side of New York City. Along the way we not only learned how to do research, but also we learned a lot about ourselves and our community. The research process engaged us in asking "why?" as Annissa suggests above; in asking questions that lead to a critical perspective—in effect questioning our surroundings and in thinking deeply about what we cared about, what we knew, and what we didn't know. Collectively we shared our desires and what got in the way of us accomplishing our dreams. We argued, laughed, and compared our experiences in our neighborhood and our perspectives on the world. In this chapter, we hope to do the same, to share the struggles and joys of doing participatory action research, and its potential for "opening eyes," as Ruby, one of the researchers, explains:

> I just see with different eyes now. Open eyes . . . like people always used to say Ruby open your eyes, open your eyes. But you never open your eyes. But then like literally your eyes are open; but your eyes are not open. And I just think that just recently I've been opening my eyes.

Here we discuss participatory action research as a process for personal and social transformation; in other words, as a process of "opening" our own eyes and seeing the world through "different eyes," coupled with a desire to open others' eyes. We propose the metaphor of opening eyes because our collective participatory process pushed us to adopt a more critical perspective on our everyday lives. This was not an easy process for any of us, but we think it is completely necessary if we are going to participate in making positive changes in our selves and our communities. The metaphor of opening eyes is also relevant to the goals of our project "Makes Me Mad: Stereotypes of young urban women of color" to "reverse the gaze," speak back to problematic misrepresentations, and untangle the relationship between stereotypes and the gentrification/disinvestment of our neighborhood.

Our discussion will touch upon three "openings." First, we discuss our experience doing community-based participatory research that provided an opportunity for us to look closely at our neighborhood, to question our surroundings (that we often take for granted), and to "see" how social/economic/political issues take shape in our neighborhood. Because how we understand ourselves is intimately bound with where we come from, opening eyes is about making sense of our everyday life experiences at school, in our neighborhood, etc. and drawing connections between our personal experiences and global economic and political processes. Our place-based research is grounded in radical and feminist geography, urban scholarship concerned with social change, activism and grassroots organizing. An investigation of place makes visible the sometimes invisible social issues that we grapple with every day. The focus of our project is upon the area of the Lower East Side, also known as "Loisaida," reflecting the Puerto Rican/Nuyorican community who live(s/d) there. Through our research, we came to "see" the profound disinvestment and simultaneous gentrifica-

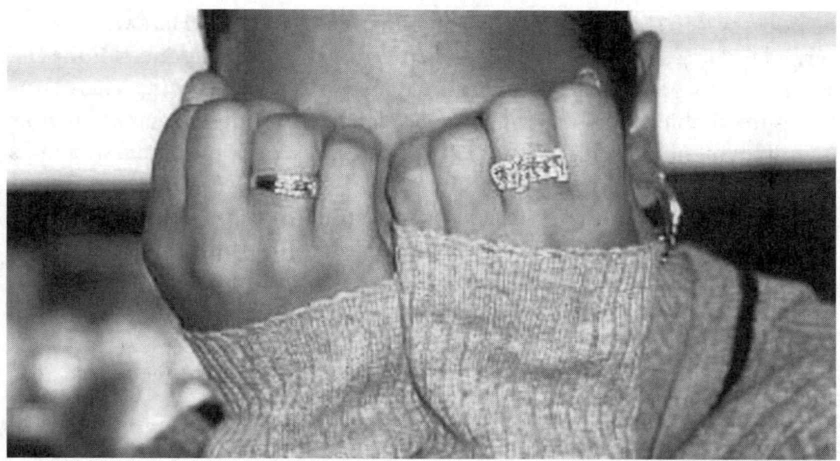

Figure 5.1 Fed Up Honey (photo credit: www.fed-up-honeys.org).

tion of our neighborhood, and the disappearance of "our" community, "our" culture, and "our" homes (Mele, 2000; Muñiz, 1998).

Digging deeper, we traced the connections between "at risk" stereotypes of young women of color as a "burden to society" or "teen moms" and the "geography of inequality" that characterizes the new, hip, trendy, whiter, Lower East Side (Lipman, 2002). Our bodies line the frontier of gentrification (Smith, 1996) and are "another front in the struggle for the direction of globalization. The stakes are high" (Lipman, 2002: 409). With a new critical consciousness, we saw our world with different eyes, as we understood the ways stereotypes of risk pathologize and target us, and justify our exclusion from the community in which we grew up, in the name of "civilizing" the neighborhood (Lipman, 2003). As we discuss later, in response we developed research products to "speak back" and intervene in the too-smooth commodified processes of gentrification, including a sticker campaign (Figure 5.7), our website, and our report.

The second opening speaks to how doing this research changed the way we look at ourselves. As our self-image was central to our inquiry, we reflected upon our personal and collective identifications, holding up a mirror and, in the words of Freire, "coming to terms with the roots of your oppression as you come into your subjecthood" (Freire, 1997[1970]: 31). In so doing, our research process awakened our critical consciousness and was personally transformative, as we shifted our understanding of ourselves and our relationship to our world. Third, we want to also invoke "vision" in terms of conjuring up a sense of possibility for a different future, a dream of quality public education, affordable housing, racial equity, and democracy—in short, vision as a catalyst for change/action. Here we are concerned with opening others' eyes and engaging the public in questioning the status quo. Is gentrification—and the displacement of working-class families—inevitable? Why are inequitable racialized group outcomes such as unemployment rates, high-school dropout figures, or home ownership rates accepted as natural (Aspen Institute, 2004)? Why are we stereotyped? And how do we also use these stereotypes to understand ourselves? Opening eyes is thus a project of poking holes in the accepted "truths," the hegemonic discourses that normalize racial disadvantages and reinforce inequalities. In this chapter, we describe our personal journey—our "praxis"—an inside perspective on the processes of doing participatory action research and its relevance for "education as a practice of freedom" (Breitbart and Kepes, 2007; Cammarota, 2007; Cammarota and Romero, 2006; Fine et al., 2004; Fine et al., 2007; Freire, 1997[1970]; Ginwright et al., 2006; Torre and Fine, 2006a; Youth Speak Out Coalition and K. Zimmerman, 2006).

These "openings" speak to the potential of participatory action research as a pedagogy of citizenship, embracing all of the loaded contradictory and political implications attached to "citizenship." We engage the term citizenship optimistically, in the sense of both feeling included and "at home," not defined by arbitrary geographic boundaries. Citizenship = being recognized as a decision maker and as an agent of change. To be counted. We propose a pedagogy of citizenship as a critical process for engaging the public, across generations, in community governance and change. Building upon longstanding traditions of asset-based community development (Kretzmann and McKnight, 1996), our approach to research is founded upon an assumption of capacity and agency. We harken back and aspire to Septima Clark's "citizenship schools," the literacy/education initiative that became a cornerstone of the Civil Rights Movement by enabling disenfranchised Southern Blacks to participate in politics. Similarly, we think participatory action research offers a process for civic engagement and reflects the promises of democracy (Torre and Fine, 2006b). By placing value upon collaboration, deliberative process, and representation, PAR offers an alternative paradigm to the neo-liberal shift in governance away from democratic decision making, the shrinking public sphere, and the prevailing emphasis upon personal accountability and responsibility (Cahill, 2007a). Instead, PAR engages the transformative potential of collective responsibility to contribute to social change. What's more, "people's ability to exercise their free agency and choose in an informed and participatory way," as political and economic theorist Amartya Sen (2004: 55) reminds us, is a "necessary condition for democracy" (Torre and Fine, 2006b: 268). In this way, PAR might be understood as a sort of "free space" for processing social inequities and reflecting critically upon the contradictions of our everyday lives (Weis and Fine, 2000), and also a process for ""practicing" citizenship.

The political potential of PAR lies in its intentional inclusion of excluded perspectives in the development of new knowledge. Inspired by the insight of Dr. Martin Luther King "that freeing black people from the injustices that circumscribe their lives, America will be freeing itself as well" (Guinier and Torres, 2002: 293), Lani Guinier and Gerald Torres argue that the experiences of marginalized people of color can be the basis for social transformation. We agree. We hope that our documentation of the pain young women of color experience when negotiating and challenging stereotypes of risk will shed light on what's wrong with our society and point toward the possibility of social change.

As a practice of decolonization, PAR is committed to "re-membering" the excluded (bodies, history, knowledge, etc.) and interrogating privilege and power (Fine and Torre, 2004). In our project, this translated into a heightened consciousness with regard to our positionality within an intersectional framework and an articulation of our social locations and relationships to privilege (Crenshaw, 1995). As a multi-ethnic/racial collective of young women, aged 16–22, of Puerto Rican, Dominican, African-American, and Chinese backgrounds, facilitated by a white woman, we found it necessary to attend to our differences and acknowledge our standpoints; in other words clarifying where we were coming from. As Omi and Winant (1994) argue, opposing racism requires that we notice race, not ignore it. Along these lines, in our project, we made an explicit decision to address issues of white privilege and everyday racism, foregrounding the questions and concerns of young women of color whose voices are too often missing in public/academic discourse (even while their bodies remain hypervisible in the public sphere). This is a conscious engagement of "working the hyphen" (Fine, 1994), where we have decided to flip the privileges usually associated with whiteness and instead design a research project that is "by" and "for" young women of color.

In our discussion, we move between theory and practice, sometimes shifting abruptly between voices. Despite our differences, most of the time we have decided to write collectively as a strategic "we," placing emphasis upon our collective "message" and upon our shared experience as young women of color. But at times we shift to our personal voices articulating our multiple positionalities and distinct points of view. This is reflective of our process that was rich with dissent and negotiation, while our shared perspective is a political stance speaking to the power of our collaboration.

The outline of the project that follows offers a broad overview of what was a deep, messy, and intense experience that has evolved over time. To begin, we will introduce broad outlines of the project and how we got started, next we will look closely at our participatory project through "the openings," along the way touching upon the underlying pedagogical principles—what we think of as the "necessary conditions" for community-based participatory action research: building a community of researchers and collective ownership over the process; facilitation; a safe space for dissent; an emphasis upon personal experience; a commitment to exploring the contradictions of everyday life; an engagement with issues of power; and an explicit consideration of the audiences and purposes of research.

How We Got Started

> We entered the room where we would be conducting our research, the room where we would be spending all our time, and I felt a sudden case of claustrophobia kick in. There was barely enough floor space for all of us to stand at the same time . . . The buzzing of the lights above was louder than our breathing. I found it to be funny yet terrifying, what if my stomach growled; as it has the habit of doing for no apparent reason at all except to humiliate me.
>
> **(Janderie, Fed Up Honey)**

The research project "Makes Me Mad: Stereotypes of young urban womyn of color" was developed starting in summer 2002. We represent three of a team of seven who worked together on the project. Our study considered the relationship between the lack of resources in our community, the Lower East Side neighborhood of New York City, and mischaracterizations of young women. When we first began our project, we did not know what we were going to research. The area of investigation was open as the study was broadly defined as "the everyday lives of young women in the city." We collectively determined the focus of the project after working together for several weeks, and after doing preliminary research on our neighborhood and our own everyday experiences. As mentioned before, the project is for and by young urban women of color and is reflective of our own concerns and the issues that personally affected us. We represent a diverse collection of personalities and backgrounds; the fact that we all felt so passionately about this topic is a testament to its likely importance to all young women affected by stereotypes that are pervasive in popular culture and the self-image issues that stem from them. This is a snapshot of our collaborative process that we think gives a sense of where we started and the evolution of our project. Along the way we share our different perspectives on what it was like to be involved in this project, our process, the challenges we faced, and the impacts of our research. To begin, Caitlin will discuss the background on the project. Then, together we—Indra, Tiffany, and Caitlin—reflect upon our processes of becoming a research collective. Next, we discuss the "Makes Me Mad" project in detail, our personal process of opening and seeing our world with different eyes, and our understanding of participatory action research as a pedagogy of citizenship.

The original intention of the research was to study and understand the experiences of young women growing up in the city. Caitlin initiated the project as part of her doctoral research at the City University of New York (CUNY). While much of the research on urban youth focuses upon young men, who are closely surveilled in urban public spaces and social research, there was very little research on young women's experiences growing up in the city. The studies that do focus on women in the city often foreground issues of fear (Madriz, 1997; Pain, 1991), and the studies on "young *urban* women" (code: Black and Latina teenagers) focus upon their bodies—teenage pregnancy and promiscuity (Harris, 2004; Leadbeater and Way, 1996; Murry, 1996; Tolman, 1996). Situating our interpretations and questions at the center of the research was a conscious political and theoretical undertaking. What are young women's concerns? Questions? How are these different from the prevailing scholarship? In fact, there is very little, if any, research from a young woman's perspective in the literature.

> Urban environments are typically characterized and described using aggressive terms, such as "loud," "violent," "dark," and "ghetto," and more often than not little attention is paid to the womyn who inhabit the city, influencing the very fiber of urban environments as mothers, grandmothers, daughters, sisters, wives, and granddaughters. This project was specifically designed to emphasize the everyday lives of young womyn to make the voice that is so often ignored the central perspective through which our community, the Lower East Side, is viewed.
>
> **(Fed Up Honeys, Rios-Moore et al., 2004)**

Young women aged 16–22 who lived in the Lower East Side neighborhood were invited to apply to be part of the project and paid a stipend for their work which initially involved a four-week commitment. We met at CUNY and at various sites on the Lower East Side. A diverse group of women reflecting the neighborhood demographics formed the research team, later self-identified as the "Fed Up Honeys":

> We are Chinese, Puerto Rican, African-American, Dominican, and Black-Latina. As diverse as we are, personalities included, we seemed to click instantly and our conversations flowed. We fed off each other's ideas and we built on them as well. We spoke of personal experiences, shared our writings and discussed world issues we felt were impacting us.

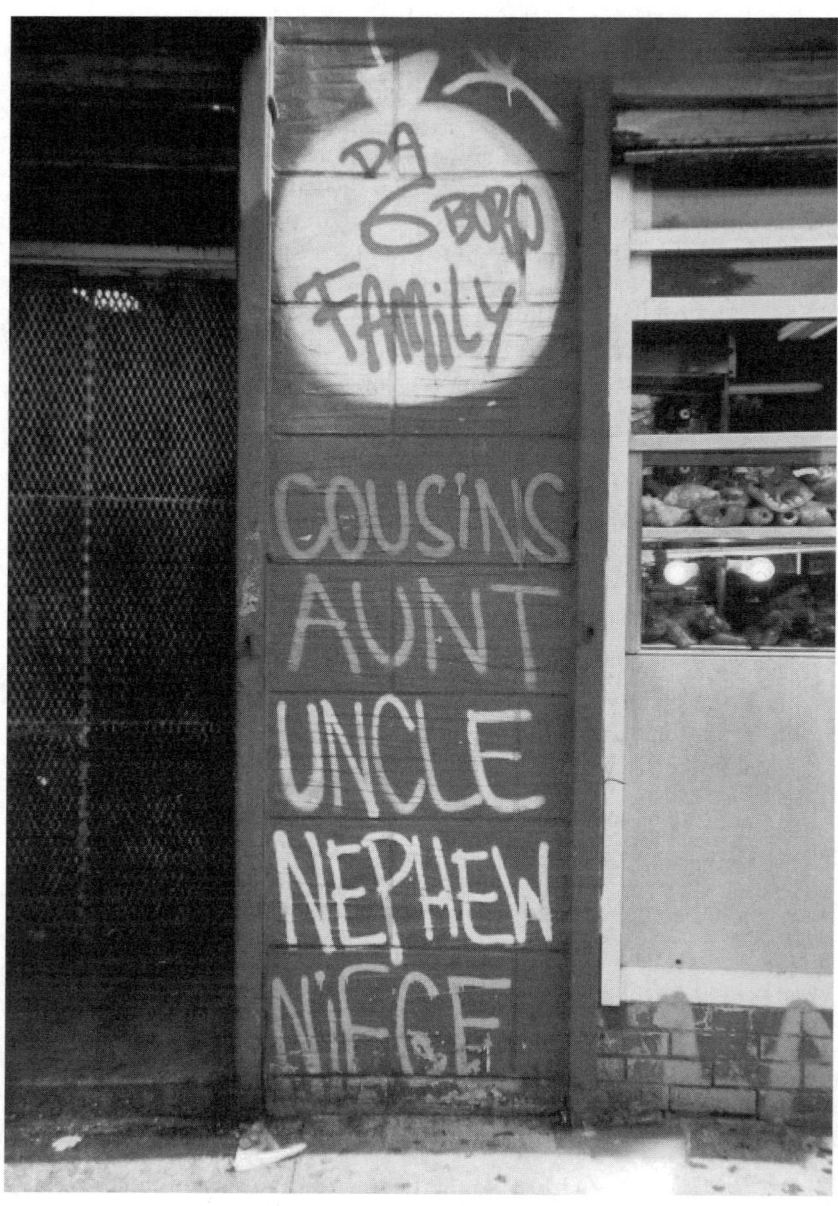

Figure 5.2 Da 6th Boro Family (photo credit: Indra Rios-Moore).

The differences between us were especially striking to all involved, as Indra (Fed Up Honey) articulates:

> We're almost like a boy band with members that meet pre-prescribed personality types that are different enough for any teenage girl to have a favorite. Jiang Na is quiet and shy with an undercover bravery of spirit; Shamara is loud and jovial but truly a sensitive person; Jennifer is also loud but is a story teller who takes guff from no one and is not a big fan of school but is an excellent business woman; Tiffany is quiet and reserves judgments but when she decides to talk she lets out pearls of true wisdom; Erica is all tough on the outside but is really very sweet on the inside with a propensity for crying; Caitlin is the kind soul that keeps us all on track and at the same time makes sure that we feel free enough to let loose—she's the glue; and I'm the crazy one, I let loose with random useless facts, make weird sounds for no good reason that anyone can discern, and am the anti-establishment representative of the group . . . All of us together make up "Fed-Up-Honeys," very different womyn with different opinions, and, though it takes time to get on the same page, when we get there we always have very interesting, fresh, new, and unique ideas to share and use.
>
> **(Cahill, 2004: 234)**

It was exciting to relate to each other across differences and to learn about new ways of seeing the world. Even though we all lived in the Lower East Side neighborhood, we lived in very different communities. We identified with multiple various ethnic and racial communities, subcultures such as hip hop culture, and geographical communities defined by their block or within particular boundaries.

Becoming a Research Collective

The way the project started set the tone for our work together. It is difficult to pull apart the pieces that made us identify our project as successful, but certainly our interpersonal interactions were critical to our feeling good about the project. Despite our cultural differences and our diverse views of the world and our environment, we just clicked. An unpredicted connection was made and soon after came a natural communication. You can't plan for something like this to happen, it just has to happen, as you do not know who will be part of the project and what they will bring to it. However, critical to this was an open and comfortable atmosphere. Early on Caitlin made us realize that we are all equal partners and our collaborative project really would integrate all of our ideas. This atmosphere of democracy and community started us out with camaraderie and respect and became a very important part of our research approach.

Our project was structured by the principles of PAR, which starts with "the understanding that people—especially those who have experienced historic oppression—hold deep knowledge about their lives and experiences, and should help shape the questions, [and] frame the interpretations" of research (Torre and Fine, 2006a).

PAR is based upon a belief in the power of "knowledge produced in collaboration and action" (Fine et al., 2003). Placing emphasis upon the democratization and redistribution of power within the research process, PAR builds participants' capacity to analyze and transform their own lives and is committed to "giving back" to community collaborators (Breitbart, 2003; Cahill, 2007b; Fine et al., 2003; Hart, 1997; Pain, 2004; Torre, 2005). PAR is not really about a choice of methods or tools for participation—we did not follow a recipe for participation—but instead it is about taking seriously the agency and decision-making capacity of all involved. We were *all* involved in *all* stages of the research process: problem identification, data collection, data analysis, and the development of research presentations.

While we knew we would be involved in every aspect of developing and creating a research project, for many of us research was not something we were totally comfortable with, and a PAR approach seemed entirely different from what we normally associated with research, as Indra and Tiffany discuss:

Tiffany: I never thought of research as a tool to talk back to the community. I always thought of it as analyzing (sometimes over-analyzing) history. Like with researching past events—something we would get in school or looking up a lot of information on a certain subject. I also thought of research being used like statistics, making observations about things and only using them for big companies or businesses.

Indra: Even though I've had past experience with research, it's still been hard for me to grasp the concept that research can be a tool for changing society, never mind being able to embrace it as a powerful tool for womyn of color in particular. For a number of reasons, namely the fact that education alone is connoted with negative feelings and failure for communities of color, research is not understood fully and used to its full merit by communities of color. Because of this relationship or rather lacking relationship with education and research, I think we didn't understand the potential impact of our work at first.

From the beginning, Caitlin made it clear that our experiences and perspectives would guide the project: "What matters to YOU?" she asked us, "what are your concerns about your community?" We interpreted the openness of the research agenda as a lack of structure, which was an unusual experience for most of us and very different from our experiences at school:

Indra: The fact that we had a very loose idea of what we were there to do gave us an opportunity to make the space our own and to express our thoughts and ideas more freely . . .

Tiffany: The unstructuredness of the project was great for me. I like not having barriers or a strict schedule of work to follow. It gave us time to get to know everyone and talk about what we wanted to do. Also it made me feel like the project was actually ours.

Indra: Because we were at CUNY, clearly an educational setting, there was potential for us to feel intimidated or feel that there were going to be specific expectations of us, but because we only knew we were going to be there to do some level of discussion and because our activities were loose enough to be group directed they resulted in shared thoughts and ideas that were particularly unique to us as a group.

Tiffany: If it was more structured it would have felt like school to me, and I know Caitlin was worried about coming off as a teacher but she wasn't. She gave us the opportunity to speak our minds about every- and anything even if it was racial . . . For me the unstructuredness helped me to develop ideas on what to do and made it easier to work knowing there were no barriers. The most important thing for me to be able to do this work was it not feeling like school.

(Cahill, 2004: 237–8)

In fact, while the project was undefined, it was not unstructured. But because it was collaborative it could not be planned in advance; instead our research evolved in a slightly messy and organic way. There was room for the unexpected to occur. Again this was a different way of working that was unsettling at first for some who were used to following directions, filling in scantrons, and who were not sure how to contribute to a very open process. The fact that we felt free and were encouraged to speak our minds on everything—including issues of race—was critical. In many of our experiences, White teachers shut down conversations involving race, but here this became our focus—looking at "at risk" stereotypes of young women of color—of us! This is an issue we were all concerned with and that we confronted every day; could this also be a worthwhile research focus?

Learning through Doing

Building a community of researchers involves paying attention both to the processes of collaboration and to the development of research proficiency among all participants (Lykes, 2001; Torre et al., 2001). The development of research skills is significant because it serves to "even the playing field." On our research team, some had more research experience than others; we helped each other and learned from each other. In addition, learning how to do research gave us a new vocabulary and tools for understanding the issues in our community.

We learned how to do research through *doing it*—in the process of researching our own everyday lives and community. In the beginning of our work together, we tried out different research methods, which included mental maps, behavior mapping, taking field notes, photography, a guided tour of places of significance in the Lower East Side neighborhood, and daily focus groups/brainstorming sessions. Through this preliminary research process we gathered a lot of data about ourselves and our community, which we then analyzed collectively, making sense of our shared experiences and where we differed. Our analysis fed into the development of our research questions and became the basis for our study. In this way our research followed a Freirian model as our process started with the critical reflection upon the conditions of our own everyday lives. Using what Freire identified as a "problem posing approach," we collectively interrogated our personal experiences and identified issues that were important to us. As Freire states (1997: 64, italics in original): "In problem-posing education, people develop their power to perceive critically *the way they exist* in the world *with which* and in which they find themselves; they come to see the world not as a static reality, but as a reality in process, in transformation." Opening our eyes and seeing the world—and ourselves—with different eyes is akin to what Freire identified as *conscientização* (1997 [1970]), a process of awakening our critical consciousness. As "subjects, not objects" (1997 [1970]: 49), we practiced a pedagogy of citizenship, transforming ourselves as we reaffirmed our capacity as agents of change (Ginwright and James, 2002).

Opening #1: Researching Our Home Community

Doing research on one's own life is personally revelatory and potentially upsetting. To carefully examine our everyday experiences, to take stock in our neighborhood know-how, and to study the familiar can be both thrilling and disturbing. In our research, we focused upon what we shared—our community. Studying the changes in our neighborhood, the Lower East Side of New York City, forced us to "see" and question how economic, political, and social disparities took shape in the everyday life of our community.

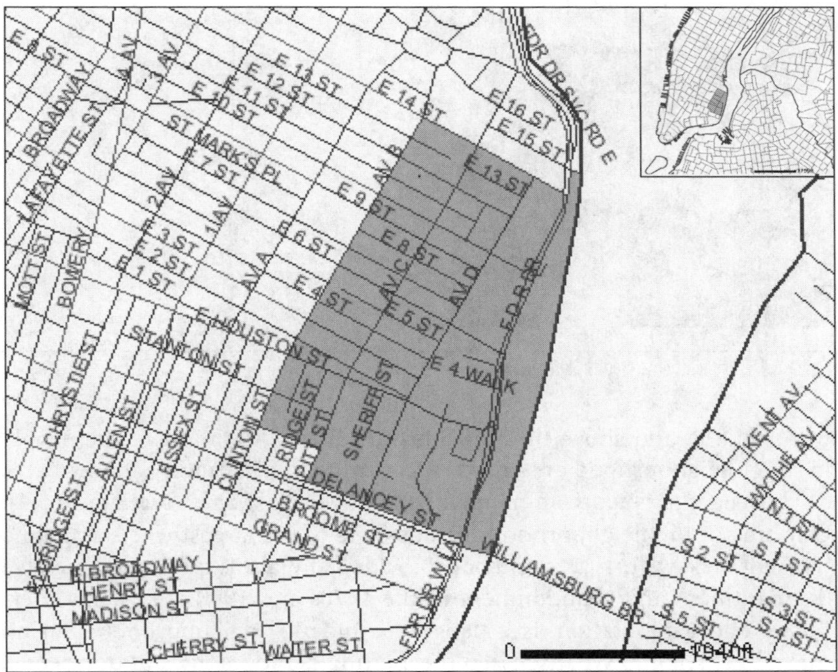

Figure 5.3 Map of Lower East Side study area.

We did a day-long "field trip" through our neighborhood that created an opportunity for us to look at our surroundings with new eyes—as researchers—analyzing and documenting block by block the environment we usually took for granted. For some of us who usually stayed in our small corner of the neighborhood it was really eye opening to walk around and see how much our community has changed. And it was especially interesting to hear about and compare experiences with the others.

We discussed the lack of support and places to go for young people. As one researcher described, "I am an interesting young woman who bores herself to delirium. Because there's nothing to do. I'm bored . . . It's like that I'm interesting is going to waste because I have nothing to do with it." We also talked about the obvious discrepancies we noticed in the community, for example, the juxtaposition between the fancy new wine bar across the street from a disinvested public elementary school, and the line of poor Black and Latino elderly waiting to get breakfast from the soup kitchen down the block from the upscale design shop. What was happening to our neighborhood? "Lowa" or "Da 6th Boro" was definitely not what it used to be. Our neighborhood/study site (see Figure 5.3) is below 14th Street, east

Figure 5.4 Loisaida (photo credit: Caitlin Cahill).

of Avenue B, and above the Williamsburg Bridge. As most of the people in "our" neighborhood are Puerto Rican and Dominican, it is known also as "Loisaida," a Nuyorican name for the Lower East Side (see Figure 5.4). Our area of the neighborhood includes one of the largest tracts of public housing in New York City, and not coincidentally, also experienced massive disinvestment and abandonment in the 1970s and 1980s. "Loisaida" definitely had a reputation as a dangerous "ghetto" neighborhood. But all this was changing. We discussed the shifting demographics of our neighborhood, which over the course of our lifetimes (the Fed Up Honeys were all born after 1980) had become both whiter and wealthier, and how this related to the gentrification of our neighborhood. Actually, some of us were not familiar with the term gentrification, and learning this new word and "naming" our experience was really important, as articulated by Janderie:

> I have become more aware of the happenings in my environment and the world . . . While engaged in a deep discussion about what has become of the Lower East Side of our childhood we spoke of how little boutiques and trendy bars were popping up all over the place of the small businesses that used to be owned by locals. I shared that since this had been happening, the building where I lived had come under new management and every few months my mother was forced to pay a higher rent. Suddenly I hear one of the girls say the word gentrification. I had never heard the word before in my life, so naturally I asked "what's that mean?" She explains to me that these yuppie ass, money having, culture seeking, white people are buying us poor people out of our neighborhood in part because they want a taste of our culture-rich environment, and the more of them who came in, the more of us are forced to leave because we can longer afford to live here. Oh! My! God! That's what was happening to me!

Placing gentrification in the larger context of the cycle of global economic restructuring and making sense of the repercussions for our families and our community was really upsetting. Most of us understood the cycle of gentrification–disinvestment as part of a broader experience of racial discrimination and social inequality that includes the violence of poverty, poor-quality education, the lack of good jobs, and the threat of displacement. Through our research we began to see what Pauline Lipman describes as the "geography of inequality" in our neighborhood, characterized by a highly stratified labor force, new forms of racialization, and "a constellation of policies that regulate and control African-American and Latino youth, in particular, and sort and discipline them for differentiated roles in the economy and the city" (Lipman, 2003: 332).

While making sense of this was painful, our research project provided a way for us to engage and use this new knowledge productively rather than be demoralized by it (hooks, 1995). Our study of our neighborhood enabled us to understand and "see" in concrete terms the impact of sociopolitical forces on our everyday lives:

> The trendy bars, the raised rent . . . the white people! There weren't this many white people in the ghetto before, then again it's starting to look less like a ghetto and more like confusion. Cute Italian and Japanese restaurants in one corner and a broke-down project building on the next. Every day I walked down the same three blocks and I found something else that hadn't been there before, like the annoying little boutique that sold hand-crafted figurines. And even more annoying was the tea shop that seemed to never have a customer inside. All I could think to myself was "can't wait to see how my neighborhood looks in ten years."

Because we had a stake in our neighborhood, we were motivated to learn more and to move forward with our research. We started a list of opportunities and issues in the neighborhood that we would return to when we developed our research questions. For example, some of the opportunities we identified included: diversity, sense of safety, knowing people, pride, tolerance, a lot of hardworking people, knowing your neighbors. Issues and problems we identified included (among others): nothing to do, outsiders taking over, garbage, expensive unaffordable housing, and misperceptions of the people who live here.

In the course of doing research on our neighborhood, we read a report produced by a local nonprofit organization that features a hypothetical profile of a young womyn that fed into all the common negative stereotypes that are prevalent in the media and in society. An example: Taniesha, whose single mother is a high school dropout on welfare, raising her and her two brothers. Taniesha, who has little supervision, drops out of high school herself, shoplifts, and by the age of 16 finds herself with a police record, pregnant, and with HIV. In other words, Taniesha was a super stereotype, an exaggerated representation of what would happen to a young woman unless this organization stepped in to put her on the path of productivity. As one researcher said, "They are saying basically that we are all these things unless we had their help, their goodwill, to save us." What a betrayal! We were enraged by the misrepresentations perpetuated as an oversimplified approach to fundraising buying into culture-of-poverty explanations to justify their existence.

We decided collectively to develop a "response" research project to speak back to stereotypes that oversimplify, reduce, and limit us. We realized that we, as the target audience for preventive and "at-risk" programming, could give a unique perspective on what we feel are our needs by refuting stereotypes directed at young urban womyn of color, identifying how these stereotypes impact us, and drawing connections between the relationship, lack of resources (or disinvestment), and misrepresentations of young womyn of color.

Reading the stereotype-saturated report was a turning point for the Fed Up Honeys because it forced us to confront what Freire calls the "the roots of their oppression," the process through which one perceives social, political, and economic contradictions of one's daily existence. In so doing, we "awakened our critical consciousness." As Annissa, one of the researchers reflects:

> I was so totally saturated by stereotypes of women of color. So saturated that I had incredibly short-sighted assumptions about the other young womyn that I was going to be writing and learning with as part of this project . . . I spent my whole childhood and adolescence isolating myself from my peers because my mother thought—and eventually I thought—that was the best way to keep myself safe from crime, pregnancy, and ignorance. I saw my own people as ignorant—I just didn't really know why I saw them as ignorant. After 22 years of tricking myself into believing that I was living above the fray, through PAR I was able to find my own ignorance and learn more about how our community arrived at its current state . . .

Our own process revealed not only how young women of color are perceived by society, but also the interrelated and complex ways in which young women identify themselves. This informed one of our research questions:

1 How do stereotypes inform the way you explain/characterize/understand yourself? your understanding of your peers? your community?

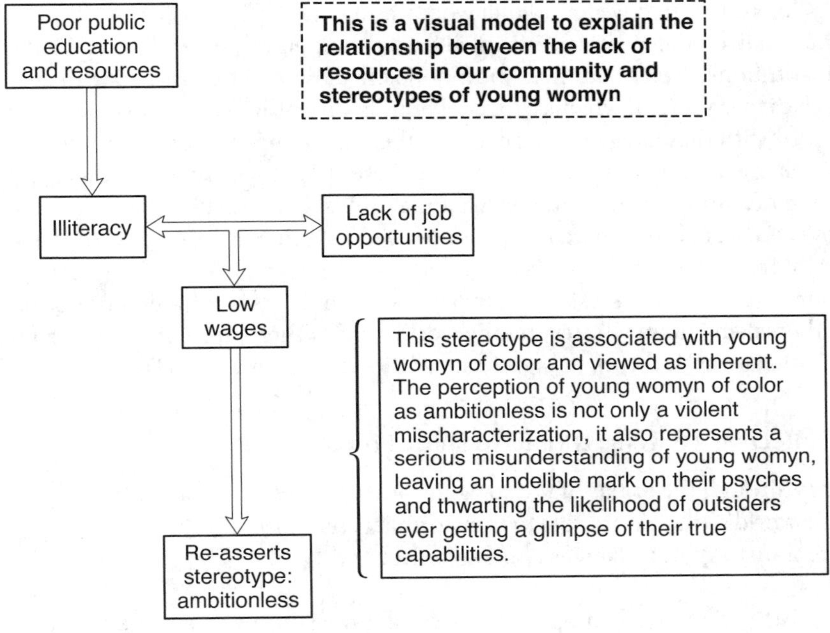

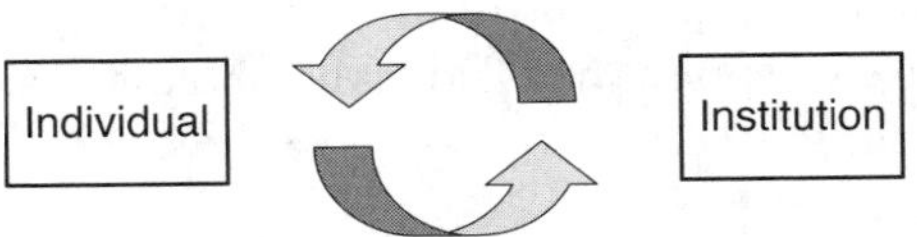

Figure 5.5 Our model (Rios-Moore et al., 2004).

Our study of neighborhood change and the disinvestment and gentrification of our community informed our second set of research questions:

2 What is the relationship between the lack of resources (for example, education) and the stereotypes of young urban women of color? In what ways does stereotyping affect young women's well-being?

Figure 5.5 presents a model from our report (Rios-Moore et al., 2004) that shows how the stereotype of young women of color as "uneducated" or "lacking ambition" is produced within a deficient public education system.

In our research we found that what was the most disturbing was when we internalized the stereotypes and when we took on responsibility for failing institutions, such as our neighborhood zoned high school, and blamed ourselves for failure. If what is expected of us is very little and we are constantly faced with these negative stereotypes, there is a danger that we will become exactly what they want us to become. These stereotypes keep us down, and then our mind set is "If that is what they think I am, that is what I'm going to be." Part of our research process involved breaking down how the cycle of reinforcing stereotypes leads to the ways we begin to explain and understand ourselves. This feeds a struggle that has some of us resisting stereotypes and others using them to interpret the world around them. It is this fierce struggle that gives our work its significance (Rios-Moore et al., 2004).

Collective Analysis: Rituals to Share Power

It is through the praxis of the struggle—through reflection and action upon the world—that we are able to transform it (Freire, 1997 [1970]). In so doing we transform ourselves, as Annissa reflects:

> By the end of our time together during the summer we came to the agreement that we wanted to provoke others into rethinking the standard negative stereotypes of young urban womyn of color that they encountered. But before we could even realize that that was what we wanted to do we had to (through angry eruptions, upset, and discussions) realize that we were living under the veil of those stereotypes ourselves. We had to touch upon some of those emotions that those oppressively heavy misconceptions had laid on us, and that was a difficult and sometimes painful process.

To face stereotypes as a collective was to come to terms with our experiences of everyday racism. This was a painful, emotionally loaded process. But as hooks (1995) argues, in order for rage to not consume us it must be engaged and used constructively, and it is this engagement that leads to social transformation. But, how do you move from the pain and personal struggle to develop a coherent analysis (Cahill, 2004)? And, keeping in mind the critique that participatory work often prioritizes consensus (Kothari, 2001), a significant challenge then is to create a safe space for sharing different perspectives, where everyone's point of view is taken seriously, even if disagreed with. This is especially important when the area of inquiry is so personal and close to home.

Indra describes our negotiated process:

> The initial process of choosing a research question/focus was difficult because it required us to have really long and heated discussions about everything and anything that happened to come up. I have never had such an intense conversational experience. It had a great deal to do with the small size of the room that we were in and the amount of hours that we were all together—but it created an environment that forced confrontation. There was nowhere to run from any disagreement. We all had to wrestle with our opinions and with our reactions to others' opinions and yet still find a way to work together, to incorporate all of our ideas, and to create something together that spoke for all of us. The fact that we were all able to do that—to disagree, to respect each other, and create research that spoke for us—I found to be truly inspiring. If it was possible for us, imagine what it can do for others . . . I will always remember the mini-explosions of thought that kept us going and forced us to confront some of the toughest and most unique parts of ourselves . . . What we realized was that not all differences of opinions need to be resolved. Not everyone has to think like you and you don't have to think like everyone. It's okay to disagree and express opposition because it helps others to see things from every angle possible. This was one of our biggest accomplishments, the ability to see the world through someone else's eyes and to let others see the world through ours.

We agreed to disagree and collectively analyze our differences as part of our process. In order to maximize the participation of all of the researchers involved, we established a series of practices, repetitive ways of working—rituals to distribute decision making and share power—that were transparent, collaborative, and facilitated group ownership and collective negotiation. Through this praxis we collectively shaped our research questions and also analyzed our data. Key rituals involved free writing in our journals and reflective note taking (see Cahill, 2007b). "Free writing" was a way for the researchers to think through individually and privately on paper issues such as "what I like about my neighborhood" or "personal experiences of racism in school." Journals thus served as a private space for reflection, for spending time thinking through and developing one's own perspective. They also served as a preparation for sharing excerpts of what we wrote with each other. This could be a way to start a group discussion or to compare perspectives with each other. The practice of journal writing established a process of moving from personal to shared experiences. As we shared our writings, Caitlin would take reflective notes on what we were saying on big sheets of paper on "our wall" (see Figures 5.6a and b). Caitlin would then check in—"is this what you were saying?" The notes

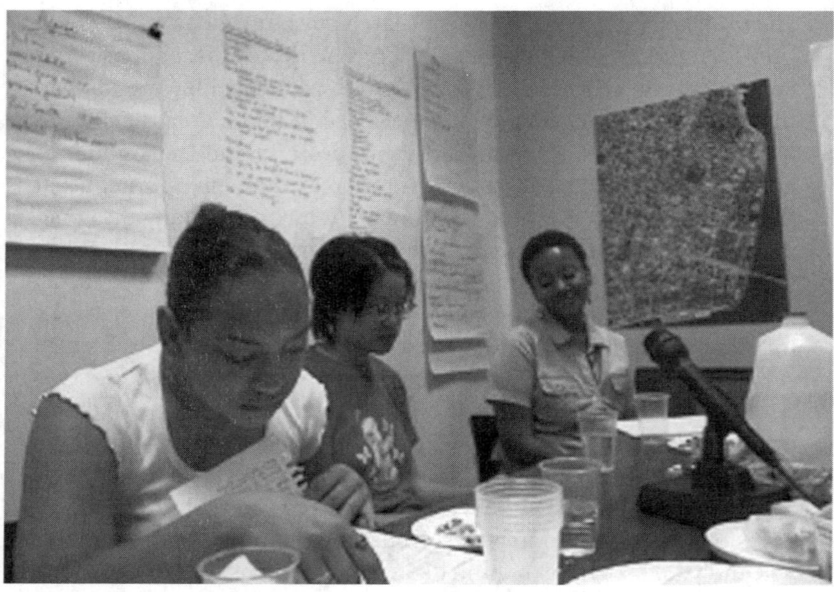

Figure 5.6a The Fed Up Honeys at work.

would serve as documentation to which we could refer back. Our collective wall was a public memory of shared knowledge production from which we could build new ideas and construct our project together.

One of the challenges in working collaboratively was making sure that everyone was involved—this involved sometimes interrupting silences ("Jasmine what do you think?"); or disrupting dominant voices by creating regular opportunities for group reflection and checking in with the group periodically ("Do we all agree? Why or why not?"). Checking in and clarifying our understanding of each other's opinions was especially important when we were trying to articulate conceptually complex ideas. It was necessary for us to "break down" and clarify the group's understanding of the sometimes abstract and theoretical interpretations offered by individual research team members. This, in turn, generated richer analysis of our data (Cahill, 2007b).

Following is an excerpt from a conversation as we started to identify our research questions. It demonstrates how we supported each other in "breaking down" and clarifying our interpretations:

Carmen: . . . I think that we should like focus a little bit on women and their relationship to the neighborhood and the challenges that they

Figure 5.6b Analyzing data on "our wall."

face because of the report that you read. It seemed that society, well like the neighborhood, puts out an image about how women should act 'cause they in a certain neighborhood. And I think that's a crime . . . so I think that then we should focus on that.

Caitlin: On kinda, what are the real challenges that women are facing in their neighborhood . . . instead of focusing on that women behave a certain way in a certain neighborhood—but instead—what are the challenges for women in that neighborhood. Is that what you're saying?

Carmen: Yeah, because like, to me, it seems that just because somebody comes that doesn't know anything about the neighborhood, and never lived here for like quite as long like we have, and get to know everyone in the neighborhood . . . That they come and they say "it seems like women in this neighborhood act like this and that." And when people see that, people be like "oh, it's true—look" and they do it. And like you know, and, that doesn't seem like it's right . . . because people are saying like—the strawberries are red. And you like . . . yeah that's true, they are red. And you're going to say it too. And that's like you're doing something and you don't know that you're doing it and yet when somebody tells you, you do it even more.

Ruby: Yeah. That's just what I was going to say. They're reacting to the stereotype. And making them true. More realistic.
Caitlin: Okay. What is the power of stereotypes? How do stereotypes become reinforced or . . .
Carmen: True.
Caitlin: Or become true?
Annissa: They become a part of—
Carmen: I didn't make myself clear before—
Caitlin: No—I think you are expressing a really complicated idea and I think we are all trying to figure out how to best say it.
Ruby: I don't want to think about something that you weren't really saying. I'm just trying to get a better idea of it.
Annissa: I think most importantly once they become marketed they become the only means for us to get the kind of attention that we need. It makes me think of minstrel shows. Black people would never run around in black face but that was the only way that they could get the money that they needed—
Ruby: That's what they have to do.
Jasmine: And now you see these rappers doing the same thing. Hos, bitches, and hos types of thing.

In our discussions it was necessary to confirm and clarify: "Is this what you meant?" For example, when early on in the research project Carmen suggested that other students at her school brought failure upon themselves, Caitlin questioned what she meant by that—"Do you mean that they don't try to succeed at school because they don't care? Or they do try but still don't succeed because they aren't capable?" And later, Indra asked Carmen why she didn't think the students cared and then, how she herself fit into this understanding as Carmen was also having a hard time in school. This process of "breaking down" served to reflect back our interpretations in a way that drew out political/social/ethical implications. Later Carmen decided to drop out of her zoned neighborhood school, which a year later was forced to shut down, and instead she chose to finish her high school education at an alternative, student-centered school. And she graduated!

Opening #2: Personal Transformation

The voice of a young womyn of color

> I am an interesting young womyn who bores herself to delirium. And a comedian who can't tell a joke. I am a responsible sister and a helpful daughter. I love to be me and yet I am different around others. I

> am extremely emotional but want to hide my feelings. I have a hard time trusting some and put too much trust into others. This leads to hurt feelings and total vulnerability. I want to be vulnerable but it makes me feel weak. I want to feel weak but no one wants to care for me. I want to care for those I love and want them to care for me more. I never believe anyone can love me as much as I do them. I want to take care of people but don't want them to need me. I am too clingy and never see friends and family. I am a complete idiot but an intelligent person. I am lacking education. I have no communication skills and I am a good listener. I am a good listener who hates to hear people speak. I am a reader who watches way too much TV. I am a good friend and girlfriend but I have few friends and no boyfriend. I am open and bold but hold my tongue when I'm hurt. I put people in their place and yet others walk all over me. I try too hard and yet do nothing at all. I am a procrastinator but I am always early. I help and help and help, and get nothing in return. I am not where I would like to be and want to be so much further. I am very opinionated and yet know nothing about the world. I know where I want to go but I am confused. I know what I want but I am confused. I know how I feel but I am confused. I know what I mean but I confuse myself. I am boring and fun, and innocent and cruel. I am trusting. I am always here. I am always there. I am always needed. I am loved and hated. I am admired. I am spiteful but not jealous. I am very jealous. I am scared of everything. My face shows bravery. I am angry. I am in love. I am confused again . . . Honestly, I am too much to put into words.
>
> **(Erica Arenas, Fed Up Honey, 2002; Rios-Moore et al., 2004)**

"This is an example of how a young womyn describing herself manages to convey the difficulty and challenge of being a contradiction . . . of being many things at once. Her words exemplify our struggle to find a voice through research" (Rios-Moore et al., 2004). As the emphasis in our project was on challenging stereotypes, in our autobiographical writings we foregrounded our contradictory selves, or, perhaps more accurately, the push and pull we experience in negotiating the contradictions of our everyday lives. For young people who at this time in their lives are investigating, "trying on," and refashioning possible selves, participatory action research offers an opportunity for critically reflecting upon the different ways we identify. The research process opened our eyes to new ways of understanding ourselves and the world.

Conscientization involves the critical reflection upon the contradictions in one's own everyday life and the transformation of oneself as part of this process. Dialogue is a key component of conscientization, according to Freire: "it is in speaking . . . that people, by naming the world, transform it, dialogue imposes itself as the way by which they achieve significance as human beings. Dialogue is an existential necessity" (Freire, 1997[1970]: 69). Through the dialogic process of collectively working through and making sense of personal and shared experiences, there is the potential for identifying new ways of being in the world. Key is the collective act of sharing and processing together our personal experiences, for example, the private pain and humiliation that comes with racism. In this way, we became aware of how our personal experiences are connected to broader social problems and at the same time we felt a sense of solidarity.

Discussing together the persuasive and dangerous characterizations they face in their everyday lives but don't often have the space to speak seriously about was cathartic or, as one researcher put it, therapeutic—"We opened up to each other and expressed ourselves passionately. It was like I was getting paid to go to therapy." The collective critical reflection process of PAR provided a space for expressing and releasing emotions and working through the pain and confusion of personal and shared experiences in a supportive setting.

Jasmine: This is good because like—this is not something that happened over a year. This is like years of stuff that's just like festering inside of people and there's no place where you can just go and have people of different . . . coming from different areas, and talk about stuff. And—

Janderie: And not let it get hostile.

Jasmine: Yeah exactly. So this is perfect. This is something that people need. Especially if they come—if they're very frustrated. Because that frustration just leads to violence.

By collectively creating a narrative framework to interpret their experiences of racism, the young women redefined "the problem" and in turn their selves (cf. Cahill, 2007a). Through the PAR process, the researchers developed a social analysis weaving together tales of discrimination, of disinvestment and White privilege. Together, the Fed Up Honeys reworked their personal stories, and created a shared space for validating experiences of structural racism and poverty (made concrete in the virtual space of their website www.fed-up-honeys.org).

Whereas at the beginning of our research process what was most remarkable to all of us were our differences, through the process of doing the research project we identified a collective identification as "young urban women of color"—a shared standpoint based on an identification of intersections of race, gender, and place. Key to our collective reconstruction of what it means to be a young urban woman of color is the bifurcated perspective of being the "other," what DuBois (1989) calls "double consciousness" (Cahill, 2007a). Acknowledging the power of stereotypes, "as expectations of who we should be or who we will be," as an "axis around which everything revolves," we identified examples of how we use, relate to, and resist stereotypes and how we "define our (them)selves against and/or through stereotypes" (cf. Rios-Moore et al., 2004), as researcher Erica Arenas explains:

> Sometimes, as a defense mechanism, people will adopt stereotypes as their own. If you take the stereotype and make it yours then there is no way that it can be used against you. When we do this we sometimes lose sight of the negativity in the stereotype and we begin to use these stereotypes as our excuses for why we are the way we are and why we do the things we do. For example: "Don't make me get black up in here" or "I'm Puerto Rican, I can't speak proper English."

As part of our research we deconstructed the stereotypes and identified everything they leave out:

- background
- struggle
- lack of support
- the inherent diversity of every womyn
- the abuse that some womyn face
- the challenges the young womyn sometimes face that leave them in compromised stereotypical situations
- the aspects of life that make this more complicated
- the true multifaceted stories of how/why negative things happen to young womyn
- the ability for young womyn to think for themselves
- everything that makes each life special and unique!

In our project we considered the ways that young women related to or challenged stereotypes. We found that the stereotypes can also be viewed as expectations of who we should be or who we will be. The lack of space to define ourselves affects not only our own self-image but also the way we perceive our peers through the stereotypes. This cycle of reinforcing stereotypes leads to the ways we, as young womyn, begin to explain and understand ourselves, and feeds a struggle that has some resisting stereotypes and others using them to interpret the world around them. In our research, we tried to untangle the ways violent mischaracterizations seeped

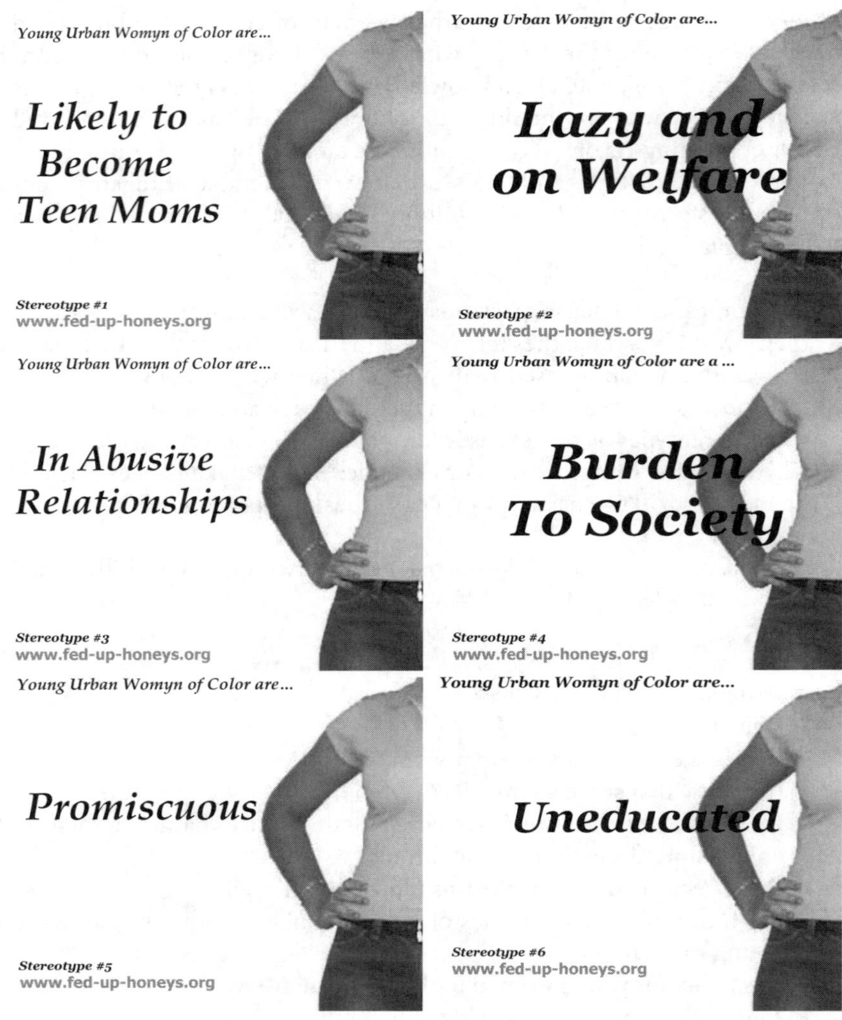

Figure 5.7 Our "stereotype stickers" (credit: www.fed-up-honeys.org).

into our consciousness, the way we understood ourselves (Rios-Moore et al., 2004). This was necessary for us to see ourselves clearly, with "different eyes," and this is also what we hoped to do in our research project:

> We are looking to plant a seed in the minds of society. We wanted our stickers to upset you to the point of inspiration. We want our beautiful, young, urban womyn of color to realize what it is we have against

> us and we hope it will give you all the motivation to go against the grain; to prove everyone wrong. [See Figure 5.7.]

Opening #3: PAR as a Catalyst for Change

> Our project is a voice for young womyn of color but it is an issue that the whole community and society needs to acknowledge and be committed to change. The first step is admitting the problem (admitting to these stereotypes), the next, which is where so many fall short, is to take action in change.
>
> **(Fed Up Honeys, 2002; Rios-Moore et al., 2004)**

According to Freire, conscientization is not "an armchair revolution." The "discovery cannot be purely intellectual but must also involve action; nor can it be limited to mere activism, but must include serious reflection: only then will it be praxis" (Freire, 1997 [1970]: 47). Freire's conceptualization of praxis, as "the reflection and action upon the world in order to transform it" (1997 [1970]: 36), places emphasis upon agency. This was also the emphasis of the "Makes Me Mad" project:

> Presumably, the main audience for our research would be people outside of our community because it would be simple to assume that these are the people that are misunderstanding us and are the main consumers of stereotypes of young urban womyn of color. But over the course of our discussions we came to the very difficult realization that we too were consumers of these negative stereotypes, so we decided that our primary audience should be our peers. If we only communicated with outsiders that presumes that our peers (and ourselves) don't have the level of agency needed to make change to the predominant perceptions of us and we strongly disagree with that belief.
>
> **(Rios-Moore et al., 2004: 3)**

The metaphor of opening eyes also speaks to vision in terms of conjuring up a sense of possibility for ourselves and also for our community: a dream of quality public education, good jobs, affordable housing, racial equity, and democracy. Reflecting upon the relationship between stereotypes and our self-identifications, we engaged in a pedagogy of citizenship, in which we collectively thought through how to make changes within both our own everyday lives and our community, as Annissa reflects:

> In a highly patriarchal society where even white womyn still face a great deal of the same limitations and misconceptions that their

> grandmothers once faced, womyn of color are all the more in need of the space and the encouragement to start shaping their paths within society. Part of the journey starts with womyn of color smashing the skewed pictures of themselves that they see being constantly portrayed and reified in the world that they live in. Participatory action research is one such method of making sure that we as womyn of color could control how our voices and our thoughts would be portrayed and interpreted through the lens of research. We crafted a project that made our voices the centerpiece and were able to develop new and innovative approaches to research that are more likely to catch the attention of our peers and urge them to re-think their own self-perceptions and those of their communities.

Personally, we changed how we viewed the world, our neighborhood, and our own circumstances. What this meant was different for each of us, but we all saw the world with "different eyes" as a result of the research process. For example, Alice understood her experiences in the Chinese immigrant community differently after participating in the project and as a result she developed a website addressing stereotypes of young Chinese women (www.fed-up-honeys.org/cn). As mentioned before, Carmen transferred from her zoned public high school to an alternative student-centered school, where she succeeded in graduating. And while some of us felt ambivalent and even angry toward our disinvested neighborhood, we decided that rather than abandon or be pushed out of our home community, we collectively developed a proposal for "Community building needs from a young womyn's perspective"—a proposal that honors our belonging and inclusion. In our proposal, we advocate for community participation in the development of our neighborhood and our own involvement. To this end, we created a concrete list of practical solutions in the conclusion of the *Makes Me Mad* report, arguing for our concerns to be taken into account (Rios-Moore et al., 2004).

If research is understood as a means "to change the world, not only study it" (Stanley, 1990: 15, cited Maguire, 2001), action must be understood as integral to the process. To this end, it is critical to address both the purpose of doing research and the intended audiences. Questions we raised along these lines included: What do we hope to accomplish with our research? Who should we "speak to"? In our consideration of potential audiences, we thought about how we could design a research project to serve "our community." With this in mind then we thought about how we might effectively reach out to our community with "our message" (Cahill and Torre, forthcoming).

Tiffany: When we decided on researching stereotypes then using it to educate the womyn in our community it seemed new, like something no one has done before. Most likely there were and are many who do this but are not recognized, but that's where our research will be different. We have explored many options to speak to our community and have come up with very effective ways like the stickers, website, and paper to reach our community. Using our research to talk to our community made me realize that research is not just words of a paper or statistics, but it can be used to empower. Research can be anything the researcher wants it to be and that is a powerful thing.

Speaking back was probably the most satisfying part of our research process—thinking about creative ways to reach out and get our message out to the public: "We call these our babies and we couldn't be more proud of our accomplishments." Seeing the results of our research and getting positive feedback has been personally meaningful to each of us. There is a concrete difference between sitting in a room "complaining" (as some would see it) and effectively exploring, researching, and developing research "products" for reaching out to our families, our neighborhoods, and society in general. We developed a few different ways of "speaking back" with our research: including a sticker campaign (see Figure 5.7), two websites (www.fed-up-honeys.org), a "youth-friendly" research report (Rios-Moore et al., 2004), book chapters (Cahill et al., 2004), and presentations at conferences, schools, and local community-based organizations.

As is evident in the title for our project "Makes Me Mad," we wanted to express our anger in order to engage others, depending on who they are, to either feel their own pain or experience the pain and guilt of acknowledging racism. With our "stereotype stickers" (Figure 5.7) we wanted to "prick the 'psychic amnesia' that has infected America" (Torre and Fine, 2006a). Each sticker features a stereotype about young urban women of color including: "Likely to become teen moms," "In abusive relationships," "Promiscuous," "Uneducated," "Lazy and on welfare," and "Burden to society." In the sticker campaign we hoped to upset and motivate "to go against the grain, to prove everyone wrong" and "to realize what it is we have against us." We created the stickers especially for other young women of color, but we posted them all over our neighborhood as we hoped to provoke the public in general into rethinking these stereotypes and how they related to the gentrification of our community. We also used the stereotype stickers to "advertise" our website.

Our website www.fed-up-honeys.org (Figure 5.8), "created by young womyn of color for young womyn of color," is a kind of one-stop-shop experience where visitors can find out about the "Makes Me Mad" research

Figure 5.8 Our website (credit: www.fed-up-honeys.org).

project. On our website you can download our study and learn more about our research. We have a page devoted to the Lower East Side that includes links to community organizations and businesses that connect to young people's interests. We have a page of resources especially for young women (links to other websites with information about health, sexuality, financial resources). We also have a "rant" page because venting was key to our own process so we wanted to create a virtual space for self-expression, where people can post their frustration. Another page includes poetry of relevance to other young people of color and features a beautiful poem about taking cold showers in the projects.

In our report *Makes Me Mad: Stereotypes of young urban womyn of color* (Rios-Moore et al., 2004), we discuss our study, how we went about it, and what we found out. We designed it to be "youth-friendly" and wrote it in a friendly personal voice to appeal to young people in particular, but with the hopes of engaging everyone in our community to take seriously the issue of stereotyping and its impact upon young people. The report includes concrete steps for making change (as mentioned previously), a list of "community building needs," and addressing the lack of resources in our neighborhood, such as education, health, and housing resources. We distributed the report in schools and youth organizations in our neighborhood, and we also shared it with policy makers. Across the country, teachers have been using our website and our study in their classrooms.

Some of our most rewarding experiences have been presenting our research at conferences and doing educational workshops in organizations and schools in our community. We find young people especially excited to talk about racial stereotyping in their schools. We have received a lot of positive feedback from young and old people and we continue to work to get our message out there in the world. We hope to encourage expression and foster a space that will give peers and youth alike a chance to voice themselves, challenge, and complicate the stereotypes and misconceptions of our peers and communities.

Through the fed-up-honeys website and our sticker campaign, we want to stress the importance of self-directed and community-supported action for change. Using the vehicles of action research, research products such as our stickers, and the website, we want to help in the process of motivating and taking part in a revitalization of active community participation. We believe that by simply living your truth and encouraging others to do the same, you can participate in your community's growth. In the process of being true to yourself and the network of people that make up your community, you can help to knock down the myths that hold down our communities.

Conclusion: A Pedagogy of Citizenship

The ultimate and most beneficial means to an end of the negative effects of such a stark lack of resources is a community that is self-sufficient and self-concerned. It is a priority to have young womyn who can feel connected and have a desire to contribute and be involved in their community. But there have to be ways to become involved in the community. Our research has identified several important ways to build a stronger and more positive community, one that is able to stand in the face of the stereotypes that its children have been pegged with (Rios-Moore et al., 2004).

When we speak of self-sufficiency, we do not condone the abandonment or disinvestment of our community. We know all too well what that is about. No, instead we are arguing for sovereignty as a "praxis of self-determination" (Tuck, 2007), a "restorative process" (Grande, 2004: 57) acknowledging the assets already existing within our community, and a recognition of our capacity to make change. Our own experiences of doing research on our communities taught us just how important it is for young people to learn about the history of their neighborhood if they are to be engaged in making or resisting changes, as Annissa argues:

> For those of us who don't know the history we just see the results of the disinvestment. We just see the results of the degradation and all we feel is that crater and that we're just sinking deeper and deeper into it. And feel incredibly helpless and at the same time, you know, like pissed off, and that you can't use your pissed-offness in any way.

Without an understanding of our personal situation we are unable to make or "see" a possibility of change. Many young people feel demoralized by the "system" taking responsibility for failing institutions, such as the terrible public schools we are forced to go to, leading to a personal sense of failure. We think it is astonishing and saddening that the only way we could break through the misconceptions and stereotypes was to become part of a participatory action research process. And the fact that we expressed interest in participating in the research project indicated that we already showed some bravery in being willing to step outside of our comfort zone. But we think that there has to be a way to reach out to people who are not yet brave enough to take such a step. How do you reach them? This is the issue that so many social justice organizations deal with: How do you reach the apathetic, those who have been sleeping for so long that they've forgotten what awake is and how uncomfortable growth can be? Or those who are so busy they have no time to reflect or participate?

Our recognition and personal experience of unconscious denial and hopelessness is what inspired us to try to wake up other young people with our research, to force them to think about stereotypes and motivate them with anger, to force them out of the comfort zone as a prelude to engagement. But this is not enough. Getting mad is a first step, but we want to convince other young people that their opinions matter, that their concerns and needs are important, that they are citizens! With this in mind, we identified many "community building needs from young womyn's perspective" in our study, including the succession of jobs that are underpaying, the lack of a living wage, overcrowded homes, the lack of financial investment, environmental justice issues, and the under-education of young people. We want to engage young people in thinking about what they need, desire, and want to change in their community. How can we develop young people's civic literacy? We want to involve young people as decision makers in our community, as agents of change (Ginwright and James, 2002). Participatory action research offers a promising process for engaging young people in community governance. That said, we realize that communities that do not value the input of adult citizens may not be inclined to value the contributions of young people (Carlson, 2005). While we are optimistic and excited about the possibilities of change, we are not naïve.

We conclude with a call for a pedagogy of citizenship as a critical process of personal and social transformation. We think this is especially important work to do now at this particular political moment. Why? Why now? Is it because young people are less engaged in civil society? Are they more alienated these days? No. We don't think so. We agree with scholars who move beyond narrower conceptions of political participation and demonstrate the diverse ways that young people are already actively involved and engaged in community struggles (Akom, 2006; Ginwright et al., 2006; Stovall, 2006; Torre and Fine, 2006a; other chapters in this volume). Nevertheless, we are very concerned about the contemporary neo-liberal political context, which puts a premium upon individual responsibility and personal accountability: "each person should be obliged to be prudent, responsible for their own destinies, actively calculating their futures" (Rose, 2000: 324). As we are staying so busy trying to get to where we want to go (to college/to a better life/to a new neighborhood/to reach our dreams), we are increasingly isolated. And so we worry that other young people who are caught up in trying to pass the test—to graduate, to get into college, or just get by—might lose sight of the big picture of racism, the lack of investment in our schools—in us!—in our education, and the violence of poverty, and the fact that very few "good jobs" are available. The "Makes Me Mad" project challenges the blame that gets projected on the bodies of young women in the form of stereotypes. We don't want young women and their/our communities to internalize and take personal responsibility for the bigger social/political problems that plague their/our neighborhoods and everyday lives (see Figure 5.5).

We are especially distressed by the fracturing and displacement of our communities and concerned about how this may impact our generation. Psychologist Mindy Thompson Fullilove's definition of "root shock" is relevant to the potential trauma of a loss of place and cultural dislocation that speaks to our experience of gentrification: "a profound emotional upheaval that destroys the working model of the world that . . . undermines trust, increases anxiety about letting loved ones out of one's sight, destabilizes relationships, destroys social, emotional and financial resources" and increases health risks (2004: 14). With this in mind, and with urgency, we want to invoke a pedagogy of citizenship as a call to arms—an embrace—of community-based collaboration and engagement in addressing social and political issues that take place on the ground in our neighborhoods. Critical to this process are the questions that Ginwright et al. raise (2006: 117): "How can civic engagement in the community shape young people's political identity and consciousness? How is space created in which to sustain political consciousness in community settings?" As Jasmine, Fed Up Honey, explains: "People, most importantly young women, do not feel invested in their community or connected to it if they don't have the positive aspects of their community, their lives and their personal strengths reinforced to them." For us, taking control of one's self-definition, one's identification is also about staking out a position in the community. A pedagogy of citizenship is founded upon this praxis, the investigation of everyday life as part of a process of identification with where you come from and your sense of place in the world. And, perhaps it may also be a basis for claiming space and rights in the larger society (R. Flores, 1997; W. Flores, 1997). We hope so.

Note

Please note, names have been changed to protect the confidentiality of those involved. In this chapter, we draw upon transcripts from our taped discussions and our unpublished and published collective writings: Cahill, 2004; Cahill, 2007a; Cahill, 2007b; Cahill and Torre, forthcoming; Cahill et al., 2004; Rios-Moore et al., 2004.

Acknowledgments

Thanks to all of the Fed Up Honeys whose thoughts/insights/voices are woven throughout our chapter. We are grateful for Julio Cammarota and Michelle Fine's incredibly insightful comments and close reading of multiple drafts of this chapter.

References

Akom, A. A. (2006). The racial dimensions of social capital: Towards a new understanding of youth empowerment and community organizing in America's urban core. In *Beyond Resistance! Youth Activism and Community Change: New Democratic Possibilities for Practice and Policy for America's Youth*, ed. S. Ginwright, P. Noguera, and J. Cammarota. New York: Routledge: 81–92.

Aspen Institute (2004). *Structural Racism and Youth Development: Issues, Challenges, and Implications*. Roundtable on Community Change Working Paper Series. Washington, DC: Aspen Institute.

Breitbart, M. (2003). Participatory research. In *Key Methods in Geography*, ed. N. Clifford and G. Valentine. London: Sage: 161–78.

Breitbart, M., and I. Kepes (2007). The YouthPower story: How adults can better support young people's sustained participation in community-based planning. *Children, Youth and Environments* 17(2): 226–53.

Cahill, C. (2004). Defying gravity: Raising consciousness through collective research. *Children's Geographies* 2(2): 273–86.

Cahill, C. (2007a). The personal is political: Developing new subjectivities in a participatory action research process. *Gender, Place, and Culture* 14(3): 267–92.

Cahill, C. (2007b). Doing research *with* young people: Participatory research and the rituals of collective work. *Children's Geographies* 5(3): 297–312.

Cahill, C., and M. E. Torre (forthcoming). Beyond the journal article: Representations, audience, and the presentation of participatory research. In *Participatory Action Research Approaches and Methods: Connecting People, Participation and Place*, ed. Sara Kindon, Rachel Pain, and Mike Kesby. London: Routledge.

Cahill, C., E. Arenas, J. Contreras, N. Jiang, I. Rios-Moore, and T. Threatts (2004). Speaking back: Voices of young urban womyn of color. Using participatory action research to challenge and complicate representations of young women. In *All About the Girl: Culture, Power, and Identity*, ed. Anita Harris. New York: Routledge: 233–44.

Cammarota, J. (2007). A map for social change: Latina/o students engage a praxis of ethnography. *Children, Youth and Environments* 17(2): 341–53.

Cammarota, J., and A. Romero (2006). A critically compassionate intellectualism for Latina/o students: Raising voices above the silencing in our schools. *Multicultural Education* 14(2): 16.

Carlson, Cindy (2005). Youth with influence: The story of the Youth Planner Initiative in Hampton, Virginia. *Children, Youth and Environments* 15(2): 211–26.

Crenshaw, Kimberlé W. (1995). Mapping the margins: Intersectionality, identity politics, and violence against women of color. In *Critical Race Theory: The Key Writings that Formulated the Movement*, ed. Kimberlé W. Crenshaw, Neil Gotanda, Gary Pellow, and Kendell Thomas. New York: New Press: 357–83.

DuBois, W. E. B. (1989). *The Souls of Black Folk*. New York: Bantam Books.
Fine, M. (1994). Working the hyphens: Reinventing the Self and Other in qualitative research. In *Handbook of Qualitative Research*, ed. N. Denzin and Y. Lincoln. Newbury Park, CA: Sage: 70–82.
Fine, M., and M. E. Torre (2004). Re-membering exclusions: Participatory action research in public institutions. *Qualitative Research in Psychology* 1: 15–37.
Fine, M., R. A. Roberts, M. E. Torre, J. Bloom, A. Burns, L. Chajet, et al. (2004). *Echoes: Youth documenting and performing the legacy of* Brown v. Board of Education. New York: Teachers College Press.
Fine, M., M. E. Torre, K. Boudin, I. Bowen, J. Clark, D. Hylton, et al. (2003). Participatory action research: Within and beyond bars. In *Qualitative Research in Psychology: Expanding Perspectives in Methodology and Design*, ed. P. Camic, J. E. Rhodes, and L. Yardley. Washington, DC: American Psychological Association: 173–98.
Fine, M., E. Tuck, and S. Zeller-Berkman (2007). Do you believe in Geneva? Methods and ethics and the global/local nexus. In *Globalizing Cultural Studies: Ethnographic Interventions in Theory, Method, and Policy*, ed. C. McCarthy, A. Durham, L. Engel, A. Filmer, M. Giardina, and M. Malagreca. New York: Peter Lang: 493–526.
Flores, Richard R. (1997). Aesthetic process and cultural citizenship: The membering of a social body in San Antonio. In *Latino Cultural Citizenship: Claiming Identity, Space, and Rights*, ed. W. V. Flores and R. Benmayor. Boston: Beacon Press: 124–51.
Flores, William V. (1997). Mujeres en Huelga: Cultural citizenship and gender empowerment in a cannery strike. In *Latino Cultural Citizenship: Claiming Identity, Space, and Rights*, ed. W. V. Flores and R. Benmayor. Boston: Beacon Press: 210–54.
Freire, Paolo (1997, 1970 original). *Pedagogy of the Oppressed*. Harmondsworth: Penguin Books.
Fullilove, Mindy T. (2004). *Root Shock: How Tearing Up Cities Hurts America and What We Can Do About It*. New York: One World/Ballantine.
Ginwright, Shawn, and Taj James (2002). From assets to agents of change: Social justice, organizing, and youth development. *New Directions for Youth Development* 96: 27–46.
Ginwright, S., P. Noguera, and J. Cammarota, eds. (2006). *Beyond Resistance! Youth Activism and Community Change: New Democratic Possibilities for Practice and Policy for America's Youth*. New York: Routledge.
Grande, S. (2004). *Red Pedagogy: Native American Social and Political Thought*. Lanham, MD: Rowman and Littlefield.
Guinier, L., and G. Torres (2002). *The Miner's Canary: Enlisting Race, Resisting Power, Transforming Democracy*. Cambridge, MA: Harvard University Press.
Harris, Anita (2004). *Future Girl: Young Women in the Twenty-First Century*. London: Taylor and Francis.
Hart, Roger (1997). *Children's Participation: The Theory and Practice of Involving Young Citizens in Community Development and Environmental Care*. New York: UNICEF.
hooks, bell (1995). *Killing Rage. Ending Racism*. New York: Henry Holt.
Kothari, U. (2001). Power, knowledge, and social control in participatory development. In *Participation: The New Tyranny?* ed. B. Cooke and U. Kothari. London: Zed Books: 139–52.
Kretzmann, J., and J. McKnight (1996). Assets-based community development. *National Civic Review* 85(4): 23–30.
Leadbeater, B. J. R., and N. Way, eds. (1996). *Urban Girls: Resisting Stereotypes, Creating Identities*. New York: New York University Press.
Lipman, P. (2002). Making the global city, making inequality: The political economy and cultural politics of Chicago school policy. *American Educational Research Journal* 39(2): 379–419.
Lipman, P. (2003). Chicago school policy: Regulating Black and Latino youth in the global city. *Race, Ethnicity, and Education* 6(4): 331–55.
Lykes, M. B. (2001). Activist participatory research and the arts with rural Mayan women: Interculturality and situated meaning making. In *From Subjects to Subjectivities: A Handbook of Interpretative and Participatory Methods*, ed. D. L. Tolman and M. Brydon-Miller. New York: New York University Press: 183–99.
Madriz, E. (1997). *Nothing Bad Happens to Good Girls: Fear of Crime in Women's Lives*. Berkeley: University of California Press.
Maguire, P. (2001). Uneven ground: Feminisms and action research. In *Handbook of Action Research: Participative Inquiry and Practice*, ed. P. Reason and H. Bradbury. London: Sage: 59–69.

Mele, C. (2000). *Selling the Lower East Side: Culture, Real Estate, and Resistance in New York, 1880–2000*. Minneapolis: University of Minnesota Press.

Muñiz, V. (1998). *Resisting Gentrification and Displacement: Voices of Puerto Rican Women of the Barrio*. New York: Garland.

Murry, V. M. (1996). Inner city girls of color: Unmarried, sexually active nonmembers. In *Urban Girls: Resisting Stereotypes, Creating Identities*, ed. B. J. R. Leadbeater and N. Way. New York: New York University Press: 272–90.

Omi, M., and H. Winant (1994). *Racial Formation in the United States: From the 1960s to the 1990s*. New York: Routledge.

Pain, R. (1991). Space, sexual violence and social control: Integrating geographical and feminist analyses of women's fear of crime. *Progress in Human Geography* 15: 415–31.

Pain, Rachel (2004). Social geography: Participatory research. *Progress in Human Geography* 28(5): 1–12.

Rios-Moore, I., S. Allen, E. Arenas, J. Contreras, N. Jiang, T. Threatts, et al. (2004). *Makes Me Mad: Stereotypes of Young Urban Womyn of Color*. Report published and distributed by the Center for Human Environments/City University of New York.

Rose, N. (2000). Government and control. *British Journal of Criminology* 40: 321–39.

Sen, Amartya (2004). How does culture matter? In *Culture and Public Action*, ed. V. Rao and M. Walton. Stanford, CA: Stanford University Press: 37–58.

Smith, N. (1996). *The New Urban Frontier: Gentrification and the Revanchist City*. New York: Routledge.

Stanley, L. (1990). Feminist praxis and the academic mode of production: An editorial introduction. In *Feminist Praxis, Theory and Epistemology in Feminist Sociology*, ed. L. Stanley. London: Routledge: 3–19.

Stovall, David (2006). From hunger strike to high school: Youth development, social justice, and school formation. In *Beyond Resistance! Youth Activism and Community Change: New Democratic Possibilities for Practice and Policy for America's Youth*, ed. S. Ginwright, P. Noguera, and J. Cammarota. New York: Routledge: 97–110.

Tolman, D. (1996). Adolescent girls' sexuality: Debunking the myth of the urban girl. In *Urban Girls: Resisting Stereotypes, Creating Identities*, ed. B. J. R. Leadbeater and N. Way. New York: New York University Press: 255–72.

Torre, M. E. (2005). The alchemy of integrated spaces: Youth participation in research collectives of difference. In *Beyond Silenced Voices*, 2nd edn., ed. L. Weis and M. Fine. Albany: State University of New York Press: 251–66.

Torre, M. E., and M. Fine (2006a). Participatory action research (PAR) by youth. In *Youth Activism: An International Encyclopedia*, ed. L. Sherrod. Westport, CT: Greenwood: 456–62.

Torre, M. E., and M. Fine (2006b). Researching and resisting: Democratic policy research by and for youth. In *Beyond Resistance! Youth Activism and Community Change: New Democratic Possibilities for Practice and Policy for America's Youth*, ed. S. Ginwright, P. Noguera, and J. Cammarota. New York: Routledge: 269–87.

Torre, M. E., M. Fine, K. Boudin, I. Bowen, J. Clark, D. Hylton, et al. (2001). A space for co-constructing counter stories under surveillance. *International Journal of Critical Psychology* 4: 149–66.

Tuck, E. in conversation with M. Fine (2007). Inner angles: A range of ethical responses to/with indigenous and decolonizing theories. In *Ethical Futures in Qualitative Research: Decolonizing the Politics of Knowledge*, ed. N. Denzin and M. Giardina. Walnut Creek, CA: Left Coast Press: 145–68.

Weis, L., and M. Fine (2000). *Construction Sites: Excavating Race, Class, and Gender among Urban Youth*. New York and London: Teachers College Press.

Youth Speak Out Coalition and K. Zimmerman (2006). Making space, making change: Models for youth-led social change organizations. *Children, Youth and Environments* 17(2): 298–314.

Response to Chapter 5

PAULINE LIPMAN

In February 2007, our Collaborative for Equity and Justice in Education (CEJE) in Chicago (teachers, high school students, university faculty, graduate students, community activists) invited the Fed Up Honeys to talk about their work. The audience, mostly high school womyn of color, responded to their research with shared experience and solidarity. They came from places across the city, small groups organized by or supported by committed teachers, and adult allies. They found themselves in a room overflowing with other young womyn like themselves who were meeting in schools and libraries and living rooms to critique the racist and sexist stereotypes fixed to their identities and to act as strong young womyn, some as school and community activists and leaders. The Fed Ups' research spoke back to labels that target them as sexually promiscuous, lazy, uneducated, a burden to society. What does it mean to critically investigate the link between those labels and that labeling and the larger economic and political structures that are redefining cities such as New York and Chicago and writing these young womyn, their mothers, sisters, brothers, and grandmothers out of their neighborhoods? What are the possibilities when those who are labeled and dismissed pack a room with others like them and share a common experience that is collectively revealed to be intricately and purposefully linked to processes of displacement, disinvestment, and domination?

In cities across the United States, neo-liberal policies are remaking the urban landscape over and against working-class communities of color. In what Neil Smith (2002) calls the "class conquest of the city," transnational,

national, and local investors joined with city government are restructuring the city as a space of financial dominance, corporate culture, upper middle-class consumption, and whiteness (Haymes, 1995; Sassen, 2006). Neo-liberal urban restructuring is driven by global economic and political processes: deregulation of national economies, global mobility of capital and privileging of financial speculation, and competition among cities for investment, tourism, and corporate and financial headquarters. In this context, gentrification, previously a relatively marginal economic sector, is now pivotal in the urban economy (Smith, 2002). Facilitated by government policy, gentrification mega-projects that combine upscale housing, retail, recreation, and leisure space generate super-profits for transnational investors (ibid.).

This process illustrates how global economic, political, and social processes are "materialized at the local level" (Sassen, 1998: 87) in people's individual experiences, in the restructuring of their neighborhoods and destabilizing of their lives. Working-class communities, especially communities of color, have faced massive disinvestment and displacement as local governments made a dramatic U-turn from social investment (always inadequate) in schools, affordable housing, and public welfare to lubrication of private development, the "boutiquing" of central city neighborhoods, and "urban spectacle projects" (Smith, 1996)—like New York's South Street Seaport and Chicago's Millennium Park and Soldier Field sports complex. In Chicago, the city housing authority has demolished 19,000 units of public housing while affordable housing has been squeezed out by gentrification that stretches from the city center to working-class areas across the city. Thousands of immigrants and working-class people of color have been, and are being, effectively expelled to disinvested and racially segregated neighborhoods and economically impoverished inner ring suburbs (Lipman and Haines, 2007).

Dispossession, displacement, and resistance are realized concretely through material practices and the constitution of subjectivities that justify/tolerate/challenge these processes in specific places. This is where the negative and destructive stereotypes of young people of color come in and why their critical interrogation and resistance is important. The construction of young womyn of color as undisciplined, lazy, sexually promiscuous, and "at-risk" is a crucial front in the dismantling of communities. Critical geographers (e.g., Harvey, 2001; Smith, 1996) point out that the relentless destruction and reconstruction of the built environment is the central logic of real estate capitalism. This is a deeply racialized process. First, landlords milk buildings for all they are worth as they systematically fail to maintain them, while complicit governments neglect infrastructure improvements in the community and enforcement of building codes. Then, when the property is thoroughly devalorized and the potential value of the land is greater than the existing structures, capital moves in again for a new round of investment, evicting the current tenants for super-profits from new development and revalorized property values. This strategy in working-class communities of color, such as the Lower East Side, is validated by reference to "bad" neighborhoods and pathologies of poverty. Capital's responsibility for (and the state's collaboration in) deindustrialization and disinvestment in affordable housing is shifted onto the backs of "negligent" tenants whose expulsion by million dollar condos and chic cafés is hailed as neighborhood regeneration. This discourse is not only racialized but also clearly gendered in the post-industrial economies of cities such as New York and Chicago, where womyn's low-paid service work is devalorized—often invisible—but essential (Sassen, 1998). Viciously stereotyping young womyn of color is an ideological lynchpin in packaging dispossession as neighborhood reclamation.

Demonization of young womyn of color and enforcement of discipline, sexual abstinence, and moral supervision can also be located in the rise of the security state. The new world order is defined by "competition, inequality, market 'discipline,' public austerity, and 'law and order'" (Duggan, 2003: x). An increasingly punitive neo-liberal state resorts to surveillance, containment, and discipline to police those it defines as irrelevant or dangerous (Harvey, 2005; Wacquant, 2001). Intensified social control is a political imperative for those in power in the face of real and future resistance to vastly shrinking public resources, a polarized labor force in which many face a future of low-wage labor or unemployment, while a handful flaunt vast concentrations of wealth and privilege, and inevitable opposition to imperialist war without end. Ideologically, the security state is buttressed by viciously racist and patriarchal images of the "urban" as danger zone and working-class people of color as the undeserving poor (Katz, 1989) who need social discipline. Regulation, containment, and criminalization of youth of color are warranted by their construction as pathological and irresponsible. Instead of resources and support, they get military high schools, surveillance, regimented curricula, and the policing of their bodies.

But working-class communities of color share dialectical histories of containment/exploitation and resistance. Stephen Haymes (1995) argues that racially segregated Black urban communities, demonized in the White supremacist cultural imagination and assaulted by political and economic violence, were appropriated by the people who lived there as spaces of survival and political and cultural resistance. The Lower East Side represents a history of multi-racial multi-ethnic struggle for economic justice, decent housing and education, and against police brutality. Significantly, womyn—Jewish, Puerto Rican, African-American, Dominican, Chinese—were often the leaders. Today, for the womyn of the Fed Up Honeys who grew up there it means "diversity, sense of safety, knowing people, pride, tolerance, a lot of hardworking people, knowing your neighbors." Bringing in that submerged narrative of Lower East Side womyn's resistance is an important grounding for a critical counter-narrative of the "Lowa" today.

We live in an urgent moment defined by global neo-liberalism and resistance in which local struggles have global dimensions. While urban youth are demonized as social problems, we in CEJE see them as future leaders of transformational social movements. We need analyses by youth and adults that connect lived experiences with the global political economy and the realities of the punitive neo-liberal state in all their racialized and gendered forms, and that are generative of social action. Participatory action research, as a form of critical democratic inquiry, is a means for people who are objectified to become subjects, actors in history. It is, as the Fed Up Honeys eloquently explain, a vehicle for us to see ourselves with "different eyes," write our own narratives, define ourselves through our own histories, material realities, community resources, impulses for solidarity. "Different Eyes/Open Eyes" demonstrates that this can be personally transformative and inspire agency.

Going back to that hall in Chicago filled with young womyn, as public text, PAR can inspire and provoke critical dialogue. But the challenge for us in our own locale is to create opportunities for young people to critically investigate their own experiences in order to "'see' in concrete terms the impact of sociopolitical forces on our everyday lives" *in order to act collectively to transform them*. This latter point is significant. We have seen young people, with eyes wide open to the social forces of domination, express powerlessness and a loss of hope. We are constantly challenged to create spaces to excavate what neo-liberal urban restructuring means in people's lives, how it constrains choices and fixes identities, while finding spaces of sustained resistance. How do we soberly assess reality and inspire hope through critical analysis and collective action? Critical social praxis requires a long view, complex analysis, collective action, creativity, and solidarity. In Freire's terms, we need to read and write the world as a dialectical process, to develop critical consciousness in order to change, and through changing, the world. This is a humbling and urgent challenge.

References

Duggan, L. (2003). *Twilight of Equality? Neoliberalism, Cultural Politics, and the Attack on Democracy*. Boston: Beacon Press.

Harvey, D. (2001). *Spaces of Capital: Towards a Critical Geography*. London: Routledge.

Harvey, D. (2005). *A Brief History of Neoliberalism*. New York: Oxford University Press.

Haymes, S. N. (1995). *Race, Culture and the City: A Pedagogy for Black Urban Struggle*. Albany: State University of New York Press.

Katz, M. B. (1989). *The Undeserving Poor: From the War on Poverty to the War on Welfare*. New York: Pantheon.

Lipman, P., and N. Haines (2007). From education accountability to privatization and African American exclusion—Chicago Public Schools' "Renaissance 2010." *Educational Policy* 21(3): 1–32.

Sassen, S. (1998). *Globalization and Its Discontents*. New York: New Press.

Sassen, S. (2006). *Cities in a World Economy*. 3rd edn. Thousand Oaks, CA: Pine Forge Press.

Smith, N. (1996). *The New Urban Frontier: Gentrification and the Revanchist City*. New York: Routledge.

Smith, N. (2002). New globalism, new urbanism: Gentrification as global urban strategy. In *Spaces of Neoliberalism: Urban Restructuring in North America and Western Europe*, ed. N. Brenner and N. Theodore. London: Blackwell: 80–103.

Wacquant, L. (2001). The penalization of poverty and the rise of neo-liberalism. *European Journal of Criminal Policy and Research* 9(4): 401–12.

CHAPTER 6

"The Opportunity if not the Right to See"

The Social Justice Education Project

AUGUSTINE ROMERO, JULIO CAMMAROTA, KIM DOMINGUEZ, LUIS VALDEZ, GRECIA RAMIREZ, AND LIZ HERNANDEZ (IN ORDER OF APPEARANCE WITHIN THE CHAPTER)

This chapter discusses the Social Justice Education Project (SJEP) and its participatory action research program offered in the Tucson Unified School District (TUSD). The discussion focuses on some of the successes and struggles of the SJEP throughout the five years in which the program has been active. We also describe the pedagogical theory driving the SJEP, which simultaneously elevates student voices, consciousness, and academic performance. The chapter concludes with student voices explaining how the SJEP and their involvement with participatory action research (PAR) influenced their perceptions of themselves as well as their capacities for social action.

Social Justice Education in Public Schools: Successes and Struggles
Augustine Romero

From the inception of the SJEP, Controlado (pseudonym) High School granted this unique social science program space within its core US History offerings. One year later, this offering expanded to the senior level US Government course. Since fall 2002, the SJEP moved from one course at one high school to five courses at three public high schools in TUSD. A key goal of the SJEP is to meet the cultural, social, and intellectual needs of Latina/o students. It attains this goal by employing a curriculum that centers on social justice, critical race theory, and Funds of Knowledge (Delgado and Stefancic, 2001; Ginwright and Cammarota, 2002; Gonzalez et al., 2005). As an extension of the curriculum, we believed that it was only fitting to use Freirean libratory pedagogy (Darder et al., 2003; Freire, 1993, 1998) as our pedagogical framework.

Moreover, our students conduct their own participatory action research (Selener, 1997; Whyte, 1991) projects on social and structural problems that limit or even prohibit their opportunities and possibilities for liberation. For example, past research foci include the inequitable reality of "a school within a school," "language or cultural oppression in education," and "the injustice of America's Immigration Policy." Our students then apply their research by presenting their findings—based on interviews and observations of their peers—to district, city, state, and national elected officials. In addition, the students present their findings throughout the community in education and political settings. The intention of the research presentations is to raise their voices and to use student knowledge to fill the social and intellectual void created by their absence in decision-making and policy-making arenas.

The following is a complete description of the SJEP. This ongoing project (currently in its fourth cohort) is broken into two-year cohorts; in the first year, the students develop and engage a curriculum that is culturally, socially, and historically relevant with the concepts of race and racism serving as primary lenses of inquiry and understanding. Throughout this year, students go through many exercises to help them contextualize and problem-pose their realities through a deeper understanding of their cultural, historical, and social realities. In year one, the students receive United States History credit for their participation in the project. The curriculum used in year one is aligned with the state's US History Standards. In year two, the students enroll in a United States Government/Chicano Studies (Noriega, 2001) perspectives course. This course satisfies the Arizona State graduation requirement. Again, the curricular framework is aligned with the state's United States Government Standards. Furthermore, Lorenzo Lopez (SJEP teacher) and I had the privilege of developing this framework from the perspective of the generative themes and social realities offered by the students in year one. Moreover, this is simply a framework, and each and every year the curriculum is modified and adapted to meet the current political climate and the needs of our current students. The point is that relevant and contemporary generative themes often become research topics that our students self-select.

The participatory action research component of the SJEP affords our students the opportunity to engage in a critical analysis of social justice issues that impact their lives and the lives of youth and other Latinas/os in their community. In this process, the students use the research methodologies within participatory action research to help them evaluate and engage the everyday injustices that prohibit and impede their movement toward reaching their full potential. Some of the students' research methods include: observations on campus and in the community, the creation of field notes, photographic and video documentation, taped interviews, and student surveys.

Over the past three SJEP cohorts, research topics focus on the social injustice that exists in the lives of the students. Moreover, the SJEP students conduct research that allows them to offer resolutions to the issues they forward in their research. Students have presented their research and resolutions at academic conferences such as the American Education Research Association, the American Anthropological Association, and the National Association of Chicano and Chicana Studies. Also, in spring 2004, the first cohort presented its research findings and its resolutions for the Hispanic and Black Caucuses of Congress; along with presentations to the Tucson Unified School Board and the Pima County Board of Supervisors. The research topics of the first three cohorts have been: The Impact of Banking Education versus Critical Education, The Media Misrepresentation of Latinas/os, Teacher-to-Student Violence, Additive Schooling versus Subtractive Schooling, and The United States Unjust Immigration Policy, to name a few.

We believe that it is important to articulate some of the successes of the SJEP. The representations forwarded by the members of cohort #1 significantly influenced Controlado officials to address the egregious physical neglects, such as replacing missing urinals in the boys' bathrooms, repairing the falling tiles in the gym ceiling, and repairing the water fountains so that water would flow. Among academic changes that the SJEP influenced at Controlado are updating the books in the library and the placement of the exceptional education students in a true classroom, rather than having them in a room that was previously the woodshop (they were placed in a room that was filled with heavy, dangerous equipment, such as saws and drills!). The SJEP influenced the expansion of multicultural course offerings at Controlado.

Another successful component of the SJEP is its multi-generational (multiple cohort) representation. There is at least one graduate from each of the previous three cohorts currently working, as student workers, with the SJEP. In addition, as students graduate from the third cohort, we plan to add members of the fourth cohort to the SJEP student-worker program. The roles played by the student workers include leading the participatory

Figure 6.1 Members of the Social Justice Education Project in Washington, DC, left to right. First row: Tela Paxson, Antia Valenzuela. Second row: Veronica Trujillo, Amanda Carillo, Yarko Ruiz. Back row: Kim Dominguez, Angel Rodriguez.

action research, documentary production, and newsletter creation. These responsibilities are critical for the SJEP; moreover, it gives our blossoming intellectuals the opportunity to assume leadership roles and the opportunity to impact the political and social landscape of their community.

In 2006, the TUSD governing board adopted, as one of its six strategic goals, the concept of intercultural proficiency. A concept that is an evolution of multiculturalism or the ability of people/students to negotiate and mediate our global world with understanding, compassion, and a sense of social justice. Due to the SJEP's success as an effective model of active multiculturalism, the district can move forward in the process and pursuit of intercultural proficiency.

Despite successes, the SJEP has faced many political intersections in which we have met opposition to our efforts. Some opposition came from Controlado teachers and administrators who felt threatened by the students' stark representation of educational injustice, albeit the clear, graphic evidence was undeniable. Once the SJEP's student-made video documentary on educational injustice reached the governing board, the principal and TUSD administration had no other choice but to make school improvements. Structural problems were slated to be fixed several years earlier. With the presentation and video, problems were made public and immediate changes were required. Other opposition has come from ultraconservative factions of TUSD's community. Representatives of these factions have made presentations to the TUSD governing board wherein they have labeled the SJEP racist, communistic, anti-American to name a few. Last, the Arizona State Superintendent of Public Instruction has made many public comments about his disdain for the SJEP, and his desire to eradicate its existence.

Despite the antagonisms, the success of the SJEP has led to its expansion to two other high schools, plus several courses at these sites. In fact, the SJEP has been requested at many more sites in TUSD, and in other districts in the Tucson area; however, at this point the SJEP lacks the fiscal capital necessary to accommodate these requests. Public dollars are unfortunately prioritized toward implementing standardized testing instead of educating active, critically minded citizens.

Participatory Action Research in the Public School Curriculum: Toward a Pedagogy of Dialogical Authoring

Julio Cammarota

In the education literature, the Funds of Knowledge (Gonzalez et al., 2005; Gonzalez and Moll, 1995; Gonzalez and Moll, 2002; Moll et al., 1992) approach circumvents the institutionalized Anglo-cultural bias in traditional schools by rendering participatory research the first step in educating Latina/o students. In this approach, teachers learn ethnographic research methods and then visit their students' households to document the cultural practices or "Funds of Knowledge" families utilize for everyday survival. Their knowledge may include informal trading, home-based manufacturing, as well as herbal remedies for illness. Once teachers observe these sophisticated forms of cultural practices that facilitate families' survival within difficult circumstances, they realize how Latina/o culture is positively linked with intellectual thought.[1] Teachers then integrate their observations into the curriculum and create lessons on such subjects as cross-border trade networks or ethnobiology. When students witness the validation of their culture within the educational process, they concatenate their identities as family members and students. Most importantly, the cultural substance of their identities feeds and sustains an academic persona. Teachers acknowledge that the students' culture contains valid and sophisticated knowledge; the students thus see themselves as knowledgeable.

In many respects, the SJEP draws from the Funds of Knowledge approach by rendering PAR as the first step in the educational process. However, students, instead of teachers, are the action researchers.[2] The sites for research extend beyond the family to include neighborhoods, schools, peers, and workplaces. The students' social contexts are key milieus for study and analysis.

The knowledge gathered in analyses is not only limited to cultural aspects, but also emerges from understanding how social relationships may impede or enhance their life chances (Cammarota, 2007). Thus, students learn how to use culture or "Funds of Knowledge" to generate more equitable social relations to ameliorate conditions and opportunities for themselves, families, and communities. Thus, the SJEP adopts a social justice orientation (Ginwright and Cammarota, 2002) in the formation of knowledge while reframing questions related to epistemology to consider the purpose and value of knowledge for underprivileged youth. If the knowledge attained by young people helps them improve their social contexts, then their learning holds a greater purpose and meaning.

A dialogical authoring process

Learning in the SJEP transpires in a dialogical authoring process,[3] in which students take ownership over their education by consistently voicing their concerns, thoughts, and opinions in the classroom. We structure most class time so that students openly and freely discuss what they want to learn, why they need to learn it, and how they will go about learning. The net effect of students actively shaping their own education is the burgeoning confidence to improve conditions within their world. By having students contribute to teaching the course, they begin to see themselves differently. They generate new perceptions and ideas about their own capabilities. No longer do they sit passively waiting to be told what to do; they realize that they too have something to offer to education and society.

Julio Cammarota asked some students if they thought the SJEP was interesting, a class they wanted to attend.

Maria: I'd only go to second period [SJEP class] sometimes and miss first and then I'd leave after second.

Vanessa: Well, first was boring.

Maria: First was so boring.

Maria: All you had to do was turn in a folder and you pass. Why go? Why go to class?

Julio Cammarota: So this class [SJEP] wasn't boring?

Maria: Well, no. Because it was . . . because it was interesting. It was interesting.

Julio Cammarota: It was interesting because you were learning about what?

Maria: It was interesting because we were learning about our school. Where we learned what was going on and we had to say everything. We got to . . . we were the ones who are putting in all the input so it was cool. We had a part in it. That's why. We had a big part and . . .

Vanessa: 'Cuz in other classes we had no part at all—we are just chillin' in the back.

Allowing students to participate in constructing the learning process encourages them to perceive education as their project, something they create. Tapping into the creative spirit of young people will render education exciting and thus inspire them to learn. They no longer feel that education is something being done to them by somebody else, but something they are doing to recreate themselves and their lived contexts.

PAR is the way students initiate dialogical authoring. Students spend most class time collectively discussing terms and concepts along with their research observations. In this way, observations become applied immediately in their education in as much as they serve as conduits for dialogue. These research-based discussions help them better understand the world in which they are situated as well as evoke ideas on how to overcome obstacles impeding their progress.

Here is an example of a class discussion based on the students' research observations. Roberta wrote in her field notes that she was watching "American Idol," and the judges told a contestant that she sang well but her heavy stature did not make her "American Idol" material. She needed to lose weight to succeed on the show. A male contestant who was also heavy in stature won while the judges did not mention anything about his weight. This observation led to a discussion about a double standard for women. Susanna wrote about an MTV show that remade or made over participants. The show is called "Made," and Susanna was concerned that the show's content advocated to young people that they not be happy with who they are and find ways to change their appearance. This observation led to a discussion about cosmetic surgery and breast enhancements. Some female students argued that men created the breast job industry so that women can make themselves more appealing for them. Others argued that breast implants are for women who want to feel better about them. Then, Corrine adamantly stated that male-dominated society created this need for women to feel better.

Whether the dialogue focuses on research observations or personal experiences, SJEP educators encourage students to frame their discussions with a social justice perspective. The intent is to help students to realize that most problems they encounter—whether they are public or private—

have a deeper or root societal origin. The SJEP takes a sociological view of human behavior and advocates the idea that negative development outcomes, including criminal behavior, violent tendencies, and substance addiction, stem from social and economic pressures (Ginwright and Cammarota, 2002). Students learn to make the connection between oppression (classicism, racism, sexism, and homophobia) and maladaptive behaviors. Therefore, long-term solutions for promoting healthy behaviors focus primarily on the root societal causes to negative outcomes, instead of the outcomes alone (Ginwright et al., 2005). This social justice perspective removes any doubt in the student's mind that she or he is to blame for her or his struggles. Unfortunately, many students learn to accept the harassment, abuse, oppression, or failure they experience as something they deserve. They blame themselves because they have not learned how to develop a "sociological imagination" for the negative forces impacting their lives.[4] PAR opens their minds to new possibilities—seeing how they are not at fault yet capable of addressing the social and economic pressures that are truly to blame. The outcomes of PAR are normally empowered students who feel they can overcome personal struggles as well as challenge oppression in society.

The following and concluding section of this chapter presents the actual voices of SJEP students. The voices emanate from young Latinas/os who represent the primary participants in the SJEP. All SJEP classes are located in high schools on the southwest section of Tucson. This area is predominately Latina/o and working class. The voices speak from locations other than high schools, specific geographical as well as social locations (race/ethnicity, class, gender, etc.). Therefore, we hear how they articulate their sense of self within these multiple locations as well as possibilities for reconstructions to generate new places from which to voice their thoughts, ideas, and actions.

Specifically, we asked the students to write statements about their experiences when participating in the SJEP and how PAR influenced their perceptions of and engagements with their social milieus. These statements testify how PAR serves as an effective method for analyzing and addressing oppressions as well as pedagogy for transforming students' consciousness and academic capabilities.

Voices of the Voiceless: "Because We Are All So Silenced!"
Kim Dominguez

I was 19 years old and presenting a documentary and research with my classmates in Washington, DC. I can remember standing in the Capitol building and staring up at a collection of paintings that depicted what I saw in my mind during history classes and history lessons I had the last 13 years of my

Figure 6.2 Social Justice Education Project student Myra Bracamonte reciting her poem “I Am What America Hates the Most” at the Batey Urbano Youth Center, Chicago, Illinois.

life in school. Images that had contributed to my racism, sexism, and colonization. Images and history stories that had created the education gap, the reason 50 percent of my graduating class dropped out before graduation, the reason my grandparents who were disciplined in school for speaking Spanish decided not to teach me the language of so many generations of family members. I was so angry and for the first time I knew what to do. At that point in my life, I wasn’t angry and lost with a map in the dark. I knew where to go and how to get there.

The Social Justice Education Project started in 2003, and I was a student in the first class at Cholla High School. I had been a good student until I started thinking for myself and disassociating from what I was learning in middle school. In high school, I started failing classes, ditching school, and making excuses not to go. I always thought back to AIMS (Arizona Instrument for Measuring Standards) testing statistics that stated brown students at my school couldn't read. I thought to myself that I knew they could read, maybe they just didn't want to read what we were given by *our* school, because our school was *their* school.

I loved writing and history, but I hated the history classes that I was forced to take in order to meet graduation requirements, and I hated reading the boring English assignments with boring typical White authors because I had nothing to write about it afterwards. In a society in which most successful people such as doctors, teachers, congressmen and women, professors, all needed education to achieve their success, our schools, communities, and institutions were setting up the youth of color and the impoverished youth to join the military or drop out of the irrelevant Eurocentric schools that supposedly lead us to a "career" after high school or maybe a community college with equally as high dropout rates.

Up until my senior year with SJEP, I didn't realize how important it was for me to graduate on time with my class, and not become another young person with a Spanish surname at Cholla High School to drop out, and at that point I didn't have enough credits to graduate. I decided to take weekend classes and after classes to graduate on time in 2003. Without the history and government classes I took with SJEP, I might have failed any other history class, and without my newfound inspiration and motivation to graduate high school, I wouldn't have decided graduating was important.

It's almost five years since I started with SJEP, and I have had so many opportunities that I never expected for my life. My class of about 15 students who were disenfranchised by our school system and labeled as "at risk," were given the opportunity not only to speak out in class and talk about our personal struggles and how they affect our education but also to create a documentary based on the research we conducted in class through filming, interviews, field notes, photography, and poetry. We also traveled to different states to educational and research conferences and shared our findings. Thinking back to Washington, DC, I was able to meet Congressman Raul Grijalva and talk with him about our research and goals and I was surprised to meet a Chicano congressman who felt the way I did about the town we lived in and the education system and feel empowered in the Capitol where I had felt so sad because of the images I saw there. Because there was a person of power who believed in social change, I could become a person in a position of power. I had the opportunity to make a presentation in Montreal, Canada, at the American Education Research Association. Other than the two-hour drive across the border to the next town,

I had never been to another country. I thought I knew I would never be in another country. I was the only young person from our group to attend and presenting was on my shoulders. I was living a dream. In a world where adults never listened to what young people had to say, I was going to be in a room full of adults and I had to speak for myself, my little brother and sisters, my classmates, the project; I felt like I had to speak for every young person in the world. I felt like my job as a young person in SJEP was to be the voice of the voiceless because we are all so silenced. I grew up in Tucson on food stamps, welfare, and Access (state health care), attended low-income schools, my father was involved with drugs and alcohol. I didn't know anyone who graduated college or graduated high school, and I never had much expectation for myself and school didn't either. I remember my school counselor telling me I'd be lucky to graduate and if I did, should try to attend community college, because it was affordable and easy.

Luis Valdez

I love knowing that without the social justice education project I would have probably gone through life as a halfway conscious, media-controlled drone. I hate how I would have turned out if I had not experienced being a part of this project. My entire outlook on life has changed. I have lived through so many experiences that molded me into who I am now. Prior to the project, I had only some knowledge of what social justice was, let alone did I even know all of the injustices that were right under my nose, and that I went through every day. I once heard someone say that a penguin does not know how cold the water he is swimming in is until he knows of the warmth of tropical waters. I have a completely new perspective on things, and I feel like every day I learn something new about the world and most importantly about myself.

I used to be semi-average kid; I was coasting through high school on grades only good enough to stay on the baseball team. I always knew that I would eventually go to college, but the plan was to coast till graduation and really buckle down when I got to community college. My academic ambition needed to be a lot stronger, but I had no real motivation other than knowing I would be grounded and off the baseball team if I didn't make good grades. This project opened up my eyes to things that everyone should have the opportunity if not the right to see, and that is the project's goal in a nutshell.

The project showed me a completely different world to the one that I thought I lived in. Some may say that in this situation ignorance is bliss, and that many would rather not know about the negativity that surrounds us. SJEP has helped me realize that things are not as sweet as we are taught by our education system and how the media leads us to believe things are. But the project did not open up this world to me in a cruel and insensitive way, because the many experiences have also taught me how to make change in the things that need to be improved. Being involved with the project also meant that I would constantly be surrounded by very positive adults that I could look up to—on nearly an everyday basis, dozens of people who have graduated college and now have very successful careers: teachers, college professors and administrators who I can identify with. These were people who work to change the structure of the entire system to make these opportunities more relevant to all people and not just the ruling class.

I have lived through life-changing experiences with this project. For one, the American history and government classes that I took opened my eyes and mind. Then I received the opportunity to work on the second documentary that the project would be producing over the summer after my senior year. I got the chance to do a lot more research on some of the things that affect my community and we came up with several ways to resolve these injustices that were researched. When the documentary was completed and summer was done, I was chosen out of the students that took part during the summer to continue with the project as a facilitator for the high school classes that the project was working with. All of this was a huge learning experience but incomparable to the events that I will remember for the rest of my life.

I have had a chance to present research in cities that I would not have seen otherwise. The project has taken me to Washington, DC, Los Angeles, San Francisco, Oakland, and San Jose. I have also had the opportunity to meet and interview one of my heroes, Dolores Huerta, who granted us an interview for the third documentary of the project, which I facilitated. The most memorable experience of all, though, has been the action that I have been involved in. The Pima County Board of Supervisors granted me the opportunity to present the project's research to them as well as suggestions on how the county can solve some of the problems that we pointed out to them.

Then in spring 2006, I had the honor of being part of some of the most exciting moments that Tucson has ever seen—in my opinion at least. I had a chance to organize and be part of citywide high school walkouts. I was also a part of the marches that took place in May. These were very exhilarating experiences for me. I may have only been one person among thousands of people walking the streets in Tucson and millions through the world, but it was breathtaking to know that every person out there felt the way I had been feeling for years. These were amazing moments that I will never forget. I do not want to know where I would be without this project. It has done so much for me, and my world revolves around this now.

Grecia Ramirez

For the longest period of time, I wanted to change many negative aspects in the Tucson community, but I felt like I needed some sort of support in order to articulate my ideas and my beliefs. I also did not have the right resources to play my role in achieving social justice, that is until I started contributing my time and effort to the Social Justice Education Project. My experience in the project has molded the person that I am today, because it has helped me understand and value the importance of education and unity—main fundamentals to achieve social change. It is very important to be aware that these factors are an important key to social change; change does not happen overnight.

The future lies in the hands of our disoriented and deprived generation, and if no one educates them, then there is not much hope for humanity. In order to educate our generation, we must work together without ethnic or racial barriers. If this difficult but necessary task is achieved, society will develop a classless and peaceful land.

During this process, I had the privilege to interview various important figures and influential people such as Dolores Huerta, co-founder of the National Farm Workers Organizing Committee (United Farm Workers Organizing Committee); Isabel Garcia, Tucson attorney/immigration rights activist; Kat Rodriguez, Director of Derechos Humanos (human rights organization); and Marco Antonio Dabdu, Nogales politician. Interacting with these people was very inspiring; during those moments I realized that, because of the passion these people demonstrated, there is hope for the future and we are not alone in the struggle for social change.

I also experienced emotional moments when I interviewed immigrants along the Nogales, Arizona, border. This unforgettable experience helped me realize how severe the human struggle for survival is. People are dying, and, without the support and compassion of society, death rates will continue to increase. Physical and mental borders are severely harmful to society in various aspects of life, from physical structure to an individual's mentality.

In this world, it is difficult to come across people who view society through the same critical lens, which makes it nearly impossible to stress how thankful and honored I am to work with such caring individuals who are revolutionizing public education in the run-down side of Tucson. They are changing Tucson's public education by creating a strong and effective curriculum. Our approach to renovating the educational process is spreading awareness, with the research executed in the form of a newsletter and documentary film. This method has engaged students in their studies while increasing their test scores and lowering dropout rates.

Figure 6.3 Social Justice Education Project students Liz Hernandez (left) and Marisela Rodriguez (right) strategizing during student walkouts to protest anti-immigration bill HR4437.

I am often irritated when I hear people ridicule the south and the west side of town, a constant reminder of how egocentric society is. But I have yet to come across a person discussing how to implement a positive change in the public school system; the project has helped turn my anger into a much more peaceful and positive approach. There is an obvious problem in Tucson's south and west public school system, and knowing that I can contribute time and effort in creating a positive change, whether it is in an individual's life or in the community, is very rewarding. Although the project has had positive outcomes, there have been various situations that have postponed and interfered with it. However, with patience, organization, and determination, together with my peers, I have kept the project operating.

Liz Hernandez

Who would consider a female minority could graduate and continue her education? Not the majority of my teachers or the administrative staff. They did not believe in a higher education for a minority, such as myself. The SJEP is a strong advocate for students of color. It was not until my junior year when I took an American History through a Chicano Perspective class,

Figure 6.4 Social Justice Education Project student Liz Hernandez leading a peaceful student walkout to protest anti-immigrant bill HR4437.

that I learned a strong sense of identity and cultural understanding. In my senior year, I took an American Government course also through a Chicano perspective named “The Social Justice Education Project” (SJEP). In this class, I gained a knowledge base, critical thinking skills, and consciousness. It was at that moment, I found a strong Chicana identity deep in my heart.

In all my four years of high school, my last two were the most valuable. It was during this time I took on the responsibility and honor to represent *mi cultura*, *mi gente*, and my identity as a Chicana, in its true light of beauty. Unfortunately, I have been conditioned by society to feel shame for being who I am. The language my parents spoke and taught me is viewed as less than beneficial. Luckily, because of the two classes, I was able to discover my missing culture. I now feel proud of who I am! There is nothing more amazing than my culture. Knowing that people who come from the same cultural background brings love and compassion to my heart.

This past spring, I was one of the key organizers for the walkouts in Tucson, Arizona. We protested the racist bill HR4437 that would criminalize my people. Along with the help of “The Riders,” a group of high school students, we made history by coming together in solidarity to help others. On April 10, 2006, The Riders and I organized the April 10 march in Tucson for K–12 students. I was a part of history, just as much as people were a part of

Figure 6.5 Social Justice Education Project Director Augustine Romero, with Social Justice Education Project student Yarko Ruiz. Yarko, first generation from Mexico, gave the commencement speech at his graduation in Tucson, Arizona.

history. We sent a loud message to the government, and we will not give up! I am thankful for the knowledge and consciousness I have received through the SJEP. Today, I am a Chicana who graduated from high school and will continue her higher education. I know there will be more Chicanos that will graduate with knowledge and critical thinking skills and consciousness with the help of the SJEP in Tucson Unified School District.

Finally, we give these poems to you. The gift we received from our education, we give back to you.

The liberation from cultural invasion

From A Xicana, a true light of beauty
Who is to Blame?
Who discovered America?

Who is the natural enemy?
There are always two parts to a story, right?
And all this time, I have heard one,
So the other side is where I'm coming from

No longer colonized by the European perspective view,
for 515 years RAZA has been silenced.
It started once upon a time with the Aztecs living in Tenochtitlan
515 years ago a man came to my land and changed her name to America.
He killed millions, he raped thousands, he used the name of God to destroy a civilization, he was a mercenary for power, he said he discovered America . . . !!!
But in reality he did not, he discovered America,
maybe for the white man but not for the brown, get it right!!!!!
His name is not Christopher Columbus.
But a banal European named, Hernan Cortez.
He is the one to blame for killing RAZA and taking
our original language, tribe, and cultural ways of living.
He burned 99.9 percent of the Aztec books.
He sabotaged, assailed, and exploited my people so
he could steal our land and mark us as slaves.
Columbus and Cortez are no heroes, they are murderers to humanity.
Let them be heroes to the white society, but not for the indigenous people.
In my point of view, Cortez must absolve Raza,
I blame him for the brain washing, the Spanish occupation, Manifest Destiny, and the oppression in America.
Tell me, what makes America so great?
The weapons of mass distraction. Or the fact that the
rich people are getting richer and the poor getting poorer.
America home of the free yet, someone is paying the cost,
the cost of death to have the American dream.
What is the American dream?
Does it even exist?
Or is it another white man's lie?
A lie that keeps people blind of the reality.
The reality that has been taken way by
The cultural invasion!!!!!!!!!!!!!!!!!!!!

Being Woman by Kim Dominguez

I
Was created in the act of oppressing women . . .
A man with a girl only 15
Mothers let your daughters become mothers way too soon
Young housewives . . . so tired of cleaning

Grandfathers make granddaughters give them a massage
Mija' take my shoes off, rub my feet
TRAIN THEM EARLY
KEEP TRADITIONS GOING
Abuse so tired of abuse
Looking at holes in the wall punched in by angry men covered with pictures of fake smiles . . .
Women seeking happiness as all the rest in this place
I'M NOT your mother
I'm not my mother
So what if I don't feel like cleaning
Washing dishes
Or peeling potatoes?
And if that means I won't be a good mom then I'll do the unthinkable and not have kids
I hear people judging me
Do they think they're jesus?
I am rude
I should wear makeup
I should lose weight
Maybe I oppress food consuming it violently, the only thing that doesn't swing
I can be in control, no talking, no sex, no apologies
When I want what I want all I need just like this world is money$$$
I HATE when people only have time for a two minute conversation and ask how you are doing . . . fine, nothing . . . thinking to myself
Do they really want to know?
I don't care I blurt out
Eviction, corruption, and mutilation of my body, house, neighborhood, relationships . . .
Life all this stress, oppress, and chores cause I'm not a man
Well good luck with that as he turns around and starts to walk away
I think walk away . . . turn away . . . run away . . .
As all men do
Men are clams
Women are crowbars
A quote by a god fearing Christian man
Am I a crowbar? Do I pry? Do I go too far? Should I wear makeup?
In the bathroom reading my seventeen, my, teenbeat, cosmo, feeling schizophrenic
I think to myself thank god for dishwashers, I'll get up and load the dishes, or throw away my magazines

A proud "feminist" who still feels fat, ugly and scared of men at the end of the day
And dreams of romance while she's sleeping

This poem is dedicated to Tim and to all over-sensitive, strong yet vulnerable girls and women who just want to go to bed without tears in their hearts, especially my mom.

The Description by Luis Valdez

What kind of world do we live in? I ask myself this question every time I step outside of my own head, open my eyes and just observe, quietly. Every time I wake up, look around my room and realize that I've been evicted again. Every time I step outside my house, and all I see is my broken down car with no money to fix it. My neighbor being harassed by the police once again because he fit "The Description."

Every time I walk outside my yard onto no sidewalk, and cracked streets, upside down signs, and a lovely bus bench which has been a broken man's home for the past four years, which comes with a complimentary grocery cart and always replaceable corporate advertisements. I ask myself every time I work for fourteen hours a day in the blistering heat, building yet another resort that I won't afford to enjoy on my slave wages. I ask myself every time I get home and turn on my television . . . all I see is pictures of them.

Those who have it all and live in peace, those who have endless beauty and extraordinary power, those who have all the money in the world and nothing to offer, but I also see me. I just happen to be hanging off the edge of the picture, or the wrong side of town, or the wrong side of the tracks. My mother cleans their houses. My father builds their town. My sister is the town slut. My brother hijacks cars, and in the news, my neighbor's mug shot . . . . because he fit the description. So I ask myself again, what kind of world do we live in? A world of the red, white, and blue, hot dogs and fireworks, huge suv's and gun clubs, racist clans, and white television, and Liberty and Justice for all.

Notes

1 Vélez-Ibáñez and Greenberg's (1992) *Funds of Knowledge* implicitly puts forward an important critique of Bourdieu's (1977, 1985) and Bourdieu and Passeron's (1977) concept of cultural capital. Bourdieu claimed that culture with real effects in the economic realm derives from the dominant class, since the dominant develops most economic institutions, policies, and practices. However, as Vélez-Ibáñez and Greenberg (1992) indicate, working-class families also maintain cultural practices that have direct economic implications. These

cultural practices, which they term "Funds of Knowledge," have been passed down from previous generations and are critical for the household economy and family survival. The Funds of Knowledge may include special bartering and trading practices or informal "home" businesses and production among a network of households. The Funds of Knowledge are forms of valuable capital, perhaps bearing more sophistication than the dominant culture because working-class practices must help families survive in economic and social conditions antagonistic toward their survival. This idea of the sophistication of working-class culture implies a postmodern perspective in that value is not only attributed to dominant practices but also to those practices aimed at helping people challenge and overcome oppressive conditions. Willis (1981) puts forward a more explicit critique of cultural capital arguing that "value" in culture is more or less relative. While a dominant culture may have cachet in certain elite realms, it may not bear the same value in different, sub-cultural or "common" levels. At the common level, sub-cultural meanings and symbols tend to hold greater value than dominant forms. Thus, capital in culture depends on the cultural bearer and the context of use—working-class meanings and symbols have value among the working class.

2 The idea of using participatory research as a pedagogical strategy for Latina/o students was prominently introduced into the anthropology and education literature by Henry T. Trueba (1991). He writes about the South San Diego Writing Project and how Chicano students "explore possible topics, research them, develop data gathering instruments . . . discuss findings and finally write cooperatively extended and complex essays" (156). He also notes the educational and developmental effects of engaging Chicano students in research. He states, "Chicano students discovered that writing was no longer a futile school exercise designed by teachers for their own purposes, but a meaningful activity and a means for exchanging important ideas" (ibid.). The South San Diego Writing Project demonstrates that grounding curricula and pedagogical activities in the students' sociocultural context through participatory research produces positive results. More importantly, research serves as the "bridge" between the sociocultural context and the classroom. For current examples of youth conducting research see Ginwright et al. (2006).

3 Drawing extensively from the work of linguistic theorist M. M. Bakhtin, Holland et al. (1998) claim that the formation of identity is a process of "authoring selves," whereby the individual communicates meaning about the self-mediated through the ideas, words, and categories of others. An authoring dialogical process increases students' power in the "authoring process" and thus their possibilities for self-determination by providing them the unique opportunity to rearticulate the mediating structures forming others' perceptions of them.

4 Mills (1959) claimed that many problems of modern society require what he termed a "sociological imagination," that no problem (no matter how small it may seem) emerges without any influence from the larger workings of societies. To understand these problems, people may need to "imagine" or at least conceptualize how and in what ways societies are structured and organized to better grasp the social relationships connected to everyday problems. The larger workings of societies may be empirically impossible to visualize in reality; however, Mills believed that our minds have the capacity to conceptually map out these workings in an abstract sense. Once we attain a sociological imagination, then we can comprehend the true complexity behind many social problems.

References

Bourdieu, P. (1977). Cultural reproduction and social reproduction. In *Power and Ideology in Education*, ed. J. Karabel and A. H. Halsey. Oxford: Oxford University Press: 485–511.

Bourdieu, P. (1985). The forms of capital. In *Handbook of Theory and Research for the Sociology of Education*, ed. J. Richardson. New York: Greenwood: 241–58.

Bourdieu, P., and J.-C. Passeron (1977). *Reproduction in Education, Society and Culture*. Beverly Hills, CA: Sage.

Cammarota, J. (2007). A social justice approach to achievement: Guiding Latina/o students toward educational attainment with a challenging, socially relevant curriculum. *Equity and Excellence in Education* 40(1): 87–96.

Darder, A., M. Baltodano, and R. D. Torres (2003). *The Critical Pedagogy Reader*. New York: RoutledgeFalmer.

Delgado, R., and J. Stefancic (2001). *Critical Race Theory: An Introduction*. New York: New York University Press.

Freire, P. (1993). *Pedagogy of the Oppressed*. New York: Continuum.

Freire, P. (1998). *The Paulo Freire Reader*, ed. Maria Araujo Freire and Donaldo Macedo. New York: Continuum.

Ginwright, S., and J. Cammarota (2002). New terrain in youth development: The promise of a social justice approach. *Social Justice* 29(4): 82–96.

Ginwright, S., J. Cammarota, and P. A. Noguera (2005). Youth, social justice, and communities: Toward a theory of urban youth policy. *Social Justice* 32(3): 24–40.

Ginwright, S., P. Noguera, and J. Cammarota (2006). *Beyond Resistance! Youth Activism and Community Change: New Democratic Possibilities for Practice and Policy for America's Youth*. New York: Routledge.

Gonzalez, N., and L. C. Moll (1995). Funds of knowledge for teaching in Latino households. *Urban Education* 29(4): 443–70.

Gonzalez, N., and L. C. Moll (2002). *Cruzando el puente*: Building bridges to Funds of Knowledge. *Education Policy* 16(4): 623–42.

Gonzalez, N., L. C. Moll, and C. Amanti, eds. (2005). *Funds of Knowledge: Theorizing Practices in Households, Communities and Classrooms*. Mahwah, NJ: Lawrence Erlbaum.

Holland, D. C., W. Lachicotte Jr., D. Skinner, and C. Cain (1998). *Identity and Agency in Cultural Worlds*. Cambridge, MA: Harvard University Press.

Mills, C. W. (1959). *The Sociological Imagination*. New York: Oxford University Press.

Moll, L. C., C. Amanti, D. Neff, and N. Gonzalez (1992). Funds of knowledge for teaching: Using a qualitative approach to connect homes and classrooms. *Theory Into Practice* 31(2), Spring: 132–42.

Noriega, C. A. (2001). *The Chicano Studies Reader: An Anthology of Atzlan 1970–2000*. Los Angeles: UCLA, Chicano Studies Research Center.

Selener, D. (1997). *Participatory Action Research and Social Change*. Ithaca, NY: Cornell Participatory Action Research Network.

Trueba, H. T. (1991). From failure to success: the roles of culture and cultural conflict in the academic achievement of Chicano students. In *Chicano School Failure and Success: Research and Policy Agendas for the 1990s*, ed. R. R. Valencia. London and New York: Falmer Press.

Vélez-Ibáñez, C. G., and J. B. Greenberg (1992). Formation and transformation of Funds of Knowledge among US-Mexican households. *Anthropology and Education Quarterly* 23(4): 313–35.

Whyte, W. F. (1991). *Participatory Action Research*. Newbury Park, CA: Sage.

Willis, P. (1981). Cultural production is different from cultural reproduction is different from social reproduction is different from reproduction. *Interchange* 12(2–3): 48–67.

Response to Chapter 6

LUIS C. MOLL

It is with pleasure that I write this brief commentary on the SJEP, whose work I have admired since its inception. As Julio Cammarota mentions in his section of the chapter, the SJEP project has commonalities with the "Funds of Knowledge" research my colleagues and I have conducted (González, Moll, and Amanti, 2005). In much of our work, we attempted to document the knowledge base of households by establishing relations of trust that would allow us to interact with families in ways that we could learn from them. SJEP also depends on developing such relations, in its case with adolescents, while displaying a deep sense of respect for their intellect, which I consider a key aspect of its pedagogy. In contrast to the dogmatic pedagogies sponsored by the state, with its stultifying testing regime and rigid curricula, the SJEP engages students in challenging, relevant, and compelling intellectual work with practical and political consequences. There is nothing "compensatory" about these efforts; it involves rigorous inquiry about issues that matter to the students and their communities.

I first came to truly appreciate the consequences of SJEP at a presentation by its students at the meeting of the American Educational Research Association mentioned by Kim Dominguez, perhaps its initial presentation at such a major conference. I was in the audience when Kim presented her work and closed the session, if I recall correctly, with a poem. What she does not convey fully in her section of the chapter is the extraordinary power of her words, the sincerity of her presentation, and the emotion of her appeal. It was a stunning performance. It conveyed the transformative potential of SJEP in its ability to engage students in serious work to help them thrive as social activists and intellectuals.

There are two additional aspects of the work, which their chapter does not necessarily feature, but on which I would like to comment. One is that through the courses and inquiry, and by deliberately creating space and time for discourse, the "dialogic authoring" that is central to its pedagogy, SJEP produces not only socially aware but also academically adept students, including in courses not associated with the project, that form part of the "regular" curriculum. This outcome involves, in concordance with the students, the development of their identities as learners, and a change in their relationship to schooling, now and perhaps in the future. As such, it deserves considerable attention and careful documentation. It may be the most important reason that some teachers and administrators set aside reservations about SJEP's critical intent, and instead of impeding have allowed it to thrive.

Richard Ruiz and I have used the term "educational sovereignty" to signify strategic conditions that schools can create to challenge the severe constraints of the status quo and offer a progressive pedagogy with potent consequences for students and teachers (Moll and Ruiz, 2002, 2005). We have cited several examples, of the many one could identify, dealing in most detail with a dual language model that facilitates the development of biliteracy in all students, even when under siege by misguided and anachronistic English-only state policies. The SJEP article mentions how it has incorporated its courses into existing school structures without compromising the integrity of the project, but they do not provide details on how such conditions were created and supported, the resistance to the program notwithstanding. This type of analysis is terribly important. It would involve studying not only how and why existing social structures accommodate SJEP, but also any influence of the project on the teachers' and administrators' thinking about education, its processes, goals, and consequences. Consider that the receiving context for SJEP consists of schools that face the usual pressures from the state to conform to its policies and mandates, and to federal regulations. What sorts of social relations must SJEP cultivate, and where does it find its allies, its resources, to establish a niche, as fragile as it may be, within these schools? It may be too early to tell whether SJEP can influence the power structure of schooling, even in contained ways, but the dynamics of this type of social work are important to understand, as part of the "sociological imagination" the project induces. The schools would be wise to listen and learn if just for the simple reason that SJEP is having success, creating new possibilities, class after class and year after year, with the same students these institutions often identify as lost causes.

References

González, N., L. C. Moll, and C. Amanti, eds. (2005). *Funds of Knowledge: Theorizing Practices in Households, Communities, and Classrooms*. Mahwah, NJ: Lawrence Erlbaum.

Moll, L. C., and R. Ruiz (2002). The schooling of Latino students. In *Latinos: Remaking America*, ed. M. Suárez-Orozco and M. Páez. Berkeley: University of California Press: 362–74.

Moll, L. C., and R. Ruiz (2005). The educational sovereignty of Latino students in the US. In *Latino Education: An Agenda for Community Action Research*, ed. P. Pedraza and M. Rivera. Mahwah, NJ: Lawrence Erlbaum: 295–320.

CHAPTER 7

Six Summers of YPAR

Learning, Action, and Change in Urban Education

ERNEST MORRELL

Being a critical researcher has changed the way I look at things in many ways. For one, I have realized that I could question any time I want if I feel there is anything wrong or when I disagree with anything. My opinion does count and should be heard because it could make a difference. I no longer read text without questioning it. Being a critical researcher also makes me feel kind of invincible. Like they say, knowledge is power and now with this brand new power there are many things that I could do to make a change where there needs to be a change. I don't know how I am going to go back to S High School and not do anything with this power. I no longer feel powerless like I used to in school. Every time the school did something I didn't agree with and didn't like, I just took it without saying anything like most kids do. That isn't going to happen anymore because now I know that my voice counts and that every person's voice should be heard. The thing is that I always wanted to do something like this, but I felt powerless. Now with this brand new power that I have acquired, I'm unstoppable. The knowledge that I have will be spread to other people and that will make the difference. That is how I have changed now that I'm a critical researcher. Now I have ambitions on how I will change things that are messing up the whole community.

(From the critical memoir about "Becoming a Critical Researcher")

One way I can bring things from the seminar to the kids at my school is to talk to my friends about what I did, what I learned, and how it's changed my views of things. Hopefully once I tell my closest friends about this they can also pass it on to other people they know. I can also share with them some of the readings that we did during the seminar. This way they can realize that Southwest High isn't the only one with problems. And the only way some of these problems can disappear or get better is to challenge authority to make them do something. In the readings the only way things got better or something was done about them was

> by letting the public know what was going on. If the people don't know what is going on how are they going to do something about it? In a way I feel I can help the situations that are going on at my school by just letting others know that there is something you can do about it. Other people at other schools similar to S.W. solved problems by challenging authority; like [our college student mentor] said, that's the only way it can be done.
>
> **(A student response to the journal prompt, "How can you bring the knowledge from the seminar back to your school?")**

Challenges in Contemporary Education and the Promise of YPAR

> My walk home is never predictable; sometimes there's a bike cop escort, sometimes there's a police car escort and sometimes there's a helicopter escort. Kids are smoking and taking things from other kids. I begin thinking, "Why are the police here and, what good are they here to do?" When I get home, I reflect on my day. I think about what I have accomplished and I can't help but to think nothing. As I drift off to sleep to the sounds of the helicopter, I see that the day is turning into night.
>
> **(From a student's critical memoir about "A Day in My Life")**

Although they are the population with the most at stake in schools, youth are rarely engaged in conversations about the conditions of schools or school reform. If they are invited to speak, this usually occurs at individual case level. Youth simply are not asked to speak as a larger collective, nor are they provided with the tools needed to amass evidence to speak about the relationships between their particular experiences and the experiences of others in similar situations. Simply put, youth do not often participate as researchers or experts in dialogues concerning the present and future of urban education. In my work with the Institute for Democracy, Education, and Access (IDEA) in Los Angeles, we created spaces where young people attending city schools can learn and utilize the tools of research as they design and carry out research projects of interest to them and their communities. Over our eight years of work, we apprenticed youth as participatory action researchers to develop academic competencies, to develop youth as engaged intellectuals, and to expand the scope of what is considered quality scholarship in the arena of educational research.

This chapter examines youth participatory action research (YPAR) in the context of a summer seminar in critical research offered from 1999 to 2004 to high school seniors in the Greater Los Angeles area. Particularly I address the following questions:

1. How were the principles of YPAR translated into a curriculum and pedagogy for urban adolescents?

2 How did students use YPAR to investigate the conditions in their schools and communities?
3 What did students produce through their YPAR projects?
4 What were the various outcomes of the YPAR projects with respect to student learning, student identity development, and changes in policy and practice?
5 How might this case study of YPAR in a summer research seminar contribute toward a framework for youth engagement, empowering education, and urban school reform?

I begin by offering a working definition of YPAR. Over the course of the six years of involvement with the project, the meaning of the term was refined, but the basic principles largely held constant. I then briefly discuss the various theories of learning, action, and change that informed the work of the seminar. Particularly, I address the influence of John Dewey, Paulo Freire, and sociocultural learning theory, on the work of the seminar. The next section offers a brief history of the summer seminar and describes the core activities as they evolved over the six years of the project. I also describe the participants of the seminar over its duration.

The heart of the chapter examines the six summers of YPAR in the seminar. I address each seminar separately, looking at how the theme translated into youth projects. I examine student work products and offer multiple examples of student work that highlight youth voice and youth textual production. When possible, I offer student voices describing how the work influenced their academic and social identities. In the final section, I consider how an examination of this work might influence conversations about youth engagement, empowering education, urban school reform, and paradigms of research in the field of education.

What is Participatory Action Research?

McIntyre (2000) identifies three principles that guide most participatory action research projects:

1 The collective investigation of a problem
2 The reliance on indigenous knowledge to better understand that problem
3 The desire to take individual and/or collective action to deal with the stated problem

Participants become researchers about their daily lives in hopes of developing realistic solutions for dealing with the problems that they believe need to be addressed. By assuming active and full participation in the research process, people themselves have the opportunity to mobilize, organize, and implement individual and/or collective action (Selener, 1997). Of course, in YPAR, *youth* are the people involved in this research process. Involving youth is significant for several reasons. First, youth, and especially youth from low-income communities, are seldom engaged as potential knowledge producers. YPAR is an approach to research for action and change that conceptualizes youth as legitimate and essential collaborators. In addition, positioning youth as researchers offers important and unique insights into some of our most serious social ills that disproportionally effect young people: ills such as gang violence, suicide, and educational injustice. If we are to truly understand how young people are affected by these social issues, and if we are to understand how to eradicate the social conditions that contribute to these issues, then we must listen to the young people who are most affected by them. Furthermore, we must equip young people with the investigative tools that allow them to collect, analyze, and distribute information about these issues from their unique perspectives as insiders.

Participatory action research (PAR) gained recognition in Latin America during the 1970s through the Symposium of Cartagena on Critical Social Science Research in April 1977 (Morrow and Torres, 1995) and the influence of Brazilian educator Paulo Freire (1970) who engaged marginalized populations of Brazilian peasants as collaborators, researchers, and activists. Freire fundamentally believed that any meaningful social transformation would only occur in conjunction with everyday people. Freire's critical pedagogy was designed to help everyday people to develop the literacy and inquiry skills that would allow them to more powerfully engage structures of power.

PAR projects are often partnerships between sanctioned institutions (universities, Institutes of Health, Bureau of Indian Affairs, etc.) and local groups (teachers, adolescents, community residents, etc.). The research itself is part of the process of empowerment. The researchers are aware of themselves as implicated agents. Designating one's project as an action research project is to make a political statement. Participatory action projects have been popular across academic disciplines, especially psychology, public health, environmental studies, women's studies, and Native American studies. Additionally, PAR projects are very likely to focus on issues of culture, gender, class, ethnicity, race, and power. Most PAR projects are conducted with or on behalf of marginalized populations (such as inner city youth) with the goal of understanding and intervening in real social problems such as domestic violence, environmental pollution, and lack of access for people with physical disabilities.

The participatory action research in almost all cases intended to inspire multiple transformative outcomes, including individual development and social action. This is important when considering its potential role in urban education, particularly when students are positioned as researchers. A major goal of YPAR is youth development, but an equally important focus is the development of students' literacies through innovating and empowering classroom curricula and pedagogies. Additionally, YPAR seeks to develop young people as empowered agents of change through a process that also addresses larger issues of social inequality.

Researchers also situated PAR in the context of democracy and the creation of a true public sphere. Both university and community-based participants were aware of who normally has the power to conduct research, and the research itself was a conscious effort to disrupt or call into question this paradigm of knowledge production. Finally, participatory action researchers challenge the notion of any research being neutral or value-free. Recently, PAR, which in some ways exists in contrast to traditional research, has been attacked as involved, interested, engaged, and, somehow less important and rigorous than research that is distanced, disinterested, and objective. Given its position on the periphery of many social science fields, researchers who engage in PAR have had to "defend" the rationale of their studies. In a meta-review of research on YPAR I found that researchers who engage in YPAR also engage in a critique of the disciplinary norms that have placed additional burdens on "engaged" researchers (Morrell, 2006). Regardless of the attacks from the more traditional core of social science research, YPAR, I argue, is an important pedagogical and social action tool that affirms youth as transformative intellectuals and involves an important and often-neglected population in the process of collecting and distributing information intended to inform, persuade, and ultimately transform oppressive social realities. I now move to a discussion of the theories of learning, action, and change that lay at the foundations of YPAR in the context of our summer research seminar for adolescents in urban Los Angeles.

Theories of Learning for Action and Change

> I grew up in a neighborhood where I couldn't walk safely to school in the morning without the fear of getting my CD player stolen at gunpoint. I saw people of my own race and those of others mistreating, beating, shooting, and trying to put each other down all the time. So I started questioning and asking why this happens in my neighborhood and hardly not in others where there are less minorities. I thought that by going to school I would come to a deeper understanding of the issues

> in my society and how to deal with them. Instead, I was learning about how the Greeks came up with the concept of democracy, the potential form of government, which would create a "utopian" society in which all men are said to be created equal. I saw no equality in the streets, schools, even in the lifestyles of my community, and the lifestyles of the rich and the famous.
>
> **(From a student memoir on "Art and Politics")**

Several major theorists influenced the work of the summer seminar and the youth participatory action research projects that are the substance of this chapter. I would like to briefly acknowledge the contributions of John Dewey, Paulo Freire, and sociocultural learning theorists, whose ideas shaped our pedagogy of YPAR. We were heavily influenced by the ideas of Dewey, who advocated that students learn best when they are investigating their own social worlds. Dewey understood that children naturally learned when they were allowed to follow their own natural curiosity about the world around them. He also understood the importance of active participation in the learning process. Further, Dewey understood the implicit motivation that children have to become more knowledgeable of and connect with the immediate world around them. Only after young people became connected to their immediate social surroundings would they be willing and able to expand their sphere to consider themselves as members of a global community. Dewey was explicitly skeptical of the pedagogies of his day, which began with distant and abstract concepts rather than local and meaningful concepts; he was also critical of rote learning that positioned youth in the roles of passive recipients of discrete bits of information. Rather, Dewey advocated a participatory social inquiry whereby young people learned relevant academic and citizenship skills as they learned to inquire about the world around them (Oakes and Rogers, 2006).

Additionally we drew from Paulo Freire (1970), who advocates for a critical education that confronts real problems that the oppressed face in their own worlds. Freire understood the connection between oppressive educational structures, the dehumanization of marginalized groups, and the reproduction of social inequality. Freire identified a banking metaphor of education in which teachers utilize their position to feed problematic information to students, who are merely passive recipients. Both the process of education and the content of banking education serve the interests of power elites, which, through this process, maintain inequitable conditions that are passively accepted by the broader public. Friere believed that it would only be through dialogic and problem-posing pedagogy that members of historically marginalized groups would come to a recognition of this oppression. Freire also believed that the process involved decentering the relationships between teachers and students and situating the learning process within a dialectic of thought and action that he referred to as praxis.

We combined these theories of the purpose or context of education with empowering theories of learning that moved away from the top-down pedagogies (what Freire refers to as "banking education") traditionally found in K–12 classrooms, in which students functioned as passive recipients and teachers as disseminators of all relevant knowledge.

In contrast to the banking education, we drew upon neo-Vygotskian sociocultural learning theorists who articulated learning as changing participation in changing communities of practice (Lave and Wenger, 1991; Wenger, 1998). Lave and Wenger, for instance, analyzed the ways in which indigenous participants become contributing members of highly functioning communities in order to develop a social theory of learning. They found that each of these communities provided spaces for legitimate peripheral participation for newcomers that allowed neophytes exposure to the practices of the community without giving them responsibilities for which they were not ready. Over time, the participation of newcomers would change; they would acquire more responsibilities associated with core membership. One way to view learning, they surmised, was to examine the changing participation over time in these communities of practice. Additionally, Lave (1996) felt that because participation changed so too would the identities of the participants change since they do different sorts of things and become fundamentally different kinds of persons.

The sociocultural learning theories appealed to us greatly because they offered a model of learning through participation in socially and culturally meaningful practices; in our case, the practice of PAR. The theory becomes strained, however, when it frames learning as a rather simple trajectory from novice to expert. When thinking about YPAR in urban educational settings, for example, it becomes clear that expertise does not simply flow from core participants to newcomers. While we, as university researchers, held important information, so, too, did the students, who experienced daily the tragedies of educational injustice. Our challenge, then, consisted of providing spaces for legitimate peripheral participation in the research community of practice while also giving youth the autonomy to pursue their interests and passions and to appropriate the tools of social science research in ways that suited their needs. Finding ways to facilitate this tricky balance while facilitating powerful learning and powerful research became the driving impetus of the summer seminar. It is toward a description of the structure of the IDEA summer seminars that I now turn.

The IDEA Summer Seminar: 1999–2004

Beginning in 1999, several colleagues at IDEA began convening a summer seminar at the University of California, Los Angeles. The seminar brought together urban students, teachers, and parents to design and carry out critical research projects on issues of immediate concern to their schools and communities. Throughout the five weeks of the seminar, the students read seminal works in the sociology of education and critical methods of educational research; they developed research questions, read relevant literature, collected data, analyzed data, and created research reports. At the end of the seminar, they presented these reports to university faculty, policy makers, and, on occasion, to regional and national conferences of educational researchers and practitioners. Students also wrote individual papers in which they contemplated the practical applications of their research to the issues in their own schools and communities.

There were multiple goals of the seminar, but two emerge as primary. The seminar space was used to help students acquire the language and tools they need to function within the academy—what I have called *academic literacy* (Morrell, 2004). Historically, students of color have not been well represented within the nation's elite colleges and universities. We envisioned critical, community-based research as a vehicle for helping our students gain the literacy tools they would need in order to be successful at these universities. We looked upon the seminar as an opportunity to demonstrate that young people of color from urban communities were indeed capable of college-level work.

A second goal of the seminar related to the research itself. We held the sincere belief that teachers, students, and parents were the most legitimate collaborators for the kind of community-based praxis-oriented research in which we ourselves were interested. In other words, the participatory research studies were not merely a context for literacy learning; the products themselves were important to the struggle for educational justice within local schools and districts as well as across the state and nation (Oakes and Rogers, 2006). The student-participants and their work influenced policy and practice across all of these settings.

Each summer, the participatory research contributed new insights along three planes. First, it helped create new knowledge relative to the core question(s) of the seminar. (For example, we know a lot more about the changing demography of LA and community-led resistance to educational inequality as a consequence of the 2003 seminar.) Second, it elaborated our understanding of the critical research process. Third, it opened up new ways to consider how urban youth could participate as powerful and knowledgeable agents in their schools and communities.

The seminar met with different cohorts of students for six summers in UCLA's Graduate School of Education and Law School. The thirty or so student participants attended all-day sessions for five weeks to earn a semester credit for a university course. As a part of the seminar, students were exposed to critical theory, cultural studies, educational sociology, legal history, social theory, and critical qualitative research methodology as they designed and conducted research related to issues of equity and access in urban schools and communities. Thus, the seminar sought to address these issues of access both in terms of course content and desired outcomes for its students.

In each seminar, students produced research papers and multi-media presentations. Individually, students wrote 1,500- to 2,000-word essays dealing with their journeys to becoming critical researchers and the implications of their seminar work for engagement in their schools and communities. Student research teams produced PowerPoint presentations, research reports, and a public presentation that showcased the tools that they developed along with their research findings. Further, the students produced short digital documentary films and materials for an electronic journal targeted toward urban teachers and parents. Student participants also presented their research to university faculty, local and state politicians, teachers, community members, and parents. This research has been presented at regional and national conferences such as the annual meeting of the American Educational Research Association (AERA) and the Sociology of Education Association. Finally, this work has been featured by local and national media, including national news outlets such CNN and NPR.

I now move to an analysis of each of the six summer seminars. In particular I focus on the ways that students appropriated YPAR to explore issues of concern to them in their schools and communities; additionally I examine the work produced by the students as academic texts and as artifacts that contribute to discourses of urban school reform. Finally, in each of these seminars I examine the relationships between involvement in YPAR and emergent identities as intellectuals and activists.

Six Summers of YPAR

Summer 1999: Language, media, and resistance

Our inaugural summer, 1999, involved 20 incoming juniors who were involved in a college access program at a local high school. These juniors, all working-class students of color, attended a bimodal high school where access and achievement were largely determined by race and class. That is, White and Asian-American students, who comprised about half of the school population, performed very well by all traditional measures; the African-American and Latino students, however, performed rather poorly. The four-year college access program (the West High Futures Project) of which they were a part existed as a university–district collaboration aimed to increase college access by developing the students' knowledge of structural inequality and educational research. By the end of their sophomore year, students were beginning to explore social theory, its explanations for school failure, and its uses for school reform. The teacher of the annual project classes (each year the students were enrolled in a special class that required their involvement in a YPAR project) asked students about issues that most concerned them and that they would want to research. Project personnel decided that it would be important to create a summer seminar space, away from the school, where the young people could apprentice to university researchers as they applied social theory to the investigation of their own social world. The goals of the initial seminar were twofold: project personnel wanted to create research artifacts that demonstrated the students' ability to engage in college level work; and the project staff wanted the students to begin taking on identities as youth researchers, which, it was believed, would help the students to more critically navigate their own educational trajectories even as they participated in larger conversations about race, class, and educational justice.

The first seminar focused on *Language, Youth Culture, and Transformational Resistance in Urban Schools.* The four research groups, which were developed based on students' interest, focused on: the potential of hip-hop music and culture to transform high school literacy curricula; the different manifestations of student resistance in urban schools; the impact of teachers' attitudes toward students' home languages on student achievement; and differences between home and school attitudes of well-educated citizens in the African-American and Latino communities. The four groups were led by the project teacher, another teacher at West High, the Latino parent liaison at West High, and me, a graduate student at the time who was transitioning from being a high school teacher to a research associate with the burgeoning institute.

Seminar participants were exposed to social theory, educational theory, and existing educational research. With the assistance of their group leaders, each research group developed research questions and designed and carried out research projects. In this particular seminar, all of the groups decided that they wanted to survey their peers to understand more about their perceptions on hip-hop culture, student resistance, language pedagogy in schools, and home attitudes toward education. As team leaders, we facilitated a workshop on survey design and helped the groups to develop survey questions that were then combined into one larger instrument (see Figure 7.1 for an excerpted version of this instrument) that was disseminated to other secondary students participating in summer projects on the university campus.

FUTURES SUMMER RESEARCH PROJECT SURVEY

Background

Name:

School attended:

Year in school:

Age:

Ethnicity:

Resistance and Education

1 Are you involved in any extracurricular activities at school? (For example, sports, clubs, theater, etc.)

2 Please list any leadership roles you have had in high school.

3 Do you belong to any cultural organizations on campus? (For example, MECHA, BSU, etc.) Please list them.

4 If you are not involved in any extracurricular activities, leadership roles, or clubs can you please explain why you have decided not to participate or any reasons why you are unable to participate?

5 Are there times you purposely don't do well in your classes? What are some of the reasons for this choice?

6 How do your feelings about a teacher affect the way you perform in the classroom?

7 Have you ever been in trouble at school for standing up for something you believe in? Explain.

8 Do you think all students have the same opportunities at school?

9 Do you think your school is designed for all students to succeed academically?

10 Do you think a student's race or culture has any influence on their ability to succeed in school?

Language and Education

Do you speak a second language? If yes, what language?

Do you speak in a different manner at home, with friends, or at school? How so?

Have you ever been made uncomfortable because of language? Explain.

How do you react in the classroom if another student speaks with an accent or another form of English?

Are students who speak non-Standard English (Ebonics, accents, etc.) treated differently in the classroom than speakers of Standard English?

Figure 7.1 Excerpts from 1999 Summer Seminar Survey.

Several of the student groups also wanted to interview teachers, so we set up an opportunity for students to talk with teachers from the California Subject Matter Projects who were participating in workshops on campus that summer.

During the final weeks of the seminar, the students analyzed the data that they had collected from their various YPAR projects and created research reports and PowerPoint slides which they presented to an audience of high school educators, parents, community representatives, and university faculty. In analyzing the student work, the sophistication of the appropriation of social theory and educational research methodologies became readily apparent. What also stood out, however, was the way that students began to talk about how they had been personally transformed by the research process. Given that YPAR necessarily means that students are researching issues that affect their daily lives, engaging in these projects also means that students have access to information that they can then use to act differently within and upon the world that they have been investigating as emergent researchers. These changing perceptions and attitudes are evidenced in the following quotes, which are taken from the final presentations in the initial seminar:

Student 1: One of the things that I learned from the interviews was that the things I wanted were immaterial. And that the people who we interviewed that wanted an education and weren't able to have one didn't have all of those things, but they still tried. I think it opened my eyes a lot more. I've seen a clearer picture of what's more important in life.

Student 2: In researching the topic, I got to research my family's beliefs on education. All this time, my mom's given me the opportunity to have a successful education, but I realize that I haven't been taking advantage of it. I've come to realize that I do want to succeed in life, but I have to have a good education . . .

Student 3: What I've learned throughout this research project is how extremely important parent's role is for us . . . why? It's not good enough if they just give us money . . . along the way, you're going to need someone to back you up, someone to guide you, that's going to help you out. To eliminate your fears . . .

In subsequent seminars we built on this dual process of individual and social transformation, allowing the students more formal outlets to discuss their developing identities as critical researchers as they also worked on participatory action research projects. We also became more deliberate about collecting data in schools and communities and allowing the young people more direct access to their social worlds as researchers and intellectuals. Toward these ends, the second summer seminar took place in downtown Los Angeles at the Democratic National Convention.

Summer 2000: Youth Access and the Democratic National Convention

The second summer seminar included 25 students from high schools throughout Greater Los Angeles. While 12 of the participants were actually returning seniors from the West High Futures Project, we recruited low-income students from other schools throughout the region. The seminar was framed inside of a larger university initiative to bring students from under-served neighborhoods into the university. Several of the highest need neighborhoods, for example, were not sending any students to the top-tiered universities in the system, including our own university. So, while the seminar still held its college access focus, we were much more explicit, in the title, theme, and syllabus, about the process of critical research for social change. In summer 2000, the seminar focused on *Youth Access and the Democratic National Convention*. As the Democratic National Convention was located in Los Angeles, the students had the opportunity to participate in the event as researchers and as interested community citizens. Students attended formal meetings and organized protests and met with elected officials and activists. The seminar probed the Democratic National Convention to explore provocative political, social, and educational issues around which students formulated research questions, collected and analyzed data, and presented their findings to a panel of university faculty and community activists. In the context of the DNC, research teams investigated youth access across five domains—the media, a livable wage, community learning resources, learning resources in schools, and civic engagement.

During the third week of the seminar, after students had been exposed to academic literature and after they had developed their research questions, we resituated the seminar from our academic context (the university) to a local context near the DNC. We chose to set up shop in a church within a local neighborhood largely populated by recent immigrants from Central America. Although this neighborhood was literally connected to downtown, its residents and its issues were largely invisible to the conveners of the convention. Throughout the week, students witnessed the incongruence between the conversations inside of this local community and the larger conversations of politics and reform taking place inside of the sanctioned spaces of the convention. As researchers, the students worked to push those in power to recognize the issues of access and equity that were largely absent from the major spaces of debate. At the same time, the students turned these critical lenses onto an investigation of equity and access in their own neighborhoods and communities, which were very similar to the neighborhood where we situated our headquarters during the week of the DNC. One of the assignments we gave the students was to document, in field notes, what they saw as they left their homes and traveled to the site of the DNC. Following is an excerpt from one student's field notes:

Observations

1 Bus line 30–1st and Broadway
2 On the bus, everybody either Latino or Black (99% Latino)
3 One young man—shoes w/no soles on bottom; worn out to the ground
Broadway and Pico
4 Venice and Figueroa (right by the Staples Center)
5 Venice and Burlington (bus stop)

Comments

1 Streets filthy until pass through Little Tokyo . . . because city has to keep up the maintenance in tourist prone area
2 People on their way to work(?), listening to music, reading the paper . . . not looking forward going to work
3 Going to work (Little Tokyo), I assume restaurant
4 Homeless all over the street, filthy street; most looked confused and had nowhere to go
5 Blocked off to public, very clean street, quiet, patriotic "mood" USA flag mural on walls of businesses
6 Residential area; again filthy, garbage on sidewalk, homeless man looking for cans along with his homeless friend . . . seemed as if they were very accustomed to that lifestyle

How does this relate to Youth Access? How is it significant?
What you're about to read is based on what I have observed almost every single day on the streets of Downtown and East Los Angeles, so if I have typed anything that needs factual evidence, you're out of luck (sorry). It was pretty obvious that the people on the bus were mainly immigrants. Most were on their way to their very low paying jobs in downtown. That alone is what is holding them back from taking the time to think about issues affecting their community because they're so caught up with working making money for their families who live in the poor neighborhoods. I also see a lack of education in the youth that I see on the bus and on the streets because of where they get

> off at their designated bus stops and what they carry with them and how they are dressed. Instead of going to school, they go work lower than minimum wage jobs. The significance is that the youth's access to learning, media, political and community issues are being denied, simply because they lack the education and the motivation from their family members to go to school. This could possibly be the reason why changes have not yet occurred in the problem cities.
>
> **(Valerie's observational notes at the Democratic National Convention)**

While experienced researchers would point to some obvious shortcomings in the field note itself, it is also possible to see how, in a relatively short time, youth can appropriate the lenses of social science research to explore the happenings in their own communities. As an apprenticing researcher involved in a YPAR project, this young woman is applying a sociological lens to explore the populations and neighborhoods she encounters on a relatively short trip between her home in East Los Angeles and the DNC in downtown LA. It is also possible to see how she begins connecting issues of race, class, and education in her analysis of the inequalities that she witnesses.

Once again, when the students returned to the university during the fourth and fifth weeks of the seminar, they brought together the data that they collected from the weeks in the field. In addition to field notes, students recorded interviews with elected politicians, community members, members of the media, leaders of activist groups, students, clergy, and university researchers. In their final projects, it is possible to see how the students are more emphatically embracing their roles as legitimate researchers and how they are reappropriating the tools of social science research to serve the more progressive needs of their YPAR projects. The following is from the written introduction of the research group that studied youth access to a livable wage.

> Picture this, a group of high school students go out in the world to do research and find out just what a livable wage is, and whether or not we need to impose one. We, as young critical researchers read, listened to speeches, followed members of the media, tallied surveys, and conducted interviews. Throughout the seminar we used different methods to come up with the answers that we were looking for. We interviewed people like KB, president of the Chamber of Commerce. She represented the business perspective of livable wages. We also interviewed RJ, who works with the Service Employee International Union (SEIU), which represents about 70,000 home workers. We interviewed residents of the Area of Los Angeles to have their personal perspectives,

Figure 7.2 Students in downtown Los Angeles interviewing media participants in the DNC.

> and we interviewed a couple advocates for workers' rights like the Green Party to see what their position was in terms of livable wages. We also conducted surveys to people walking in the area of Westwood in order to see how much money people were spending on necessities like food, clothing, and shelter. Then we asked them their zip code to see whether or not people were spending more money on basic necessities according to the area in which they reside. We tried to see how much coverage the press was giving to the issues of livable wages, but we concluded that there was more focus on the speeches inside the Democratic National Convention and the possible violence that protesters might ignite.

The obvious passion and anger comes through in this introduction. It is also possible to see the extensive mixed method research design that the students developed to further understand the context of the livable wage debate. Rather than focus merely on the perspective of economists, business elites and politicians, the students took to the streets and asked people how much money it cost them to live. Additionally they talked to representatives of organizations who worked with people who were not earning a livable wage. Finally the students were able to critique the lack of information in the media about millions of working poor in America during the

DNC. However, for the four days we spent downtown, all of the major daily newspapers we surveyed contained stories about violence and protesters.

Summer 2001: What does every student deserve?

In summer 2001, the seminar focused on an *Educational Bill of Rights*. The seminar theme built on a grassroots effort to establish a set of conditions that every California student deserves. The student participants in the seminar examined the status of these rights within urban schools across Los Angeles. The seminar sought to answer the following questions:

- What does every student in California deserve?
- What inequalities arise in the experiences of California's students?
- Why do these inequalities arise? (What is our explanation for the inequality?)
- What can youth do? How can they use research to play a part in legal advocacy?

From these basic rights and from conversations with members of local community organizations an Educational Bill of Rights was developed. It contained the following:

> Every student in California has a fundamental constitutional right to an adequate education. Every student has a further right to educational opportunities equal to those provided to most of the students in the State. Students, parents and members of the community at large have a right to know what they may expect California's system of public education to provide for each student in California, in accord with these fundamental constitutional principles. These abstract rights must be understood as giving to every student in an elementary or secondary school in California a right of access to each of the following:
>
> 1 A school program that prepares all students to graduate from high school qualified for a 4-year state university, a living wage job, and active participation in civic life.
>
> 2 Adequate learning materials and resources, including:
>   - Materials necessary to advance the instructional program recommended in the state curricular framework;
>   - Textbooks, workbooks and other instructional materials that can be taken home;
>   - Books that can be borrowed from the school library;

- Computers and internet access at the school site;
- Laboratory equipment and supplies necessary for rigorous science instruction;
- Suitable chairs, desks and other classroom equipment.

3 A suitable learning environment and school classrooms, buildings, and facilities that enable learning and health, including:
- School facilities located within a reasonable commuting distance of one's home;
- Clean, uncrowded, well-lighted classrooms and other instructional spaces with adequate ventilation and necessary heating and air conditioning, reasonably maintained and free of vermin, mold and other health hazards;
- Adequate laboratories and studios for students to complete rigorous work in science and the arts;
- Bathrooms and sanitary facilities that are unlocked, accessible, well-stocked and maintained in decent, safe, and sanitary condition;
- Outdoor space sufficient for exercise and sports;
- Adequate school nursing services;
- Adequate lunch periods with nutritious food;
- Educational programs during "off-track" periods.

4 High quality teachers and counselors, including:
- Teachers adequately trained to teach the subject;
- Teachers who have a caring attitude towards students;
- Teachers who receive ongoing professional development and training;
- Teachers who have sufficient time to devote to each student's development—hence access to classrooms with a reasonable cap on class size;
- Counselors who are trained in college admissions;
- Counselors available at regular intervals throughout the school year.

5 A course of instruction that will enable all students to who wish to do so to compete for admission to any public university in the state and participate actively in California's civic life, including:
- Access to challenging curriculum in elementary and middle school that prepares students to enroll and succeed in college preparatory curriculum in high school;
- Access to A–G course sequence;
- Access to AP courses regardless of which "track" or which part of the school the student is enrolled in;

- Access to the full array of curricular and extra-curricular options offered across the entire school calendar. No student can be denied access to any program offered in the school because of their assignment to a particular "track" in a year-round school.

6 Fair and authentic assessment that is used to measure and improve the quality of education students receive and supplementary educational services that respond to identified student needs, including:
- The right of parents/students to waive out of any standardized test;
- The right for students who waive out of the standardized tests to demonstrate their competence through authentic assessment for the purpose of graduation, state scholarship funds, and college eligibility.

7 Instruction taught in the language approved by students and their parents, and instruction provided in a manner that prepares all students to participate in a diverse democratic society.

8 A safe and supportive school environment, including:
- Protection from harassment or abuse of any kind, from any person, including those persons designated to provide school security;
- A fair and nondiscriminatory disciplinary system.

9 Easy and immediate access to current, reliable information on the performance of the school in delivering each of the rights herein listed, including:
- Access by both parents, guardians, and students to accurate information about the individual student's preparation for, and completion of, requirements for college eligibility;
- Access by parents, students, the press and the public to information on the performance of the school and the facilities and services available to all students within the school, including racial and ethnic minorities, and students assigned to curricular tracks, compiled and distributed so as to permit meaningful comparisons of school performance as to each of the rights listed herein.

10 The right of students and parents to associate, organize, protest, and petition—without threat of retaliation—to insure that their rights as herein enumerated are being met, including:
- The right for students and parents to be heard by site principal and district administrators;
- Access to mediation services to resolve conflicts with teachers, principals, or other school personnel.

- Access to an ombudsperson who will advocate on behalf of students and families in their interactions with schools, districts, and the state.

The goal of the seminar was to utilize YPAR to flesh out each of these student rights. Particularly, we wanted the assistance of the student researchers to determine: (1) whether or not students attending local schools actually had access to this right; (2) what it might look like to have access to this right; and (3) how student-initiated research might be used as an assessment and advocacy tool in the continual struggle for student rights.

Each of the five research groups addressed one educational right and designed research projects to be conducted in the local schools. One major shift in the 2001 summer seminar entailed our transition into local schools as primary sites of research. Our students visited several schools in the city where they conducted interviews with teachers and students, and where they conducted school site observations of classroom instruction, curricular materials, and larger school culture issues. This shift in focus had several powerful effects. The schools visited were the same schools that seminar students attended, so the return as student-researchers changed the power dynamics between student and school. Also, the change in venue put students in direct contact with their peers in interesting and mutually pedagogical ways. As our students collected data and learned about the experiences of their peers, other students learned about the YPAR projects of the seminar and they witnessed youth taking action in their city schools. Additionally, the presence of youth researchers on these school campuses impacted the school campuses. Administrators, teachers, security guards, and others in power at these schools participated in conversations with our student researchers that forced them to think differently about their norms and practices at these schools. After our visits, we invited the school leaders to attend the final presentations. We also at this time developed a website that maintained the student reports from the seminar. I would argue, though, that the very visits to school campuses served as a catalyst for conversations and action.

In their final reports, students spoke eloquently about the lack of access to basic student rights. The quality of their arguments and analyses is evident in the following two excerpts from student reports:

> We asked students if they were able to learn in English only classes and to explain why or why not. Responses varied. Some ELL felt that they were learning, however, the students may have had a different understanding of what "learn" meant. Some of the students equated learning with learning English instead of learning the subject matter. Lucy

> (CHS): "I think if English is spoken to us in English only classes then we learn more, because if Spanish is spoken to us and if we respond/talk in Spanish then we're never going to learn English." Lucy's statement reflects the attitudes of assimilation that many minorities internalize. Kris Gutierrez (2001) offers a similar explanation: "the rush to replace Spanish comes at the expense of substantive learning and literacy development."
>
> **(Excerpt from the data analysis section of a student research paper on bilingualism, p. 17)**

> Once a universal definition of computer literacy and access is engrained in California policy, schools can begin to organize themselves to effectively prepare their students for the changing technological needs and advances of today's society. Schools could now realize the need for computer labs that would be open until evening hours so as to afford students greater access to the Internet and technology as well as computer courses that support students as creators of more technology and advancements. Such courses should not discriminate against students due to their economic, language or ethnic background so as to provide more innovators that can create technology sensible to the great diversity of people in American society. It would also be necessary for even teachers to demonstrate some level of computer literacy in efforts to receive and renew their teaching credentials. Such a definition of computer literacy and the skills necessary of all high school students would also facilitate legal action by the schools that are not receiving the same access as other schools. Provisions in the Williams v. State of California case or new cases can be inserted to accommodate these newly defined rights and necessities of all high school students.
>
> **(Excerpt from the conclusion of the student paper on access to computer resources)**

In addition to producing quality reports, however, the student research projects also served as a catalyst for advocacy for a Student Bill of Rights. Largely upon the momentum from the summer seminar, community advocates found a state assembly member to sponsor legislation supporting a Student Bill of Rights. The assembly bill (AB-2236) was fiercely fought in committee, where it died, but not before busloads of teachers and activists descended on the State Capitol to argue for its passage. This process also formulated a community of advocates, attorneys, and educational researchers who continue to struggle for educational equity in the state and across the nation.

Summer 2002: Bottom-up accountability in education

> Although policymakers argue it costs too much money to establish equity between California schools, schools in disadvantaged and impoverished areas of the state deserve the same opportunities as those in wealthier areas of the state. Schools in economically disadvantaged areas of the state are not afforded the same opportunities as those in wealthier neighborhoods. Teacher quality directly correlates with the economic situation of the students that attend the school—the poorer the student, the more unqualified the teacher—and striking differences exist between the amount of educational resources found in urban schools compared to suburban schools. As today's job market increasingly requires more intellectual ability, the acquisition of a good education is imperative for one to participate in their community's affairs and contribute to America's ever-changing society. However, the substandard conditions that exist in California's urban schools make it difficult for students that attend these schools to become democratic citizens. The quality of instruction these students receive deters them from reaching their full potential as students and achieving their rightful place in not only this state, but this country as well.
>
> **(From student essay on inequitable resource distribution in California's schools)**

The 2002 summer seminar focused on Equity and Access in California's Public Schools. The central question of the seminar dealt with how students (and parents) could contribute information about school conditions to the state-mandated School Accountability Report Cards (SARCs).[1] This question embodies three sub-questions:

(a) What are the conditions of learning in urban schools across Los Angeles?
(b) How can students access and contribute information about these conditions?
(c) How can students, working in conjunction with parents and community advocates, pressure their schools and districts to include student-generated data in the official SARCs?

The seminar divided students into four student research teams, each focused on one core condition of schooling—quality teachers, a rigorous curriculum, adequate learning materials, and a positive physical and social school environment.

The research continued upon the theme developed in summer 2001 of collecting data in schools that could be used by grassroots advocates to hold schools and educational systems accountable for ensuring a quality education for all students. The seminar also emerged in the context of debates about No Child Left Behind (NCLB) legislation and the increasing pressure put on schools and students to perform on high-stakes tests, which became the primary evaluator of school quality. While the tests were given increased prominence, very little was said about the inequitable conditions of students in schools and who were taking similar tests under the guise of educational equity. Local organizations and concerned litigators, students, parents, educators, and university researchers sprang into action to draw attention to the unfair focus on testing outcomes to the exclusion of conversations about educational inputs. It was in this context that the theme for the 2002 seminar emerged. The explicit focus entailed working with student researchers to develop tools that students and parents could utilize to hold their schools accountable for delivering a quality education. The general consensus was that any conversations about student performance indicators were premature until the state seriously took account of its gross inequities in terms of quality education students received.

In defining our final projects, we made some substantive changes that reflected the ways that young people had transformed our research process. Most notably, we changed the format of the research project to include a section on the "politics of implementation," in which the research groups could talk more pragmatically about how they planned to act upon the findings of their research studies. Often, conclusions in traditional academic texts do not include practical steps for individual and collective action. We found that the students wanted to use their research to educate multiple publics, but they also wanted to outline ways that they could more systematically act upon the data that they collected, as shown in the description of final research projects below.

As a research group, you will prepare a report that has the following components:

1 *Introduction/Problem/Question/Significance/Indicators*: How are you defining your particular issue or concept? Why is access in this domain important? What are some traditional indicators that have been used to address this problem and what story do they tell? How will the student gaze (via critical research) add to this issue?
2 *Methods/Justification/Assessment Tools*: What tools and methods did you use to conduct your research? Why did you choose (or develop) these particular tools and methods?

3 *Substantive Analysis*: Explain how you have used your assessment tools to determine quality related to your particular topic. What have you learned about the schools that you visited as a result of your research? What does this tell you about what students can contribute to bottom up school accountability?
4 *Analysis of the Process*: What insights (about critical research for social justice) have you gained from this experience? What were some logistical challenges that you faced? How did you address these difficulties? What advice would you offer to others who want to create bottom up accountability systems in urban schools? How has this process changed you?
5 *Politics of Implementation*: What are some ways that you can imagine your research (including the tools and analytic strategies) being used in official (i.e. SARC) and unofficial (local, parent-, and student-centered) spaces? What are strategies you would recommend to young people who experience substandard or inadequate conditions in their schools?
Appendix: Include any and all assessment tools.

In the final projects and presentations, I noticed a change in tone from one of a traditional researcher to a more grounded research-activist, which is more in line with the YPAR tradition. One can notice this dual identity manifesting itself in this write-up from the group charged with studying the social and physical ecologies of Los Angeles schools:

> Our research group, over the past six weeks, has implemented analytical strategies and tools to find both the physical and social problems plaguing schools. Our strategies have included interviews, surveys, group discussions, field notes, and exploring school campuses inside and out. Our tools have included video and audio recorders and writing utensils such as pencils, pads, and laptops. Through the insertion of the bottom up accountability structure, whereby students and community members are actually conducting the research themselves, community based organizations can create a more forceful approach to change. Rallies, protests, walk-outs, sit-ins, marches and all traditional approaches will have concrete documented evidence, rather than a media's two minute portrayal. This evidence becomes profoundly original because it is designed and implemented by the organization itself. It is the multifaceted tools of inquiry and the genuineness of the inquiry that allow for bottom up research methodology to be so effective for this type of group. It is critical for these organizations to engage in this type of research and documentation because

it will make community based organizations politically competitive with those politically empowered organizations that use more traditional research techniques.

(Excerpt from final paper of the social and physical ecology group)

Summer 2003: An oral history of youth of color's experiences in LA schools

In summer 2003, the seminar focused on the historical struggle for educational justice in post-*Brown* Los Angeles 1954–2003. Seminar participants examined the experience of communities of color in Los Angeles schools and their efforts to realize *Brown*'s promise of education "on equal terms." Each student research team focused on one of the post-*Brown* decades and produced a portrait of student and community life in Los Angeles that drew from oral history interviews, yearbook and document analyses, and analyses of statistical databases such as the US Census and demographic data on the composition of Los Angeles public schools.

This seminar pushed us methodologically to consider the intersections between historical research and participatory action research. That is, we had to articulate to ourselves and our students why it was important for young people to become involved in historical research. Together we came up with the idea of critical public history, where youth could work to uncover voices largely absent from traditional historical narratives of the experiences of communities of color in the city schools. By capturing these voices students would be making history in the sense that they would be developing their own historical counter-narratives of the schooling experiences of students of color. They would also be making history in the sense that they would be positioning themselves as authentic creators of historical knowledge.

The youth researchers accessed historical archives, visited school sites, examined demographic data, and collected dozens of personal stories that they then made into a mixed-method report that included the analysis of oral history interviews and census data on the correlation between changing demographics in Los Angeles communities and changing educational policies and academic outcomes in Los Angeles schools. In their final papers, young people were able to show how they added to, and in some cases amended, the dominant narratives of life in Los Angeles schools. For instance, they were able to document pockets and communities in Los Angeles that were at one time more racially integrated than they are currently. They were also able to uncover a very rich tradition of student resistance that goes beyond the well-known Chicano Blowouts of 1968. Finally, the students were able to make connections between historical research and action for educational justice. These connections are evident in these extracts taken from the conclusion of a student research report:

What needs to be done to realize education on equal terms?

- People need to be informed about the inequalities in education.
- A study of all schools around the country should be done to show individuals how corrupt the system is and how it oppresses minorities.
- Schools should value the cultural capital of students from diverse backgrounds.
- Students need to do research, like what we've done here, to show that students do not have access to education on equal terms.
- Students and parents need to spread the word about inequities in education.
- Students and parents need to join together and demand what they want.
- Students need to speak up for themselves, but peacefully.

What is the role of critical public history in pushing this agenda forward?

- It encouraged people to realize that they are important and can make a change in society.
- It allows people to gain consciousness of the fact that if things aren't fair, it's okay to stand up against what's not right.
- It presents data that shows discrimination and unequal educational opportunity.
- People who read critical public history reports and attend critical public history presentations could be inspired to conduct their own research to add on to the research we've done.

What role can young people play in this struggle?

- Start standing up and complaining, letting others know they aren't happy with the way things are, and that they won't rest until a change is made.
- Start complaining to those in authority who can actually do something about it, not just to each other.
- Uncover problems and gather data to reveal the problems.
- As students start to realize the truth, they try to seek the truth. Many individuals begin to question their schools, districts, and other structures.
- Young people can demand understanding. Once every adolescent

demands their right to equal knowledge, the system will have to give in.
- Enlightening their parents and their school peers by actually doing research before (They can't go out saying things they know nothing about and have no evidence to back it up) and show it to everyone and hold protests like Chicanos in the '60s.

How can we work together to rebel?

- By joining classes like this seminar.
- Rebelling without committing a crime.
- Not giving into where society is trying to place us.
- Refusing to be average and working class.
- Striving for excellence.
- Revealing the situation to society and making people aware of the injustices going on, or in other words, to educate people.
- Gather and protest. Protesting without causing violence or disaster.
- Voting against the public officials who make decisions that go against education on equal terms.
- Young people can go to school and attain everything that is available to them. They can be great. In the meantime, adults can continue doing critical public history and informing people of what is really going on.

(Excerpt from conclusion of the 1950s research group)

Summer 2004: Critical citizenship

In summer 2004, the seminar focused on *Urban Youth, Political Participation, and Educational Reform*. Students explored:

(a) What it means for urban youth to participate powerfully in civic life;
(b) How urban youth can learn to participate in such ways; and
(c) What civic lessons young people now learn in and outside of urban schools.

Each student team developed tools for examining civic education at a high school site and a community center in a local neighborhood. These tools included survey instruments, interview and focus group questions (or protocols), and rubrics for examining books and other curricula.

Again, we pushed forward with the theme of working in local schools and communities, but we added the dimension of work in local community organizations. Young people were able to talk with leaders of local community organizations about the connections between YPAR and advocacy, for instance. The students also used their research to make explicit recommendations for transforming school curricula to encourage more radical and engaged models of citizenship. Through their demographic data, which they imported into Geographic Information Systems (GIS) software, they were able to show the consequences of inability to impart a radical civics education in inner city Los Angeles schools. Through their survey data (of over 500 students) they showed that students actually wanted this kind of civic education, and by exploring the various ways that communities and community organizations teach about engaged citizenship (ranging from mural projects to marches) the student groups made suggestions to the local schools on how they could tap into these community contexts to reformulate their civic curricula.

YPAR, Youth Engagement, Empowering Education, and Urban School Reform

Although an important goal of YPAR is to conduct educational research that leads to school change, it is necessary to analyze the effect of the process of YPAR on the student-researchers. Across each of the six seminars, students repeatedly spoke to the impact of the critical research process on their trajectories as intellectuals and activists. As Lave (1996) predicts, becoming participatory action researchers, for the students, meant becoming different, and hopefully more empowered, kinds of persons. Critical educators, I argue, have a dual responsibility to both improving the educational system as well as humanizing individual students in this process. While the outcomes of the various research projects on the structural conditions of urban schools in Los Angeles are difficult to discern, the outcomes for the students are clear. Students felt enabled by the opportunity to participate in research projects and they became different kinds of people because of their involvement in these projects.

YPAR also offers a powerful model of youth engagement, one that affirms the legitimate role that young people can and should play in the process of collecting and analyzing data that reveals the contemporary conditions of urban schools and communities. Further, student researchers are very powerful rhetorically when they present their research findings in public. On the one hand, they serve as inspiration to parents, teachers, and community members who continue to struggle on their behalf. On the other hand, student researchers who bring data and personal experiences in urban schools to critique current practices are very difficult to argue with. For those interested in changing the current conditions of schools, it is imperative that young people play a central role. Further, youth engagement not only helps to further the cause of urban reform, but also it develops important civic skills in the youth themselves. YPAR, at once, serves as a context for youth involvement and youth leadership development. I have written elsewhere about the relationship between YPAR and literacy development (Morrell, 2006), but here I focus on the significance of apprenticing young people as action researchers on the development of our future leaders.

Finally, it is important to consider the significance of youth-initiated research to our very paradigms of educational inquiry. When the young people most implicated by the inequitable conditions of schools develop the tools and capacities to conduct educational research, they ultimately ask fundamentally different questions in fundamentally different ways. The educational research community would benefit greatly from increasing the opportunities for young people to develop YPAR projects in their schools and communities. We desperately require their passion, their purpose, and their unique positioning if we are to create a knowledge base from which to advocate more powerfully for educational justice.

Note

1 The state mandates that each school develops and provides a SARC that includes required elements (e.g., standardized test scores, teacher certification information, etc.), but that can be supplemented with locally generated information.

References

Freire, P. (1970). *Pedagogy of the Oppressed.* New York: Continuum.

Lave, J. (1996). Teaching, as learning in practice. *Mind, Culture, and Activity* 3(3): 149–64.

Lave, J., and E. Wenger (1991). *Situated Learning: Legitimate Peripheral Participation.* Cambridge: Cambridge University Press.

McIntyre, A. (2000). Constructing meaning about violence, school, and community: Participatory action research with urban youth. *Urban Review* 32(2): 123–54.

Morrell, E. (2004). *Becoming Critical Researchers: Literacy and Empowerment for Urban Youth.* New York: Peter Lang.

Morrell, E. (2006). Critical participatory action research and the literacy achievement of ethnic minority groups. *55th Annual Yearbook of the National Reading Conference*: 60–78.

Morrow, R., and C. Torres (1995). *Social Theory and Education: A Critique of Theories of Social and Cultural Reproduction.* Albany: State University of New York Press.

Oakes, J., and J. Rogers (2006). *Learning Power: Organizing for Education and Justice.* New York: Teachers College Press.

Selener, D. (1997). *Participatory Action Research and Social Change.* Ithaca, NY: Cornell Participatory Action Research Network.

Wenger, E. (1998). *Communities of Practice: Learning, Meaning and Identity.* Cambridge: Cambridge University Press.

Response to Chapter 7

JOHN ROGERS

Student 1: I liked when the principal [of Global Studies Academy] said that he wanted his teachers to make mistakes.
Teacher: What did he mean by that?
Student 1: That teachers need to try out new things so that they can learn.
Student 2: Isn't that like what Freire said?
Student 3: Yeah, remember that quote: "There's no teaching without learning."
Student 1: See, those other teachers [at Johnson Continuation School] weren't really teaching because they weren't learning.

This dialogue took place as students in our summer seminar tried to make sense of how contrasting approaches to teaching and learning impact students at risk of dropping out of high school. The 2007 seminar represents the seventh time that Ernest Morrell and I have taught a course in sociology of education to Los Angeles youth. For the past few weeks our student research teams have traveled to schools across Los Angeles to talk with students and educators about why so many youth have become disengaged from their education and what can be done to foster engagement and academic success.

During the seminar, student researchers have listened as young people their own age have spoken about the lack of caring teachers or relevant curriculum. They also have observed a few stunning counter examples—classrooms alive with the exchange of ideas. Analyzing these stories, the seminar students are beginning to formulate on-the-ground theories of the conditions and beliefs that shape how teachers and students relate to knowledge and to one another. It is too early to tell exactly what conclusions the students will draw, but not too early for me to conclude that the seminar students once again will author profound and important insights.

As Freire and our students remind us, young people are not the only ones who learn through participation in our summer seminars. Teachers learn as well. Daily engagement with youth who are at once novice researchers and students in the schools we are studying creates an environment of heightened reflexivity for seminar teachers. Our students approach us with fundamental questions that push us to define who we are and what we do: What is research? When is it critical? Why are schools unequal? Can schools be made more just? Does research have a role in this?

In addition to posing questions, the seminar students also position their own work in ways that push us to think about how we conduct research. They introduce their survey by telling potential research subjects: "We are students like you . . . We are struggling to survive just like you in this educational 'guerilla' warfare. We want to make changes that are more than just upgrading the school lunch. We want to conduct and disseminate research that will help to set things right in our community!" The questions and statements of our students prompted us to reflect on whether our core understandings of critical sociology bear what William James termed "cash value" for young people who, because of their class and race, are consigned to poorly served schools.

This summer, our students have deepened our understanding of the seminar's theme of engagement in several ways. First, the seminar students have reminded us of the important connection between identity and student engagement. Young people want to express and examine their identities in the context of school. When this occurs, creative intellectual work often results. Over the course of our seminar, students have written a "critical ethnography" about a day in their school life. Young people who had never before written an extended essay have produced pages of luminous text. They also have become very conscious in their classroom observations of how rare it is for teachers to invite students to examine life in their communities.

The seminar students also have encouraged us to think further about the relationship between student engagement and student power. The seminar students surveyed other youth about whether they could act collectively to improve their school and community and whether they felt engaged in their education. Only one in three surveyed students agreed with the statement: "I am able to make changes at my school." Further, the survey revealed a strong relationship between students' opportunities to participate in social action and students' sense of engagement in their schooling. These survey results echo the experience of several seminar students who have become increasingly engaged in the research as they recognize its potential power to determine policies that can impact their community. A turning point for some seminar students came when they traveled to the Los Angeles Unified School District Board of Education to meet with district officials about their research. The opportunity to interview *and* share insights with the Superintendent, Board President, and other officials, gave the students a tangible sense that their ideas mattered. It has provided powerful motivation for the students as they have turned to the arduous tasks of data analysis and writing.

Finally, the ways that seminar students participate in research pushes us to think generally about what it means to be engaged in research. Our students do not look upon educational inequality as merely a subject of intellectual interest. Studying schools such as those they attend, the students understand racially biased policies as personal attacks on themselves and their communities. Conversely, when they encounter positive models of education, the students often express anger that such learning is not available at their own school. The students approach to research is critical in the sense that it foregrounds concerns with inequality and asserts a prevailing state of crisis that demands immediate attention. These are insights that researchers need to be reminded of again and again. There is no more powerful prompt for such learning than youth engaged in participatory action research.

CHAPTER **8**

Faith in Process, Faith in People:

Confronting Policies of Social Disinvestment with PAR as Pedagogy for Expansion

CHIARA M. CANNELLA

> The naming of the world, which is an act of creation and re-creation, is not possible if it is not infused with love . . . love is an act of courage, not of fear
>
> **(Freire, 2000: 71)**

Participatory action research (PAR) as pedagogy is an act of courage. The choices PAR practitioners make often sacrifice the easier ways of doing their work—youth development, research, teaching—in favor of an approach that embodies their ideals. This work is unwelcome in many circles, in which the mandate is to ensure youth development programs can verify their intended "outcomes" are attained, and research is "scientifically based." These narrowly defined requirements can be hard to extract from the fabulously complicated work discussed in this volume. Of course, there is research going on, and it clearly has an impact on participants. But these processes of collaborative inquiry and action are not neatly quantifiable; different participants learn different things, and do not necessarily correspond to what the pre-determined "goals" were. Yet, in this context, that variation attests to, rather than casting doubt on the value of the work. The adult organizers of these projects do so because of their beliefs about learning and about youth, and because PAR as pedagogy confronts constrictive patterns of schooling that are destructive to both young people and their construction of knowledge.

For practitioners committed to equitable education of young people in disenfranchised urban communities, the projects discussed in this volume address two major concerns: societal disinvestment in the education of huge portions of the nation's children; and schooling based on constricted notions of learning, meaning, and the purpose of public education. As pedagogy, PAR confronts both of these patterns in public schooling, creating a space where a theory of expansive learning is visibly enacted through substantive investment in the learning of all participants.

Under the major themes of respectful investment in young people and a spacious understanding of processes of learning and identity construction, these projects are marked by several characteristics that differentiate them from what many American schools have come to look like. Each of these characteristics is not just a strategy for effectiveness; rather, it is a way that project organizers and participants align their actions with principles of humanizing education. As such, each is a form of expansion: expanded notion of learning, expanded engagement of identities, expanded idea of educational goals.

Models of Expansion

First, all of the participants in these projects are learning, and all are teaching. Some begin with more socially recognized knowledge—and thus socially conferred power—but in each case, intentional effort is made to dislodge the hierarchy of which knowledge is worth more than the others. The adults here, including university-affiliated researchers, teachers, administrators, and practitioners, all position themselves as learners in these groups. While not denying their formal educational training, the project design purposely privileges the knowledge and meaning-making of the young people with whom they work. Gonzalez (2005: 42) argues that

> The border between knowledge and power . . . can be crossed only . . . when lived experiences become validated as a source of knowledge, and when the process of how knowledge is constructed and translated between groups located within nonsymmetrical relations of power is questioned.

The authors in this volume describe deliberate disruptions in power dynamics of conventional models of learning and teaching. As a result, they create room for young people to expand their own sense of themselves as teachers, as bearers of knowledge, and as constructors of social meaning.

In addition to learning and teaching, however, PAR also gives collaborators a chance to *unlearn*. As a process of inquiry into dominant narratives and destructive paradigms, increasing awareness of our own filters presents the chance to unlearn those that dehumanize others and ourselves. The young people in this volume cite the opportunity to first recognize negative characterizations of themselves and their peers they may have eventually believed (Cahill et al.). They unlearn that the way their school functions is the only way a school could ever be (Romero et al.). Through affirmation that they have intellectual insight and perception, they unlearn to suppress their intellectual identities. They unlearn to just reconcile themselves to reality because there is nothing they can do. These lessons of unlearning open possibilities for dialogue and for action.

Second, these projects embrace the complexity of human identity. Each of these projects invites participants to articulate and embody who they are as whole people—their gender, race, ethnicity, geography, languages, and politics. Inherent in this is a recognition that these facets of identity are not separate from processes of learning and teaching. Rather, our subjectivities serve as the basis for who people are, how they make meaning as they learn, and how they embody knowledge as teachers. Graduates of the Social Justice Education Project (SJEP) in Tucson cited three aspects of the program as having significant impact on their decisions to remain in school: SJEP pedagogy, curriculum, and types of interactions and relationships developed among teachers, parents, and students. These three categories reflect the breadth of human need—social recognition and affiliation, camaraderie and support, intellectual challenge and exploration, and opportunities to express and experience mutual respect. The projects described here do not view students as floating minds to absorb material. Project design reflects that students inhabit multiple politicized spaces; these spaces will affect how students appropriate and re-create meaning from the material offered. Kendra Urdang of the *Echoes* project refers to this in describing the research process as pushing participants to "reevaluate [their] comfort zones, be them political, social, or poetic" (p. 26). This work can engage all these angles of human experience and challenge participants to express themselves intellectually, artistically, and emotionally.

Third, these projects are making long-term investments in participants. Of course these projects are intended to offer everyone involved the chance to think, see, and act in ways they have not previously had the chance to do. Thus they have the hope that participants will learn, change, and grow in ways they have not previously experienced. The projects do intend to "have an impact" in the lives of participants. But there is no predetermined list for what it is participants must learn, how they will change as a result of these projects. In some cases, there is a general goal of what that impact might be. Projects here hoped to foster expansion of academic engagement, civic identity, and social activism for example, because the organizers know these to be crucial for young people's fulfilling development. But there is no test here that determines whether young people have fulfilled specified qualifications to an acceptable level by the end of the term.

Project organizers also recognize that this impact might not manifest fully for many years, and that this impact is not a static product. In recognition that people evolve and re-invent themselves as learners and thinkers throughout their lives, PAR as pedagogy does not require demonstrations of particular behavior to prove that the process of inquiry is valuable to participants. Particularly, given the complexity of topics youth engage with—institutionalized racism, educational inequity, political disenfranchisement—young people cannot be expected to sum up what they learned on a test at the end. These organizers realize that collaborators will engage with ideas, appropriate meaning, and enact it in their own lives according to their own schedule; as Gonzalez, Moll, Tenery, et al. (2005: 107) describe, "transformation does not have a time frame." These projects instigate a smorgasbord of ideas, and it is up to each individual to eventually incorporate these into their own understanding of the world as it makes sense to them. For many of the youth participating in PAR projects, the "impact" of becoming a researcher might not be identifiable for years—or might not be neatly definable, ever.

In particular, these projects show how PAR can be engaged as a pedagogy of expansion—expanded social agency, civic activism, intellectual and academic identities. This expansion seeks to compensate for the constricting environment that young people increasingly experience in their schools. This constriction reflects a lack of faith in students and their teachers. This lack of faith marks the educational policies that PAR as pedagogy successfully counters. It explains impoverished notions of learning and deficient investment in the education of American youth. This fundamental lack of confidence in what it means to learn and how schools might go about teaching, undergirds the educational policies to which students are increasingly subjected. Federal educational policies are increasingly encroaching on the classroom practices of teachers across the United States (Orfield, 2004), and they are imbricated with an underlying philosophy of learning that explicitly neglects to invest in youth and their teachers—failing to demonstrate any faith in their ability as learners, and questionable in its treatment of their humanity. This work embodies—and intends to communicate to youth—faith in young people's abilities to construct the meaning and knowledge that they need to enact just social action. These projects invest time and social resources in young people because the organizers have confidence that the youth will take this experience and create something with it. This faith in young people—faith in people at all—serves as a foundation for teaching and research documented in this volume. It is this faith that allows these projects to confront and counter several destructive patterns in education and youth development.

Culture of Constriction: Federal Education Policy

This federal policy is currently enacted by the No Child Left Behind (NCLB) Act of 2001—federal legislation that mandates a system of accountability for US public schools. The NCLB professes to improve educational opportunity for those students from groups (minoritized racial and ethnic categories, those from low-income urban communities) who have historically been awarded lower rates of achievement in schools (US Department of Education, 2001). There is, in fact, much evidence that the NCLB is not improving achievement (Lee and Orfield, 2006), and in some cases actually exacerbates inequitable resources in schools (Valenzuela et al., 2007). The resultant enforcement of high-stakes testing, standardization, and accountability undermines holistic investment in quality education (Rothstein and Jacobsen, 2007). In addition, the learning environment fostered by these policies is marked by a constricted notion of learning and knowledge, particularly in those schools already determined to be "failing" or "underperforming" (Diamond and Spillane, 2004).

The NCLB is purported to ameliorate the vastly differential achievement levels of students from "disadvantaged" backgrounds; indeed the appropriation of the name "No Child Left Behind" from the Children's Defense Fund (CDF) decades-old motto implies that the legislation's intent is aligned with the CDF's own work for just treatment of children. Yet Gary Orfield of the Civil Rights Project at Harvard University argues that the NCLB's methods instead ensure that the legislation will not improve access to high-quality educational resources for all American children. The Civil Rights Project analyzed not only the state goals of the legislation, but also "what the law actually means in action, whether it is workable and effective as it is now implemented, and what the impacts at the state and local level imply for ultimate success" (Orfield, 2004: 3). The project set out to test whether the goals of the legislation actually align with what actions it requires of states, localities, schools, and teachers. The data are not promising (Sunderman and Kim, 2004). Lee and Orfield's (2006) comprehensive report about changes in math and reading test scores since the implementation of NCLB finds, among other things, that:

1 NCLB did not have a significant impact on improving reading and math achievement across the nation and states. Based on the National Assessment of Educational Progress (NAEP) results, the national average achievement remains flat in reading and grows at the same pace in math after NCLB as before;

2 NCLB has not helped the nation and states significantly narrow the achievement gap. The racial and socioeconomic achievement gap in the NAEP reading and math achievement persists after NCLB;
3 NCLB's attempt to scale up the alleged success of states that adopted test-driven accountability policy prior to NCLB, so-called first generation accountability states (e.g., Florida, North Carolina, Texas) did not work.

As a result, there is a gap between what NCLB professes to value and how the regulations of the legislation programs must be run. Research is increasingly finding that, in fact, the administrative, testing, and pedagogical practices encouraged and in some cases required by NCLB actually undermine efforts at increasing educational attainment of those students with low test scores (Diamond and Spillane, 2004; McDermott and Hall, 2007; Valenzuela, 2000; Valenzuela et al., 2007). The means by which states and districts are to enact the Act will debilitate efforts to provide children from diverse backgrounds with the most appropriate pedagogical and administrative resources (National School Board Association, 2004).

Of all the approaches one could take in efforts to address inequitable school achievement, the NCLB is rather selective in its repertoire of strategies. The strategies it does allow embody "a vision for achieving progress in education through increased control and standardization" (McDermott and Hall, 2007: 9). This results from several ideological assumptions apparent as the basis for NCLB, all of which reflect on how the legislation conceptualizes students and teachers; the process of learning; and the purpose of public education. More specifically, this legislation relies on the following beliefs, without which there is no way of justifying its requirements:

1 Standardized tests are a good measure of how well schools are doing; factors such as graduation rates, disciplinary reform, community partnerships, teacher retention, and holistic assessments are not relevant indicators of quality education;
2 All children should be expected to meet the same goals by the same time; these goals are quantifiable and accurately represented by two or three numbers;
3 The amount of funding districts spend per child does not affect the educational attainment to be expected;
4 Class size, teacher qualification, teacher turn-over rate, physical school conditions, availability of health care, distance required to travel to school, and disciplinary policies that impede students' opportunities to attend class are also all irrelevant in determining what their required level of attainment will be;

5 Teachers' opportunities for collaboration, peer mentorship, constructive evaluation, experimentation, reflection, and community involvement do not affect student learning;
6 Motivation is the main factor limiting the ability of schools to teach better and students to attain higher scores; increasing motivation through threats will improve instruction and student achievement.

Each of these beliefs is apparent in how the Act requires state systems of accountability to come to bear in classrooms and schools. Furthermore, each reveals the underlying antagonism toward students' learning processes.

For example, the main mechanism for school improvement under the NCLB is increased accountability. The practices of standardized testing and high-stakes accountability created and maintained by NCLB are predicated on the assumption that student achievement is low because of a lack of motivation among teachers and students, and, to some degree, administration. People achieve or fail because of motivation. According to this logic, in order to improve achievement, we should reward those who succeed and punish those who fail.[1] If the only thing standing between failure and success is motivation, then increased accountability should increase achievement. When we finally institute policies that threaten to withhold funding and recognition, then teachers and students will finally become motivated, and real change will take place. Gary Orfield (2004: 3) describes this policy as relying on "the threat of punishment and the loss of both resources and the best students" as "strong incentives that will produce improvement at the school level." This logic also assumes that there are no other relevant factors affecting school achievement and failure such as students having access to high-quality educational resources, and teachers having the resources to provide them.

This attitude can only exist alongside denial of the results of volumes of research that recognize the complex yet addressable factors that affect students' achievement (Davidson, 1996; Delpit, 1995; Demmert and Towner, 2003; Gay, 2000; Gilmore, 1985; Imber, 2003; Ismail and Cazden, 2005; Ismat, 1994; Klug and Whitfield, 2003; Ladson-Billings, 1989, 1995; Lipka and McCarty, 1994; Lowell and Devlin, 1998; Mehan et al., 1994; Noguera, 2002, 2003; Valdez, 1996; Valenzuela, 1999). The attitude requires one to refuse to see a connection between the social, historical, political, economic, environmental context of schooling and the actual achievement levels of students. This marks a failure on the part of policy makers to recognize that students are complex beings, affected not only by the sheets of paper in front of them and threats from the front of the class, but by the evidence of investment in them that their society makes apparent to them.

In fact, it is not motivation that has been missing this whole time. Rather, the structures of public schools and the pedagogical practices encouraged, mandated, and often required, impede students' access to rich learning environments. Rather than increasing comprehensive social investment in quality education (smaller schools, apprenticeships, peer-teacher mentoring, respectful and constructive discipline policies, neighborhood investment, economic revitalization), the NCLB institutes a policy of threats and punishments. This results in an educational environment that undermines students as capable learners in need of equitable access to places to learn. The choice of the NCLB's accountability system betrays a lack of faith in teachers' and students' processes of learning.

Implications of Testing

I could choose any one of these sample assumptions to illustrate how NCLB's lack of faith and disinvestment in students as learners actually plays out in classrooms; each embodies an ideological distortion of what education should entail. But I select just standardized testing as perhaps the flagship example of how this policy of constriction obstructs students' opportunities for construction of meaningful knowledge. Under this legislation, states decide on one assessment that will be administered to all students in the state. Standardized tests are the only acceptable tools to determine what and how much students have learned. Under NCLB, standardized tests and other easily quantifiable measurements are assumed to be accurate indicators of what students have learned. These policies do not recognize that there are some skills standardized tests do not measure reliably, and some students who are less likely to display their knowledge through such narrow means of exhibition.

Good assessment tools reflect the subject matter and the values of the curriculum (Darling-Hammond et al., 2004; Gunzenhauser, 2003). There are many types of tools of assessment. Students may engage in discussion, answer specific oral questions, write about research, figure problems on paper, teach lessons to classmates, or integrate learned facts into a story, song, or poem. And students may also take a written test. Different methods of assessment are appropriate for different subject matter, different learning targets, and different students. We would not measure students' knowledge of multiplication tables by asking them to perform a dance; neither would we ask students to demonstrate their understanding of rhythm in poetry by administering a multiple choice test. In both cases, the subject matter and assessment tools would not be properly aligned. Standardized tests may be used as one tool in a collection of methods teachers and schools have for assessing students, for some kinds of information.

An ideal learning environment situation would allow teachers to use many kinds of assessment tools to evaluate what students have learned and where they need special attention. Unless students should be offered a variety of means of demonstrating their skills, knowledge, and understanding, from mathematical computation to broad concepts in history and science, our understanding of their learning will be incomplete and distorted. The National Education Association refers to the NCLB system as plagued by an "over-reliance" on testing (National Education Association, 2004), to the neglect of other ways that students may demonstrate knowledge. The legislation holds students accountable

> based just on two test scores on one day . . . In basing accountability just on test scores, NCLB limits how tests scores are utilized, basing everything on a snapshot on one day of what percent of students are proficient. Growth or value added models are not allowed.
>
> **(National Education Association, 2004)**

Further, the high-stakes aspect of the accountability system distorts the value and meaning of standardized tests, effectively reducing the range of student knowledge to narrow conceptions of learning and demonstration of knowledge (Gunzenhauser, 2003; Neill, 2006).

The School Redesign Network at Stanford University found particularly problematic the application of this high-stakes testing to high-school graduation requirements (Darling-Hammond et al., 2004). They cite research demonstrating that requiring a particular test for graduation results in lower graduation rates, especially for students of color. The American Psychological Association's Standards for Educational and Psychological Testing state that, because of the inability to prove strong enough validity and reliability of any one single test,

> In educational settings, a decision or characterization that will have major impact on a student should not be made on the basis of a single test score. Other relevant information should be taken into account if it will enhance the overall validity of the decision.
>
> **(American Educational Research Association, 2000)**

Researchers working with students from ethnic and economic minority backgrounds, in particular, contend that conventional means of assessment, including pencil-and-paper tests, are inaccurate measurements of the full range of student knowledge (Klug and Whitfield, 2003: 179).

The increase in use of high-stakes standardized tests mean that groups of students who currently do not do as well in school will be further disenfranchised (Diamond and Spillane, 2004; Ladson-Billings, 2006; Valenzuela,

2000). The implications are particularly stark for students from disenfranchised ethnic, economic, cultural, and geographic groups, specifically targeted by the legislation for improved services:

> High stakes-testing, which relies on multiple-choice or piece/parts thinking instead of holistic approaches to demonstrating knowledge, reinforces . . . notions of inferiority. Unwilling to admit that children learn differently, and that varied ways of learning may be culturally reinforced, the dominant culture insists on using the results of high-stakes testing to determine which schools are getting it "right" and which are performing "poorly." Students from low socioeconomic levels, students whose first language is not English, and students who have learning difficulties repeatedly make up the majority of students who fail to achieve the level of average on these tests.
>
> **(Klug and Whitfield, 2003: 149)**

Yet states and districts are limited to administering tests that are easily quantifiable and conveniently, if misleadingly, compared, regardless of their appropriateness to subject matter and their impact on classroom practices.

The Department of Education has attempted to cast critics of this legislation as being summarily opposed to testing and standards, and resistant to efforts to identify and address the achievement gap. Former Secretary of Education Rod Paige, who oversaw the implementation of the policy, has stated that "anyone who opposes annual testing of children is an apologist for a broken system of education that dismisses certain children and classes of children as unteachable" (US Department of Education, 2002). The department's explanation of NCLB's testing requirements adds that

> when we do not know whether or not a child is learning, how will we ever provide that child with a quality education? President Bush and the US Congress have challenged educators to set high standards and hold students, schools and districts accountable for results. The stakes are too high to not do a good job of measuring student performance.
>
> **(US Department of Education, 2002)**

But the assumption that standardized tests are a legitimate basis for judging the success or failure of schools and teachers remains a foundation of educational policy.

In addition, the Department of Education (DOE) denies that the need to pass tests above all other demonstrations of learning will result in a narrowing of curriculum, or that "testing promotes 'teaching to the test.'" And NCLB legislation does not explicitly require a narrow curriculum and limited demonstration of success. But increased pressure for students to score well on tests means that teachers focus teaching energy only on subject matter in the test, and generally according to testing formats (Gunzenhauser, 2003). Since the only acceptable assessment is the same standardized test, then the pressure on teachers to focus mainly—or only—on material in the test is overwhelming (Rothstein and Jacobsen, 2007). School district administrators consistently focus on how curricula must be aligned with the tests students will take. Therefore, educational goals shift from providing fertile environments for learning to a static list of goals states must apply to all students. This results in a narrowing of the range of information teachers offer students, and fewer teaching and measurement strategies used in the classroom (Rothstein and Jacobsen, 2007).

The apparent bias in the legislation toward certain types of teaching is evidenced further by news reports of misconduct among NCLB administrators (Manzo, 2007). Evidence has arisen that DOE officials pressured states to adopt some assessments over others, in some cases refusing to award funding until they switched to the preferred assessment tool (Schemo, 2007b). In May 2007, the DOE inspector general requested that the Justice Department launch an investigation into how Reading First, a major component of NCLB, is run. The inspector general found several cases of "conflicts of interest, cronyism and bias in how federal officials and private consultants operated the program and awarded . . . grants" to states to fund reading programs (Schemo, 2007a). The *New York Times* reported the House Representative George Miller, Democrat of California and chairman of the education committee, as saying that Reading First "'officials and contractors created an uneven playing field that favored certain products,' particularly those that emphasized phonics" (Schemo, 2007a).

The Inspector General issued a report finding that Reading First officials and paid consultants "unfairly promoted" certain "outdated assessments," including Dynamic Indicators of Basic Early Literacy Skills (DIBELS). The creators of the DIBELS test have received hundreds of thousands of dollars in royalties from their tests and curriculum, the use of which "grew exponentially through the [Reading First] program" (Schemo). Officials from Kentucky applied for Reading First funding several times, but did not receive any funding until they "surrendered to pressure from federal officials to drop the testing instrument it was using in favor of" the promoted assessment, DIBELS. The Secretary of Education created an oversight committee for the Reading First program.

While the legislation may attempt to remain pedagogically neutral for the purposes of retaining state and local control, it is clear that this is not the actual effect in classrooms; the types of teaching and learning that occur in classrooms are markedly different—not in quality but in orientation—

because of NCLB mandates. And we can, perhaps, allow that standardized curriculum makes sense for standardized testing (though I am still thinking on how the kickbacks help . . .). But the Department of Education argues that NCLB provides the additional funding to meet the educational needs of students who are not doing well on tests. This funding? Grants such as those cited above that were mishandled by Reading First officials. So the legislation is requiring equal achievement, but not providing the funding. As we have seen, NCLB strategies for improvement are selective: increased accountability, but biased awarding of grants; equal standards for achievement, inequitable access to resources. Of all the approaches to school reform, NCLB does not include those that invest faith or funding in students (unless a portion of that funding will get kicked-back to phonics cronies).

Inequitable Resource Distribution

Six years after implementation of NCLB, the school funding for poor and racially marginalized children continues to be inequitable. Urban public schools are renowned for the deficient academic and social resources they provide for their students. Despite a pretense of meritocracy, research demonstrates again and again that discrepancies in allocation of resources directly limit the opportunities poor children and children of color have for success in school and beyond (Bhimji, 2004; Fine, Burns, et al., 2004; Noguera, 2001; Noguera and Akom, 2000a, 2000b; Orfield, 2004; The Education Trust, 2003; *What You Need to Know and Do to Truly Leave No Child Behind [R]. An Action Guide*, 2003). Contrary to the myth that all children have the same opportunity for educational and professional success, The Education Trust (2003) has found that "differences in achievement and attainment between groups of students often have roots in differences in the availability of educational resources," not motivation. Nonetheless, the same standards apply equally to all students.

Better educational resources are generally available to students of higher socioeconomic status (Anyon, 1994). Fine et al. (2003) found that, in American public schools, a student's class predicts the quality of schooling she or he will receive. This is most apparent in the drastic discrepancies between public school funding in poor and working-class neighborhoods versus middle- and upper-class communities; there are also notable differences between schools serving mostly children of color versus schools serving mostly white children. The Education Trust has found that

> Nationally, districts with the highest child poverty rates have $966.40 fewer state and local dollars to spend per student compared with the lowest-poverty districts. That translates into a total $24,160.07 for a

> typical classroom of 25 students. Districts with the highest minority enrollments have $902.23 fewer state and local dollars to spend per student compared with the lowest-minority districts. That translates into a total $22,555.85 for a typical classroom of 25 students.
>
> **(The Education Trust, 2003)**

These funding disparities result in inequitable resources: salaries for qualified teachers,[2] appropriate school and class sizes, updated curricula, books, computers, science and art supplies, and even basic school conditions such as functioning heat, air conditioning, drinking fountains, adequate desks and chairs, toilet paper, soap, and vermin-free buildings (Orfield, 1994). In Los Angeles, woefully underfunded compared to districts in wealthier suburbs, many urban schools are so overcrowded that they have no cafeteria, auditorium, or computer lab. A lack of space causes scheduling problems, leaving some students unable to graduate on time because they cannot take the required courses to earn a diploma (Bhimji, 2004).

In addition to financial disparity, urban schools in low-income neighborhoods fare worse on other measures of opportunity. For example, The Education Trust has found that "secondary classrooms in the Nation's high poverty schools are nearly 80 percent more likely to be taught by underqualified teachers, than secondary classrooms in the Nation's low poverty schools" (The Education Trust, 2003). In addition, while most students are able to recover from one year of poor quality instruction, few can ever recover from three years of inadequate instruction (Fine et al., 2003). Given the paucity of prepared teachers in high poverty schools, it is no wonder students' test scores lag increasingly behind year after year. While the myth of meritocracy places the blame for the "achievement gap" with students, and sometimes their parents, communities, and teachers, such inequitable funding makes the term "opportunity gap" (Torre and Fine, 2006) much more accurate. Rather than tolerating the illusion (or perhaps *de*lusion) that such disparate funding can result in equal opportunity, policy makers consistently disregard evidence that a web of factors affects student performance: "to begin to understand achievement gaps among their students, states and districts should look at the distribution of qualified teachers [and] challenging curricula as well as funds" (The Education Trust, 2003). These disparities amount to such variation in opportunity for learning, individual students can hardly be judged for failing to meet the same standards of achievement.

The Impact on Learning

These disparities are not lost on students. Several seminal studies have considered the ways in which curricular practices impact not only the content knowledge students learn, but also the social roles they learn to assume—as well as how these become facets of their identities. Students in certain environments have vastly richer opportunities to learn than others, as measured by teacher behavior, time spent on content material, depth and quality of instruction, and future educational and professional value of learning material (Anyon, 1994; Mehan et al., 1994; Oakes, 1985). This social and instructional climate students experience has a profound impact on how they think of themselves as students and as members of their community.

Children learn much more than academic content knowledge during their time spent in school. Aside from the immediate family, schools serve as the main socializing mechanism for most students.

The ways that schools socialize students include allowing them particular subject positions—of being active contributors to their educational process, or of being passive receivers of information and discipline.[3] These subject positions have lasting effects on how children grow to think of themselves—of their social roles and identity construction—in their community and society. If vast segments of children in this country are educated in impoverished atmospheres, and thereby socialized into truncated notions of their potential social value, the impact will be detrimental for the country as a whole. And a great deal of research indicates that spending many years attending impoverished schools does affect how students think of themselves: as being valued in their society, as having important ideas to contribute, as being worthy—or not—of the social investment of good education (Fine and Burns, 2003; Fine, Burns, et al., 2004). Through time spent in schools, children also learn how to participate in social institutions—how to be in relation to other people and systems, and what social roles they might choose to adopt.

Schools are the places where children learn how to interact with people—adults and peers—and to participate as active (or apathetic) members of their community and society. Flanagan and colleagues argue that

> Schools are like mini polities where children can explore what it means to be a member of a community beyond their families, where they learn they are the equal of other citizens [or not] . . . Schools are settings where children develop ideas about the rights and obligations of citizenship.
>
> **(Flanagan et al., 1999)**

This process of socialization has direct consequences for how children grow up to think of themselves as active members of their communities—their self-concept and social identities.

Many scholars have found that, rather than investing in the capacity of young people to become social actors capable of improving their communities, the structure and practices of many urban schools undermine students' healthy development (Anyon, 1994; Fine, Burns, et al., 2004; Fine, Roberts, et al., 2004; McLaren and Gutierrez, 1994; Oakes, 1985; Valenzuela, 1999). Particularly in the current setting of NCLB, a lack of abundant learning experiences sentences children in *some* schools to truncated learning opportunities. This research demonstrates that impoverished and negligent schools can actually impede youth's ability to navigate entry into productive and fulfilling adulthood, serving to reinforce and exacerbate the social challenges students face. O'Donoghue's (2006) work emphasizes how public schools in low-income communities specifically do not foster social agency among students; rather, she has found that urban schools place "an emphasis on hierarchical control and order, limited conceptions of citizenship, and 'high-stakes' accountability policies" which "often fail to provide empowering civic learning" (229). Standard educational practices and structures—which are so common and unquestioned as to seem natural—are actually often counterproductive to the responsibility schools bear to socialize all children into productive and fulfilling adulthood. Youth end up alienated from the institutions alleged to serve them (Ginwright and Cammarota, 2006; HoSang, 2006; Males, 2006), which may ultimately influence their stance toward other social institutions.

PAR Instead

The pedagogies represented in these projects engage students in vastly different subjectivities than those they are generally allowed in school. Their approach to PAR addresses these shortcomings in public systems of education. Instead, PAR as pedagogy invests in youth as resources worthy of commitments of time, energy, and faith. In his review of literature on "Social Capital, Civic Engagement and Positive Youth Development Outcomes," Nicholas Winter (2003: 11) echoes research discussed above, in arguing that

> the institutions with which an individual is involved are vitally important to understanding that individual's involvement with public life. These institutions are the place where people learn the skills that foster participation and position them to be recruited into an activity. In addition, institutional involvements are an important mechanism for the creation and reinforcement of psychological identity.

Whereas schools foster negative association toward public institutions for many youth, youth development programs may be positioned to compensate, and can serve as key sites for increasing the social capital of youth.

O'Donoghue (2006), for example, argues that community-based youth organizations (CBYOs), of which these projects are examples, hold the potential to serve as "alternative sites for civic development . . . contexts within which urban youth can transform themselves into powerful public actors and effect change on the very social, political, and economic contexts that contribute to their marginalization" (230). Youth development programs can cultivate those skills and subject positions that promote a transition to fulfilling adulthood and civic agency.

By facilitating increased social investment in young people, PAR as pedagogy is a form of activist youth development, which can help compensate for the community engagement and activist identity that schools and other social institutions fail to foster. Ginwright et al. (2005: 33) have found that "for youth in communities, social capital is closely linked to connections with community-based organizations, intergenerational partnerships, and participation in broad networks of informational exchange about political issues, ideas, and events." Good youth development programs can increase community social capital, leading to more effective civic activism (Ginwright and Cammarota, 2006; Gutierrez, 2005; Kirshner, 2006; Lewis-Charp et al., 2006; Morrell, 2004, 2006; O'Donoghue, 2006; Strobel et al., 2006; Winter, 2003; Young, 2001; Youniss et al., 2002).

Ernest Morrell has argued that "engaging youth as critical researchers" of their own educational system allows them to build "efficacy . . . [and gain] confidence and tools needed to advocate for educational justice" (Morrell, 2006: 118). This is a good example of the impact that becoming researchers can have on youth, particularly when the topic is one of direct relevance to their lives; by the time the project ended, participants "had become powerful researchers and advocates for social change. Even though their research revealed gross inequities in access to learning resources, the group left the process with a sense of urgency to work for social change" (Morrell, 2006: 123). Jennifer O'Donoghue (2006: 232) describes "public efficacy" as "the extent to which young people see themselves as capable of affecting or influencing both the [youth organization] and the broader community." This term describes the process through which individuals come to conclude that

> Their actions have effects . . . in helping individuals . . . Instead of thinking of society as determined by impersonal forces, youth recognize that their agency gives them responsibility for the way society is and for the well-being of its members.
>
> **(Youniss et al., 1997: 626)**

The voices young people project in this volume exemplify how PAR can offer opportunities for this type of activism.

Kris Gutierrez (2005) describes how collaborative research can offer youth the chance to envision new possibilities for themselves through orientation to an *imagined but possible future*. As youth come to recognize that the world is composed of historical actors, and that their communities are shaped by such historical acts, they can come to see themselves as potential social actors as well. Gutierrez's program focused specifically on enhancing academic possibilities for youth whose parents did not attend college, but the mechanism of expanding youths' conceptions of their social agency parallels that in activist youth development. Through this process of re-envisioning who they are and might become academically and beyond, she argues they can see themselves as—and thus become—conscious social actors (Gutierrez, 2005). In both cases, the essential element is for youth to come to view themselves as capable and vital actors in history and social change.

Research Value of YPAR

And of course, PAR is not only a pedagogy. It is also a research method that bears tremendous potential for countering the volume of conventional social science research. Counter-narratives are needed, partly because people need to create them, but also because others need to hear them. This is not about just telling your story, but about conveying an experience grounded in one's sociopolitical context. As a research method, PAR confronts the social exploitation of research conducted on people that is of no direct benefit to them and, all too often, is of professional and economic benefit to the researchers and their affiliated institutions. It helps to fill what Cammarota (this volume) describes as the intellectual void that occurs when people's voices are left out of the research and thus policy decisions that affect their lives and opportunities. In addition, the data gleaned from conventional research tends to disregard how people make sense of their own lives (Gonzalez, Moll, and Amanti, 2005), without which any research will be hard-pressed to inform effective action.

As a research methodology, PAR allows young people to create counter-narratives to the dominant characterizations about the sources of their educational "failure." These characterizations are justified by research methods that are based on the same ideological assumptions apparent in the NCLB legislation, the same underlying assumption of positivism and empiricism in scientific research: what is *real* can be observed, even by an outsider with no emic understanding. It can be evaluated as true. This occurs when educated, privileged people, self-righteous in the ability of their tools to reveal truth, presume their systems of classification are adequate to explain all instances of human experience (Scheurich, 2002). These are instances in which people with social power observe "others" either with the intent to learn about them (traditionally so they may be catalogued or contained), or with the intent to create programs that will change them. Both cases rest on repressive treatment of one group over another.

David Smith has argued that the question of where problems are identified and located is one of the significant obstacles to research's ability to constructively illuminate social dynamics for the purpose of social change. He argues that "a well-noted practice in educational research of all types" has been to "locate the problem in those who are powerless to resist . . . [in] the disenfranchised victims themselves" (Smith, 2002: 178). It might be noted that this has historically meant that students and their families and communities have been the locus of deficiencies; however, the current climate of hostility toward teachers, and their increasing deprofessionalization, means that teachers (especially those in overcrowded, underfunded urban schools) are now viewed as an additional site of dysfunction in American schools.

Those people who create knowledge—knowledge about others through the documentation of their culture—also define *what* and *who*—constitute a problem. Participatory research with young people can help address these common problems in educational research design to bring about more holistic understandings of how schools actually function in the lives of students (Ginwright et al., 2005; Lomawaima and McCarty, 2002). Smith argues this is one of the strengths of ethnography and, I argue, of PAR as well: to "provide a framework for allowing significant problems to arise from the context, to name them and then to locate them in their social context" (Smith, 2002: 177), rather than allowing "problems" to be considered atomistically, and thus positioned in, or ascribed to, those people most disenfranchised from the system of naming.

Participatory research models actively privilege "those who have not had a voice in the past," which is one means of consciously legitimating "new information that is grounded on a different ontological reality" (Guajardo and Guajardo, 2002: 282). Gonzalez (2005: 43) describes the ways that "engendering dialogues of historical consciousness has a profound effect on interlocutors." By shifting power to study and learn to all participants in a project, the opportunity to create knowledge became a collective tool of inquiry, rather than a tool used by some to wield power over others. This design has significant social implications, given the cycle of educational disenfranchisement that both informs and is supported by exclusionary research practices.

This is a crucial shift in orientation for education of disenfranchised young people, given the power vested in the role of socially sanctioned namer, definer, and creator of knowledge. When this process of knowledge- and meaning-making becomes inclusive,

> When the observed become part of the process of observing, the reality and story of people, cultures, and communities will be told in a very different way, with different vigor, indeed, with a different voice. This in turn surfaces and creates a different power dynamic.
>
> **(Guajardo and Guajardo, 2002: 284)**

This power dynamic may result in increased social efficacy and civic agency among members of disenfranchised communities. PAR methods often provide unprecedented investment of social resources and context for engaging in critical analysis of social phenomena affecting disenfranchised communities. This investment in young people's collective agency communicates confidence in young people's abilities to engage in processes of collaborative inquiry and then act in ways that improve their communities.

Conclusion

PAR as pedagogy is messy. Not all students learn the same things. The curriculum changes in ebbs and flows, necessarily being recreated by participants in processes of ongoing inquiry, reflection, and reformulation. As a result of this irregularity, the impact on students is not easily quantifiable—in fact, it might not be apparent at all until months or years later. But PAR as pedagogy acknowledges that rich learning—learning that affects students' thinking and ways of seeing the world far into the future—requires a long-term investment. Results do not necessarily manifest right away, but will evolve and surface in new incarnations as students grow. While this volume cannot document the long-term effects, that is a symptom of both depth and breadth of these projects. And in the meantime:

> "We all make decisions together as a team, no researcher knows more than another, and no one is any more or less valuable than another. We are a unit that works together." (Tuck et al.: pp. 67–8)

> "Our research process awakened our critical consciousness and was personally transformative, as we shifted our understanding of ourselves and our relationship to our world." (Cahill et al.: p. 91)

> "Knowledge is power. Our identities, the options available to us and our education are extremely powerful. Education can determine our lives. Education can create change." Maria (Tuck et al.: p. 64)

> "My experience in the project has molded the person that I am today, because it has helped me understand and value the importance of

> education and unity—main fundamentals to achieve social change . . . These factors are an important key to social change; change does not happen overnight." Grecia (Romero et al.: p. 143)
>
> "In a world where adults never listened to what young people had to say, I was going to be in a room full of adults and I had to speak for myself, my little brother and sisters, my classmates, the project; I felt like I had to speak for every young person in the world. I feel like my job as a young person in SJEP was to be the voice of the voiceless because we are all so silenced." Kim (Romero et al.: p. 141)

These projects created alternative spaces for young people to construct meaning and knowledge, and stand in harsh contrast to federal educational policies, as enacted by NCLB's attempts to simplify—simplify learning into numbers, simplify school environments into categories of "achieving" or "failing," simplify teacher education into a series of tests, and simplify the growth and identities of students. All of this simplification is ultimately unrealistic. These policies neglect the multitude of factors that affect student learning, and are impervious to the notion that the purpose of schools stretches beyond what can be measured by a standardized test.

Each of these projects *embraces* complexity. The SJEP in Tucson incorporates regional history into the curriculum, asking students to make connections between time, place, and subjectivities. *Brown* and *Echoes* authors describes their projects as using their differences rather than ignoring them—an ambitious task, yet the only task realistic enough to support young people in navigating a society that both constrains and manipulates those differences. Through inviting students into alternative learning processes, PAR embodies a faith in young people's intellect and humanity. This faith defies the policies of punitive accountability and standardization that undermine young people in their efforts to become educated, active members of their communities. In this volume, we hear stories that evidence the potential youth have to become critical social agents, and how PAR can serve as an activist pedagogy, investing young people's creation of their own vision of justice.

Notes

1 I am borrowing the terms "fail" and "failure" from the NCLB and its surrounding discourse. My use of this term does not indicate agreement that these terms are adequate or appropriate descriptions of student learning or of schools.

2 The term "qualified teachers" is problematic; recent national policies have sought to disregard certain qualifications, such as experience, in exchange for other types, such as passing tests. My use of this term is in no way an advocation for that use of this term, which depro-

fessionalizes experienced, competent, and committed teachers. Rather, I use the term "qualified" or "prepared" to describe teachers who have the educational background, cultural understanding, and compassion to teach students from any background. In addition, while I may not agree with the standards used to determine "qualification," the concentration of "under-qualified" teachers in schools serving high proportions of students of color and poor students reveals institutional priorities.

3 This does not mean that students are actually passive receivers of information; people reconstruct, appropriate, and resist the roles offered to them. But I am most interested here in how institutions structure and allow participation. How students respond to these practices is considered elsewhere.

References

American Educational Research Association (2000). *Standards for Educational and Psychological Testing*. Washington, DC: American Educational Research Association.

Anyon, J. (1994). Social class and the hidden curriculum of work [1980]. In *Transforming Urban Education*, ed. J. Kretovics and E. J. Nussel. Boston: Allyn and Bacon: 253–76.

Bhimji, F. (2004). "I want you to see us as a person and not as a gang member or a thug": Young people define their identities in the public sphere. *Identity* 4(1): 39–57.

Darling-Hammond, L., E. Rustique-Forrester, and R. Pecheone (2004). *Multiple Measures Approaches to High School Graduation*. Palo Alto, CA: School Redesign Network, Stanford.

Davidson, A. L. (1996). *Making and Molding Identity in Schools: Student Narratives on Race, Gender, and Academic Achievement*. Albany: State University of New York Press.

Delpit, L. D. (1995). *Other People's Children: Cultural Conflict in the Classroom*. New York: New Press.

Demmert Jr., W. G., and J. C. Towner (2003). A review of the research literature on the influences of culturally based education on the academic performance of Native American students. Final Paper. Oregon: Northwest Regional Educational Lab., Portland, OR.

Diamond, J. B., and J. Spillane (2004). High-stakes accountability in urban elementary schools: Challenging or reproducing inequality? *Teachers College Record* 106(6): 1145–76.

The Education Trust (2003). *Education Watch for The Nation: Key Education Facts and Figures Achievement, Attainment and Opportunity*. Washington, DC: The Education Trust.

Fine, M., and A. Burns (2003). Class notes: Toward a critical psychology of class and schooling. *Journal of Social Issues* 59(4): 841–60.

Fine, M., J. Bloom, and L. Chajet (2003). Betrayal: Accountability from the bottom. *VUE: Rethinking Accountability* 1: 12–23.

Fine, M., A. Burns, Y. A. Payne, and M. E. Torre (2004). Civics lessons: The color and class of betrayal. *Teachers College Record* 106(11): 2193–223.

Fine, M., R. A. Roberts, M. E. Torre, and J. Bloom (2004). *Echoes of Brown: Youth Documenting and Performing the Legacy of* Brown v. Board of Education. New York: Graduate Center, City University of New York: Distributed by Teachers College Press.

Flanagan, C., B. Jonsson, L. Botcheva, B. Csapo, J. Bowes, P. Macek, et al. (1999). Adolescents and the "Social Contract": Developmental roots of citizenship in seven countries. In *Roots of Civic Identity: International Perspectives on Community Service and Activism in Youth*, ed. M. Yates and J. Youniss. New York: Cambridge University Press: 135–55.

Freire, P. (2000). *Pedagogy of the Oppressed*, trans. M. B. Ramos. New York: Continuum.

Gay, G. (2000). *Culturally Responsive Teaching: Theory, Research, and Practice*, vol. 8. New York: Teachers College Press.

Gilmore, P. (1985). "Gimme room": School resistance, attitudes, and access to literacy. *Journal of Education* 167(1): 111–28.

Ginwright, S., and J. Cammarota (2006). Beyond resistance! Youth activism and community change: new democratic possibilities for practice and policy for America's youth. In *Beyond Resistance! Youth Activism and Community Change: New Democratic Possibilities for Practice and Policy for America's Youth*, ed. S. Ginwright, P. A. Noguera, and J. Cammarota. New York: Routledge: xiii.

Ginwright, S., J. Cammarota, and P. A. Noguera (2005). Youth, social justice, and communities: Toward a theory of urban youth policy. *Social Justice* 32(3): 24–40.

Gonzalez, N. (2005). Beyond culture: The hybridity of Funds of Knowledge. In *Funds of Knowledge: Theorizing Practices in Households, Communities, and Classrooms*, ed. N. Gonzalez, L. C. Moll, and C. Amanti. Mahwah, NJ: Lawrence Erlbaum: 29–46.

Gonzalez, N., L. C. Moll, and C. Amanti (2005). Theorizing practices. In *Funds of Knowledge: Theorizing Practices in Households, Communities, and Classrooms*, ed. N. Gonzalez, L. C. Moll, and C. Amanti. Mahwah, NJ: Lawrence Erlbaum: 1–28.

Gonzalez, N., L. C. Moll, M. F. Tenery, A. Rivera, P. Rendon, R. Gonzales, et al. (2005). Funds of knowledge for teaching in Latino households. In *Funds of Knowledge: Theorizing Practices in Households, Communities, and Classrooms*, ed. N. Gonzalez, L. C. Moll, and C. Amanti. Mahwah, NJ: Lawrence Erlbaum: 89–118.

Guajardo, M., and F. Guajardo (2002). Critical ethnography and community change. In *Ethnography and Schools: Qualitative Approaches to the Study of Education*, ed. Y. Zou and E. Trueba. Lanham, MD: Rowman and Littlefield: 281–304.

Gunzenhauser, M. G. (2003). High-stakes testing and the default philosophy of education. *Theory into Practice* 42(1): 51–8.

Gutierrez, K. (2005). Intersubjectivity and the grammar of the third space. Paper presented at the conference for the Sylvia Scribner Award Address, April 13, 2005. Montreal: American Educational Research Association Annual Conference.

HoSang, D. (2006). Beyond policy: Ideology, race and the re-imagining of youth. In *Beyond Resistance: Youth Activism and Community Change: New Democratic Possibilities for Policy and Practice for America's Youth*, ed. S. Ginwright, P. A. Noguera, and J. Cammarota. New York: Routledge: 3–20.

Imber, M. (2003). Teach the student, not the test. *American School Board Journal*, 190(9), 60–2.

Ismail, S. M., and C. Cazden (2005). Struggles for indigenous education and self-determination: Culture, context, and collaboration. *Anthropology and Education Quarterly* 36(1): 88–92.

Ismat, A.-H. (1994). Culturally responsive curriculum. *ERIC Digest*, Appalachia Education Laboratory, Charleston, WV. Available online http://ezproxy.library.arizona.edu/login?url=http://search.ebscohost.com/login.aspx?direct=true&db=eric&AN=ED370936&site=ehost-live

Kirshner, B. (2006). Teaching and learning in youth activism: A case for youth-centered apprenticeships. In *Beyond Resistance: Youth Activism and Community Change: New Democratic Possibilities for Policy and Practice for America's Youth*, ed. S. Ginwright, P. A. Noguera, and J. Cammarota. New York: Routledge: 37–58.

Klug, B. J., and P. Whitfield (2003). *Widening the Circle: Culturally Relevant Pedagogy for American Indian Children*. New York: Routledge.

Ladson-Billings, G. (1989). A tale of two teachers: Exemplars of successful pedagogy for black students. Paper presented at the Educational Equality Project Colloquium "Celebrating Diversity: Knowledge, Teachers, and Teaching," New York, May 4–5, 1989, sponsored by the Spender Foundation; Chicago, IL. and the National Academy of Education, Washington, DC.

Ladson-Billings, G. (1995). But that's just good teaching! The case for culturally relevant pedagogy. *Theory into Practice* 34(3): 159–65.

Ladson-Billings, G. (2006). From the achievement gap to the education debt: Understanding achievement in US schools. *Educational Researcher* 35(7): 3–12.

Lee, J., and G. Orfield (2006). *Tracking Achievement Gaps and Assessing the Impact of NCLB on the Gaps: An In-depth Look into National and State Reading and Math Outcomes*. Cambridge, MA: Civil Rights Project, Harvard University.

Lewis-Charp, H., H. Cao Yu, and S. Soukamneuth (2006). Examining youth organizing and identity-support: Two civic activist approaches for engaging youth in social justice. In *Beyond Resistance: Youth Activism and Community Change: New Democratic Possibilities for Policy and Practice for America's Youth*, ed. S. Ginwright, P. A. Noguera, and J. Cammarota. New York: Routledge: 21–36.

Lipka, J., and T. L. McCarty (1994). Changing the culture of schooling: Navajo and Yup'ik cases. *Anthropology and Education Quarterly* 25(3): 266–84.

Lomawaima, K. T., and T. L. McCarty (2002). *Reliability, Validity, and Authenticity in American Indian and Alaska Native Research* (No. EDO-RC-02-4). Charleston, WV: ERIC Clearinghouse on Rural Education and Small Schools and Washington, DC: Office of Educational Research and Improvement (ED).

Lowell, A., and B. Devlin (1998). Miscommunication between aboriginal students and their non-aboriginal teachers in a bilingual school. *Language, Culture and Curriculum* 11(3): 367–89.

Males, M. (2006). Youth policy and institutional change. In *Beyond Resistance: Youth Activism and Community Change: New Democratic Possibilities for Policy and Practice for America's Youth*, ed. S. Ginwright, P. A. Noguera, and J. Cammarota. New York: Routledge: 301–18.

Manzo, K. K. (2007). Reading rituals. *Education Week* 26(25): 27–9.

McDermott, R., and K. Hall (2007). Scientifically debased research on learning 1854–2006. *Anthropology and Education Quarterly* 38(1): 9–15.

McLaren, P., and K. Gutierrez (1994). Pedagogies of dissent and transformation: A dialogue about post modernity, social context, and the politics of literacy. *International Journal of Educational Reform* 3(3): 327–37.

Mehan, H., L. Hubbard, A. Lintz, and I. Villanueva (1994). *Tracking Untracking: The Consequences of Placing Low Track Students in High Track Classes*. Washington, DC: National Center for Research on Cultural Diversity and Second Language Learning, and Santa Cruz, CA: Office of Educational Research and Improvement.

Morrell, E. (2004). *Becoming Critical Researchers: Literacy and Empowerment for Urban Youth*. New York: Peter Lang.

Morrell, E. (2006). Youth initiated research as a tool for advocacy and change in urban schools. In *Beyond Resistance: Youth Activism and Community Change: New Democratic Possibilities for Policy and Practice for America's Youth*, ed. S. Ginwright, P. A. Noguera, and J. Cammarota. New York: Routledge: 111–28.

National Education Association (2004). Testing plus: Real accountability with real results. Washington, DC: National Education Association. Available online at www.nea.org/accountability/testplus.html. Accessed March 25, 2004.

National School Board Association (2004). *Ensuring the Goals of No Child Left Behind: Recommendations for Legislative and Regulatory Changes*. Alexandria, VA: National Schools Boards Association.

Neill, M. (2006). Preparing teachers to beat the agonies of No Child Left Behind. *Education Digest* 71(8): 8–12.

Noguera, P. A. (2001). Racial politics and the elusive quest for excellence and equity in education. *Education and Urban Society* 34(1): 18–41.

Noguera, P. A. (2002). Beyond size: The challenge of high school reform. *Educational Leadership* 59(5): 60–3.

Noguera, P. A. (2003). The trouble with black boys: The role and influence of environmental and cultural factors on the academic performance of African American males. *Urban Education* 38(4): 431.

Noguera, P. A., and A. A. Akom (2000a). Disparities demystified. *Nation* 270(22): 29.

Noguera, P. A., and A. A. Akom (2000b). The opportunity gap. *Wilson Quarterly* 24(3): 86.

O'Donoghue, J. (2006). "Taking their own power": Urban youth, community-based youth organizations, and public efficacy. In *Beyond Resistance: Youth Activism and Community Change: New Democratic Possibilities for Policy and Practice for America's Youth*, ed. S. Ginwright, P. A. Noguera, and J. Cammarota. New York: Routledge: 229–46.

Oakes, J. (1985). *Keeping Track*. New Haven, CT: Yale University Press.

Orfield, G. (1994). Asking the right question. *Educational Policy* 8(4): 404–13.

Orfield, G. (2004). *Introduction: Inspiring Vision, Disappointing Results: Four Studies on Implementing the No Child Left Behind Act*. Cambridge, MA: Civil Rights Project, Harvard University.

Rothstein, R., and R. Jacobsen (2007). A test of time: Unchanged priorities for student outcomes. *School Administrator* 64(3): 36–40.

Schemo, D. J. (2007a, April 21, 2007). Justice Dept. is asked to investigate reading plan. *New York Times*: 12.

Schemo, D. J. (2007b, March 15, 2007). Oversight is set for beleaguered US reading program. *New York Times*: 25.

Scheurich, J. J. (2002). The destructive desire for depoliticized ethnographic methodology: Response to Harry F. Wolcott. In *Ethnography and Schools: Qualitative Approaches to the Study of Education*, ed. Y. Zou and E. Trueba. Lanham, MD: Rowman and Littlefield: 49–54.

Smith, D. M. (2002). The challenge of urban ethnography. In *Ethnography and Schools: Qualitative Approaches to the Study of Education*, ed. Y. Zou and E. Trueba. Lanham, MD: Rowman and Littlefield: 171–84.

Strobel, K., J. H. Osberg, and M. W. McLaughlin (2006). Participation in social change: Shifting adolescents' developmental pathways. In *Beyond Resistance: Youth Activism and Community*

Change: New Democratic Possibilities for Policy and Practice for America's Youth, ed. S. Ginwright, P. A. Noguera, and J. Cammarota. New York: Routledge: 196–214.

Sunderman, G. L., and J. Kim (2004). *Inspiring Vision, Disappointing Results: Four Studies on Implementing the No Child Left Behind Act*. Cambridge, MA: Civic Rights Project, Harvard University.

Torre, M. E., and M. Fine (2006). Researching and resisting: Democratic policy research by and for youth. In *Beyond Resistance: Youth Activism and Community Change: New Democratic Possibilities for Policy and Practice for America's Youth*, ed. S. Ginwright, P. A. Noguera, and J. Cammarota. New York: Routledge: 269–86.

US Department of Education (2001). *No Child Left Behind Act of 2001*. Retrieved April 26, 2004, from www.ed.gov/policy/elsec/leg/esea02/index.html

US Department of Education (2002). *Testing for Results: Helping Families, Schools and Communities Understand and Improve Student Achievement*. Retrieved March 30, 2004, from www.ed.gov/nclb/accountability/ayp/testingforresults.html

Valdez, G. (1996). Con Respeto*: Bridging the Distances between Culturally Diverse Families and Schools: An Ethnographic Portrait*. New York: Teachers College Press.

Valenzuela, A. (1999). *Subtractive Schooling: US-Mexican Youth and the Politics of Caring*. Albany: State University of New York Press.

Valenzuela, A. (2000). The significance of the TAAS Test for Mexican immigrant and Mexican American adolescents: A case study. *Hispanic Journal of Behavioral Sciences* 22(4): 524–39.

Valenzuela, A., L. Prieto, and M. P. Hamilton (2007). No Child Left Behind (NCLB) and minority youth: What the qualitative evidence suggests. *Anthropology and Education Quarterly* 38(1): 1–8.

What You Need To Know and Do to Truly Leave No Child Behind [R]. An Action Guide (2003). Washington, DC: Children's Defense Fund.

Winter, N. (2003). *Social Capital, Civic Engagement and Positive Youth Development Outcomes*. Washington, DC: Policy Studies Associates.

Young, I. M. (2001). Equality of whom? Social groups and judgments of injustice. *Journal of Political Philosophy* 9(1): 1–18.

Youniss, J., S. Bales, V. Christmas-Best, M. Diversi, M. W. McLaughlin, and R. Silbereisen (2002). Youth civic engagement in the twenty-first century. *Journal of Research on Adolescence* 12(1): 121–48.

Youniss, J., J. A. McLellan, and M. Yates (1997). What we know about engendering civic identity. *American Behavioral Scientist* 40(5): 620–31.

An Epilogue, of Sorts

MICHELLE FINE

June 2007

Dear Tenure and Promotion Committee:

I received your request to assess the scholarship of Assistant Professor H. I understand that your Personnel Committee has some questions about Youth Participatory Action Research (YPAR). Is this scholarship rigorous? Is there an intellectual tradition within which this work is situated? What about bias? Why are so many of the articles co-authored with high school students? Isn't this just community service?

This request for *paradigmatic translation* comes to me often. I am a Distinguished Professor, trained in experimental social psychology, with an interest in participatory methods and ethnography, a commitment to mixed methods and long involved with social research for social justice. I am happy to answer your questions, although I admit I tire of them. I have decided to publish this response so that it might be systematically slipped into the personnel files of faculty who engage with YPAR, to dispense with questions about intellectual tradition and departures, objectivity and bias, validity and generalizability, what it means to "be of use" as a public intellectual.

To contextualize the journey on which we are about to embark, it may be important to remind Committee Members that YPAR is typically undertaken as critical scholarship, by multi-generational collectives, to interrogate conditions of social injustice through social theory with a dedicated commitment to social action (see Torre and Fine, 2006). Such work is increasingly scrutinized in the neo-liberal academy, no matter what the methods or how many authors. If undertaken by scholars who are of color, queer, Muslim Americans, dissenting, Marxist . . . the heat rises. As higher education turns rapidly to the Right, as corporate influence and conservative government interests infiltrate, the democratic and public aspects of the university curdle. "Rigor panic" sets in.

Across the nation, YPAR has been mobilized in varied educational policy struggles for adequate schooling, finance equity, immigrant rights, alternatives to high-stakes testing, affordable housing, against violence against girls and women, for the rights of queer youth, and for books not bars/the abolition of jails and prisons (see Ginwright; Morrell; Cahill et al., all in this volume). Many of these projects have been launched from community-based organizations, with some home-grown at the intersections of universities, high schools, and communities. Over the past decade, the PAR Collective has sprung up at the Graduate Center, CUNY, just as YPAR has flourished at the Graduate School of Education at UCLA (see Morrell, this volume; Oakes et al., 2006), San Francisco State University César Chávez Institute for Public Policy (see Ginwright, this volume), University of Arizona (see Cammarota, this volume), and at varied other community-based and university settings across the nation and the globe. These projects join with a critical gaze on institutions where (in)justice reigns and human spirits are mangled, in the name of schooling, criminal (in)justice, or youth development.

Committed to radically reconceptualized notions of *objectivity*, *validity*, and *generalizability*, across sites, participatory action researchers vary wildly but together we deliberately refuse neutrality and seek, in the words of Baldwin quoted by Ginwright, "to make the world a more human dwelling place." Toiling with the words of Reverend Desmond Tutu in our collective veins, we recognize:

> If you are neutral in situations of injustice, you have chosen the side of the oppressor. If an elephant has its foot on the tail of a mouse and you say that you are neutral, the mouse will not appreciate your neutrality.
>
> **(From http://thinkexist.com/quotations, accessed June 2, 2007)**

And so I offer this text to clear the air a bit, and invite reflection on PAR as serious and engaged research.

In the remainder of this letter I offer a brief tutorial about the intellectual legacy of PAR. We begin with the most often asked query—But is it rigorous? Let us read together, the Webster's dictionary definition of rigor:

> **1 a** (1): harsh inflexibility in opinion, temper, or judgment: SEVERITY (2): the quality of being unyielding or inflexible: STRICTNESS (3): severity of life: AUSTERITY **b**: an act or instance of strictness, severity, or cruelty
>
> **2**: a tremor caused by a chill
>
> **3**: a condition that makes life difficult, challenging, or uncomfortable; *especially*: extremity of cold
>
> **4**: strict precision: EXACTNESS <logical *rigor*>
>
> **5 a** *obsolete*: RIGIDITY, STIFFNESS **b**: rigidness or torpor of organs or tissue that prevents response to stimuli **c**: RIGOR MORTIS.

PAR as Epistemology

Allow me to clear up some misconceptions about participatory action research. *PAR is not a method.* Scholars of participatory action research have relied upon and utilized surveys, logistic regressions, ethnography, public opinion polls, life stories, testimonies, performance, focus groups, and varied other methods in order to interrogate the conditions of oppression and surface leverage points for resistance and change.

PAR is, however, a radical *epistemological challenge* to the traditions of social science, most critically on the topic of where knowledge resides. Participatory action researchers ground our work in the recognition that expertise and knowledge are widely distributed. PAR further assumes that those who have been *most* systematically excluded, oppressed, or denied carry specifically revealing wisdom about the history, structure, consequences, and the fracture points in unjust social arrangements. PAR embodies a democratic commitment to break the monopoly on who holds knowledge and for whom social research should be undertaken. As Anisur Rahman has written:

> The distinctive viewpoint of PAR [recognizes that the] domination of masses by elites is rooted not only in the polarization of control over the means of material production but also over the means of knowledge production, including . . . the social power to determine what is valid or useful knowledge.
>
> **(Rahman, 1985: 119)**

While the processes of PAR have been grossly appropriated by the International Monetary Fund, World Bank, oil and pharmaceutical companies to try to co-opt "locals" to "buy into" corporate takeover of lands and resources, critical participatory projects are designed to unveil the ideological and material architecture of injustice. Firmly situated with a human rights framework (see De Jesus and Lykes, 2004), critical PAR projects seek to investigate and interrupt what Antonio Gramsci called the "passive revolution":

> The ... "passive revolution" ... qualif[ies] the most usual form of hegemony of the bourgeoisie involving a model of articulation whose aim is to neutralize the other social forces ... enlarging the state whereby the interests of the dominant class are articulated with the needs, desires, interests of subordinated groups.
>
> **(Mouffe, 1979: 192)**

These projects introduce *empirical evidence* as tools in ideological struggle:

> the objective of ideological struggle is not to reject the system and all its elements but to rearticulate it, to break it down to its basic elements and then to sift through past conceptions to see which ones, with some changes of content, can serve to express the new situation.
>
> **(Mouffe, 1979: 192)**

The essays published in this volume capture elegantly the politics, process, curricula and the practices necessary to engage what Gramsci calls *rearticulation*—breaking down hegemonic beliefs into their basic elements and then creating novel conceptions to express new situations. Participatory action researchers create the spaces, the methods, and the praxis by which rearticulation occurs. Indeed, when critical legal theorist Mari Matsuda asks, in the title of her book, *Where Is Your Body?* (1996), YPAR scholars are among the few in the academy who know just where they stand.

At base, the five projects profiled in this book engage multiple generations of researchers mobilized to shatter what Hannah Arendt called the "lying world of consistency" that underlies oppressive social arrangements. Like Arendt, Jesuit priest and activist scholar Ignacio Martín-Baró argued that a central task for critical social researchers is to *uncover the collective lies* that have been told about a people's history and to excavate *untold stories* so that people could critique the past and reimagine the future:

> In El Salvador the established power structure has concealed reality and systematically distorted events, producing a Collective Lie ... The Lie ... consists in constructing a reality that is ideologically compatible with the interests of the dominant class ... [with] at least three consequences: the country's most serious problems have been sys-

> tematically hidden from view; the social interests and forces at play have been distorted; and people have internalized the alienating discourse as part of their personal and social identity . . . Given the . . . Lie, there arises a need to increase critical consciousness through a process of de-ideologization—to which social psychologists can and should be contributing . . . public opinion surveys can play a small yet significant role . . . shaping a new collective identity.
>
> **(Martín-Baró, 1994: 189)**

By intent, PAR facilitates such de-ideologization; the projects profiled in this book lift up multiple stories and counter stories dwelling within complex institutions, challenging hegemonic stories and privileging those perspectives that mature on the bottom of social arrangements, where the lies, the ghosts, the buried memories, the disposables, the traitors, and the silences gather (see Harris et al., 2001). Shattering the silence and lies that protect systems of miseducation as if failure were predominantly the fault of students, these projects take up the challenge that Franz Fanon identified when he wrote "[a] society that ossifies itself in determined form . . . [is] a closed society where it is not good to be alive, where the air is rotten, where ideas and people are corrupt" (Fanon, 1967: 182, 224–5). PAR floats new air into unjust systems, circulating possibilities for different tomorrows.

~

Energized by the political urgency of the times, participatory methods respond to crises in politics—immigration politics, violence against women, school push outs, denial of educational quality, the school to prison pipeline, a Youth Bill of Rights—by deliberately inverting who frames and who is framed as the problem; who constructs research questions, designs, methods, interpretations, and products. Researchers from the bottom of social hierarchies, the traditional objects of research, re-emerge as subjects and architects of critical inquiry. Contesting collective lies about meritocracy and who's "at risk," some work with privileged allies (see Torre et al., this volume), some in quite diverse collectives (see Cahill et al., this volume), and some in deep solidarity with similarly situated others (see Tuck et al.; Romero et al.; and Morrell et al., all in this volume).

An Intellectual Tradition: Social Research for Social Change

Buried in the rigor question lies a doubled doubt: is PAR really just a sophisticated form of community service? Or, as the concern is often delicately cloaked, does PAR grow out of an intellectual tradition? While I bristle at this questioning, for its reluctance to see PAR as research and for its dismissal of community engagement as central to the mission of university life, I reference here what I know best—the long and often buried scholarly tradition of action research and research for social change within the discipline of social psychology. I write as the academic grandchild of Kurt Lewin, who trained Morton Deutsch, who has been my primary mentor. And it is through this line of scholarly DNA that I situate PAR within a legacy of rigorous research for social justice.

With long roots in Africa, Asia, Central and South America, PAR was born in the soil of discontent, understanding critical inquiry to be a tool for social change (Brydon-Miller, 2001; Lykes and Coquillon, 2007; Martín-Baró, 1994; Rahman, 1985; Rahman, forthcoming; Sherif et al., 1954). In the United States, PAR can be traced back to the early writings of Kurt Lewin, who first coined the term "action research" in his 1946 paper "Action Research and Minority Problems." He defined action research as "comparative research on the conditions and effects of various forms of social action and research leading to social action" and delineated "a spiral of steps, each of which is composed of a circle of planning, action, and fact-finding about the result of the action." Lewin encouraged a generation of scholars, laboring in the shadow of World War II, to apply the theoretical and empirical tools of social science to the urgent problems of global oppression, social violence, prejudice, and injustice.

Kurt Lewin is but one in a long line of researchers who have dedicated themselves to research that would reveal and challenge social injustice; research designed to provoke action for a more just distribution of resources and dignity. One need only review the archives of William James (James and Kuklick, 1987), W. E. B. DuBois (1990), and Gordon Allport (1986), the mid-century writings of Lewin (1946: 48) and Sherif et al. (1954), the later writings of Carolyn Payton (1984), Martín-Baró (1994), James Jones (2004), M. Brewster Smith (1986), Brinton Lykes (2001), and Patricia Gurin et al. (2002), or the files of the Psychologists' League or the Society for the Psychological Study of Social Issues, to discover a strong strain of disciplinary commitments to justice studies.

And yet, as Morton Deutsch and Robert Krauss have argued, social scientists—and social psychologists in particular—retreated from social research for social change in the 1950s, seeking refuge in the experimental laboratory, fleeing the chill of McCarthyism. Deutsch and Krauss wrote:

> More and more social psychologists, in the past decade, have turned their attention to carefully controlled laboratory studies, neglecting investigations of social behavior in natural settings . . . Often the light is brighter and vision is clearer in the laboratory; yet the remarkable things that people do as participants in laboratory experiments,

> to be seen in perspective, must be viewed from the outside. Knowledge must be sought even where the obstacles are considerable and the light is dim, if social psychologists are to contribute to an understanding of the human problems of their time.
>
> **(Deutsch and Krauss, 1965: 215–16)**

PAR picks up where Lewin left off, where McCarthyism petrified/froze the field. Seeking knowledge where the light is dim, the projects in this volume resuscitate analyses of oppression, power, and justice within academic inquiry. Each in its own way documents and contests the multiple and complex layers of ideological and material oppression that Deutsch theorized:

> Oppression is the experience of repeated, widespread, systemic injustice. It need not be extreme and involve the legal system (as in slavery, apartheid or the lack of right to vote) nor violent (as in tyrannical societies). Harvey (1999) has used the term "civilized oppression" to characterize the everyday processes of oppression in normal life. Civilized oppression "refers to the vast and deep injustices some groups suffer as consequences of often unconscious assumptions and reactions of well meaning people in ordinary interactions which are supported by the media and cultural stereotypes as well as by the structural features of bureaucratic hierarchies and market mechanisms."
>
> **(Deutsch, 2004: 3–4)**

The chapters in this volume reveal how structural and "civilized" oppression scars communities and youth; how negative ideologies (Cahill et al.) and material deprivations (Morrell; Tuck et al.) intersect with denial of respect (Torre et al.) and denial of ethnic history (SJEP), yielding devastating consequences for communities of poverty, leaving scratch marks on the soul of youth (Cannella), and yet fanning the flames of resistance (Ginwright).

Designed to "awaken a sense of injustice," Fed Up Honeys, CREDD, *Echoes*, SJEP, and IDEA document and mobilize subterranean pools of shame and despair by aggregating and making public the collective troubles among very differently positioned youth. Revealing the common, public roots of these "private" troubles (Mills, 1959), PAR demonstrates the *differentiated* consequences of social oppression and the *common* commitments to change.

In the United States, PAR can trace some of its inspiration to the historic work of social researchers who have collaborated in key legal decisions of the twentieth century. Across the second half of the twentieth century, we find many examples of such collaborations—including Kenneth Clark (1963) and Stuart Cook (1984), and their courageous posture in the *Brown v. Board of Education* case (see Fine, 2004 for review), the ground-breaking amicus brief crafted by Fiske et al. (1991) on sex stereotyping in the workplace, Craig Haney's legal work on the death penalty (1997), and the extensive research agenda spearheaded by Patricia Gurin and colleagues (2002) in the recent University of Michigan Affirmative Action case. *Brown v. Board of Education*, *Price-Waterhouse v. Hopkins*, and *Grutter v. Bollinger and the University of Michigan* were *nation-building* legal cases, infused with strategic and passionate social science evidence and theory.

While much is known about social research dedicated to legal change, historic bits of evidence help us understand how some critical researchers used community forums to agitate for change. Horace Mann Bond (incidentally, Julian Bond's father), a brilliant African-American educator who worked closely with Thurgood Marshall , understood that community could also be a site for the performance of critical inquiry. Combining humor and a sharp analysis of what he considered racist and classist "science," Bond conveyed a powerful critique of IQ testing.

> In 1959, Bond wrote to a friend that Thurgood Marshall who by then had been dubbed "Mr. Civil Rights" had taken to calling Bond "Mr. Toilets." The curious honorific owed to Bond's daring idea that just as White southerners were willing to base school policies on a simple correlation of intelligence test scores with "race," Bond was willing to offer his own educational proposals based on a correlation of a different sort. In 1959, Bond announced that he had discovered an "easy, economical way to search for 'Talent' or at least 'talent' as measured by the national merit Scholarship Corporation." Bond published a study based on data from his old home city, Chicago, and his old home state, Kentucky, and found a simple rule that seemingly explained how to find National Merit Scholarship winners: "More toilets, more talent; fewer toilets, less talent; lowest percentage of toilets, no talent at all." If the government were serious about finding academically talented youngsters, "instead of providing scholarships," it would "subsidize the building of two-holers, three-holers or even eight-holers." Bond argued that this was not an unreasonable proposition for "The House with Three Toilets is, of course, symbolic of occupational status, socioeconomic success and a host of other indicators of successful test performance."
>
> **(Jackson, 2004: 9)**

Like Bond, the YPAR scholars in this volume seek provocative means to awaken a sense of injustice and provoke social action. Performances, sticker campaigns, youth led protests, policy rallies, video, presentations at national conferences and school boards, joining with other youth researchers to craft a Youth Bill of Rights . . . all reflect a sense of responsibility and urgency, to contribute the tools of social theory and research to broad-based struggles for social justice.

These young people labor in the legacy of activist-research collaborations including: the Highlander Center, involved in participatory research with youth, elders, and the struggles of residents in Appalachia; the Paolo Freire Institute working globally on critical education; the Harvard University Civil Rights Project, bringing together policy analysts, organizers, journalists, and researchers on critical issues of racial injustice in education; the Applied Research Center, where organizers, writers, and activists gather social research to support their campaigns for racial justice; the Rockridge Institute directed by George Lakoff which works to reinvigorate both a vision and language for a social justice of inclusion; the Center for Policy Studies in Washington, DC, which produces critical work on economics, prisons, and social well-being with a particular analysis by race and class; the Poverty and Race Research Action Council; Mort Deutsch's International Center for Conflict and Cooperation and their international collaborations. Critically engaged social researchers, then and now, have understood their responsibility to situate themselves, among other actors, in civic struggles for justice, through the courts, community organizing, the streets, performance, scholarship, and public writing. Youth PAR walks in the footsteps of these intellectual and political ancestors, accompanied by a richer, more diverse (and younger!) collective of researchers, spanning age, generation, history, and perspective.

Objectivity and Bias, Validity and Generalizability

We come now to the question of whether or not YPAR researchers really care about traditional features of social inquiry, in particular objectivity and bias, validity and generalizability. While some would differ—and argue that these concerns are constraining hold overs and fossilized features of modernist science—I will try to make the argument that YPAR done well deepens the very social practices of objectivity, validity, and generalizability.

On objectivity

> [T]here is not just one legitimate way to conceptualize objectivity, any more than there is only one way to conceptualize freedom, democracy or science. The notion of objectivity has valuable political and intellectual histories; as it is transformed into "strong objectivity" by the logic

> of standpoint epistemologies . . . Might should not make right in the realm of knowledge production any more than in matters of ethics.
>
> **(Harding, 1987: 138)**

Sandra Harding, Patti Lather (1985), Jill Morawski (2004), Edward Sampson (1983), and others argue that elite interests have, for too long, masqueraded as scientific objectivity. By writing from a "God's eye view" (Harding, 1987), researchers who presume to excise themselves from the research often unwittingly project their fantasies and anxieties onto the bodies and psyches of those they study. While some critical researchers and PAR practitioners have therefore abandoned the notion of objectivity entirely, I find myself leaning on the writings of philosopher Sandra Harding, who argues for *strong objectivity*:

> To enact or operationalize the directive of strong objectivity is to value the Other's perspective and to pass over in thought into the social condition that creates it—not in order to stay there, to "go native" or merge the self with the Other but in order to look back at the self in all its cultural particularity from a more distant, critical, objectifying location . . . Strong objectivity requires that we investigate the relation between subject and object rather than deny the existence of, or seek unilateral control over, this relation.
>
> **(Harding, 1987: 151–2)**

Strong objectivity is exercised when researchers work diligently and self-consciously through their own positionalities, values, and predispositions, gathering as much evidence as possible, from many distinct vantage points, all in an effort to *not* be guided, unwittingly and exclusively, by predispositions and the pull of biography (see Fine, 1994; Morawski, 2004). Reading through the chapters on CREDD, IDEA, SJEP, *Echoes*, and Fed Up Honeys, we can hear intentionally difficult conversations about power, perspective, difference, shame, anger, and critical consciousness. These are the discursive journeys toward strong objectivity.

In each of these chapters, it's at once refreshing and exhausting to read how researchers across generations, locations, and status *deliberate deeply* within and across differences, *seeking dissent* and *exploring competing interpretations* of the evidence. As the cases elaborate, youth and adult researchers generate varied interpretations of many sorts of empirical materials, and together try to determine the contours, the consequences, and the vulnerabilities of unjust formations. In PAR collectives, these rugged deliberations are fundamental to method; a crucial element of question generating, data gathering, analysis and conversations about products and actions. Biases are not to be denied, but displayed, dissected, challenged, and pooled. Objectivity is neither disregarded nor simply assumed by virtue of distance. Strong objectivity is engaged as a social practice of relentless deliberation among collectives of researchers working through differences.

On expert validity

Classic social science is measured, in part, by the extent to which "experts" consider the design and constructs to be valid. I want to pause for a moment to consider how PAR transforms and deepens this notion of expertise.

PAR stands on the epistemological grounds that persons who have historically been marginalized or silenced carry substantial knowledge about the architecture of injustice, in their minds, bodies, and souls; in ways that are conscious and floating; individual and collective. This is a position that has been advocated by Gloria Anzaldúa, Patricia Hill Collins, Mari Matsuda, and bell hooks.

I want to tie this commitment to *plural and subjugated expertise* to the traditional standard of expert validity because participatory action research projects are designed expressly around a set of processes to *honor and develop these varied bases of knowledge* in youth and in adults, explicitly troubling hegemonic and hierarchical assumptions about who is the expert. As María Elena Torre and colleagues detail in their chapter, the *Echoes* collective brought together young people, elders, educators, and activists from honors classes, special education, and the Gay/Straight Alliance, civil rights activists, poets, dancers, feminist lawyers, historians, journalists, and youth who have spent too much time in the disciplinary office. The research space was designed as a messy contact zone, to recognize and elevate the deep and varied local knowledges of those who live/work/survive on the bottom, middle, and tops of their high schools, with educators, activists, and civil rights activist elders.

As we trained together in research camps practicing and inventing varied quantitative and qualitative methodologies, our multiple forms of expertise sat in conversation, percolating social analyses much more dense, splintered, and textured than any single perspective could birth. Indeed, the graffiti wall may be the most vivid chronicle of our many contentious debates, a visual sketch of conversations and contestations between researchers and between researchers and respondents to the survey. The delicate practice of joining these varied bodies and diverse forms of expertise around the same table, to generate questions, gather and analyze data and determine products, created a dynamic plurality of expertise, coalescing around points of agreement, dissensus, and surprise. Collective expertise was chiseled and achieved—not determined *a priori*, by race, class, age, gender, status, or standardized test scores. As new bodies were brought to the table as researchers, a transformative sense of expertise evolved.

Thus, I want to suggest that expert validity deepens through the practice of PAR, in several ways. First, PAR collectives include wide-ranging forms of contextualized expertise, born in experience and analysis, breathing in bodies often disregarded by social scientists except as objects. Borrowing from Giyatri Chakravorty Spivak, in PAR "the subalterns speak." And they get a hearing. That is, the very people invited to the table represent a wide swath of perspectives, biographies, and standpoints. As Luis, a member of SJEP, writes: "I love knowing that without the SJEP I would have probably gone through life as a halfway conscious, media-controlled drone."

At the same time, in some of these collectives, youth of privilege are also present and they too engage a deep process of de-ideologization, reflection, and consideration of how their privilege rides on the backs of others' exclusion. They move through guilt or alienation and into shared responsibility for change . . . but it takes time. Sometimes it takes quite a while for more privileged and traditionally "smart" youth to understand that there are many ways to think about a problem; that their perspective is not the only one, or even the most productive one; that their working with other youth is not charity *for*, but struggle *with* (Torre and Fine, this volume). In these messy dialectical relations, however, new knowledge is born.

In the *Echoes* project, for instance, in the bouillabaisse of this extremely diverse collective of youth, drawn from the "tops" and the "bottoms" of their desegregated high schools, working with assorted adults, a radical critique of the continued unfulfilled promises of *Brown v. Board of Education* was launched. Only when the elite students heard and saw the evidence on thousands of surveys did they *believe* the stories of marginalization voiced by their co-researchers; and only when the historically marginalized students realized that their privileged allies listened intently—and learned—did they believe that collective change was possible. We built a social psychological space for respect, difference, interrogation of power, exchange, and hybrid forms of collective knowledge.

Thus, as important as the *who* is the *how* of PAR. *Intentional and sustained deliberative processes*, among participatory researchers broadly defined, take up competing ideas and wrestle interpretations until well-developed, complex analyses emerge. When very different kinds of persons and texts come together, around a table, for the purpose of social analysis, the nearly invisible but ruthless threads of injustice come to light. For instance, as the Fed Up Honeys read real estate ads and articles about gentrification, wrote biographies of miseducation, and reviewed social service documents written to "help" them—framing them as "at risk"—the Honeys decided to tell their own stories and map their own geographies of the Lower East Side as they knew it. Shocked to see themselves referenced as "at risk," they launched a sticker campaign, writings, presentations, and a website informing readers and audiences that "at risk" is a victim-blaming ideological decoy placed on the bodies of young womyn of color to deflect attention away from practices of miseducation, gentrification, racism, the greed of global capital, and misogyny. In their analyses, the Fed Up Honeys came to see the material deprivations to which they had been subjected, and they railed against the ideological representations of them as "risky," which lubricated the move to sell their apartment buildings out from under them.

Thus on the basis of "who" carries expertise, and dedicated processes engaged to generate multiple interpretations, PAR projects sharpen the range and chisel the focus of expertise, strengthening and democratizing expert validity.

On construct validity

Just as PAR collectives mark a radical intervention into research conceptions of who holds expertise, PAR methods encourage a radical rethinking of constructs and causality. Cook and Campbell (1979) define construct validity as the means to assess the extent to which theoretical notions are indeed meaningful and valid and to determine how cause relates to effect. Both of these concerns are central to the critical aims of PAR. Recall, in *Echoes*, the youth early on corrected our (not very) construct(ive) frame of "*the achievement gap*" and told us, "We're willing to work on this project, but you have to call it *the opportunity gap* project and not *achievement gap*. Achievement puts the blame on us, and opportunity returns the blame to the system." They were indeed trying to assure that our constructs were valid, and our causal analyses were meaningful. That is, they wanted to be sure that we were not, inadvertently, attributing blame to the victims of miseducation and not thereby denying the collateral consequences of finance inequity or under-resourced schools.

Indeed, each of the YPAR projects discussed in this volume reports a critical moment of construct rebuilding, when key hegemonic constructs, for example "merit," "intelligence," and "risk," had to be unpacked and retheorized. CREDD writes: "Part of the reclaiming has to do with taking back words and languages that have been used against us, for example: (un)intelligence, (limited) capacity, and discourses of (trickle down) power and democracy."

Similarly, many of the projects worked hard to clean out the shame and help youth contest and recast dominant formulations of causality. "Part of the recovery has to do with tapping into parts of us that have been discouraged in our schooling . . ."

Renaming constructs, restoring integrity to self, refusing shame and returning the analytic and political gaze back on inadequate educational systems—this is the work of construct validity.

In the SJEP, the *Encuentros* mark a powerful moment of reconstructing the role of parents in school reform. In these moments, Arizona youth as "blossoming intellectuals" present critical analyses to their parents and then the SJEP staff educate the parents about their rights. In these encounters, the construct of parental responsibility is dramatically transformed from non-questioning supporter of schools to active, engaged, and questioning participant in the process of school change:

> The basis of these encounters is helping parents shift their frame of reference in regards to their position within the educational hierarchy. Many, in fact nearly every one of our parents operated on the notion that the education system and the administrators and teachers within the system could not be questioned or should not be questioned. The SJEP set that way of understanding on its head by proclaiming that parents have every right to question and critique the schools, the administrators, the teachers and the staff.
>
> **(Romero, 2007, interview)**

Indeed, in all of these projects, commonsense constructs—dropout, risk, intelligence, parental support, shame—and the arrows of causality are forcefully and collectively reconsidered.

On generalizability

In 2005, we met in New York City and brought together the *Echoes* collective and the Arizona youth research collective. At first, they presented timidly to each other, stretching across east and west, north and south, New York City and Tucson, immigrants and those who have been here too long . . . Twenty minutes into the session a young person from Arizona, listening intently to Amir's description of special education as a space for Black boys, in the basement, gasped, "Your special education is in the basement? Wow, all the way across the country, and ours is too."

In that moment, across very different settings, groups of youth, ancestral biographies—the blades of racial and class oppression, the stains of high-stakes testing, the marks of labeling—moved across the nation. This was a moment of generalizability, possible when we gather youth researchers from across sites and settings to consider the ways in which their works reveal deep, entrenched forms of oppression and resistance and the ways in which their works illuminate some profoundly and painfully predictable strategies by which elites are eating the young.

Within each project we hear distinct and amazing insights particular to local context. But it is also the case, as Shawn Ginwright notes, that *across* projects we witness stunning, shared lessons about oppression, resistance, youth resilience, collective possibility, disappointment, despair, and desire, that bleed across zip codes. I am tempted to call these latter insights a form of *generalizability*.

To think about generalizability in ways that are expansive rather than formulaic and dependent on sample size, I have come to rely on Cindi Katz's notion of *counter-topographies*. In her article, "On the grounds of globalization: A topography for feminist political engagement" (2001) Katz traces the long arm of globalization as it shapes growing up in the Sudan and in Harlem, New York. She invites readers to theorize *across* longitudes and latitudes, seeking the common residues of globalization, identifying shared forms of resistance and yet never flattening the enormous variation that characterizes each local space. With a fine ethnographic eye that penetrates deeply within each site, Katz calls for social analyses that trace globally, and dig locally, through a "spatialized understanding of problems." She argues that

> any effective politics challenging a capital inspired globalization must have similar global sensitivities, even as its grounds are necessarily local. This is different from a place based politics . . . Built on the critical triangulation of local topographies, counter-topographies provide exactly these kinds of abstractions interwoven with local specificities and the impulse for insurgent change.
>
> **(Katz, 2001: 1235)**

With Katz's thinking in mind, I want to suggest that rather than defining generalizability as a direct and technical extension of a finding or set of findings (dependent on your N), PAR (and YPAR in particular) encourages us to consider two novel conceptions of generalizability.

> **Theoretical generalizability** refers to the extent to which theoretical notions or dynamics move from one context to another. To what extent can we glean lessons about social oppression and forms of resistance from across the five cases described in this volume?
>
> **Provocative generalizability** offers a measure of the extent to which a piece of research provokes readers or audiences, across contexts, to generalize to "worlds not yet," in the language of Maxine Greene; to rethink and reimagine current arrangements. To what extent have these cases instilled in audiences a sense of urgency, pressing the question, What must we do?

On theoretical generalizability

In 1991, I published a book called *Framing Dropouts*, on the social psychological contexts and dynamics of inner city public high schools that produce extraordinarily high rates of dropouts. Concerned that in the typical neighborhood high school in poor communities of New York City, only 20–40 percent of the 9th graders survive to senior year, I designed an ethnographic analysis to study how "dropouts" were produced. Spending a year in high school, attending classes, working in the office, visiting the homes of graduates, current students and dropouts, conducting interviews, focus groups, surveys, and archival investigations, I generated a portrait of an institution that was producing, seamlessly, the mass exodus of Black and Brown youth of poverty, with an ideology that justified their exit as if sad, but inevitable. I searched to find the villain who was tossing bodies out the window, and I sought the gangs of disruptive youth who were actively tossed. But I found neither. Instead, I witnessed a slow drip feed of youth out of the doors of the school, who were thereby exiled (more or less permanently) out of the fantasy of the American dream.

The book gained popularity among critical theorists in education, urban educators in particular. And so I lectured nationally. One evening, after a detailed presentation on the book and its methods, an educator from rural Maine stood to say, "The same thing happens here." I could not imagine what she meant. The original school was located in the heart of Manhattan, with students drawn from Central and East Harlem. With its largely Jewish faculty and Black and Latino student body, I could not believe that here, in White, rural Maine, "the same thing happens." And yet this educator expanded on her initial observation—"We also have a practice of throwing out some students, as if it were inevitable or for their own good. It's a broad based theory of disposability; that many, maybe most of our students—the poor ones at least—won't make it, and then we design schools to make it true." I credit this unnamed woman with the inspiration for theoretical generalizability. There was nothing in the stubborn particulars (Cherry, 1994) of the New York City setting that would have suggested easy transfer. And yet a theory and practice of disposability traveled easily up Route 95 to rural Maine.

To consider a different, much more provocative example: In 1973, Phil Zimbardo and colleagues published the Stanford prison study. White college undergraduate males were placed in a hypothetical prison and randomly assigned the role of prisoner or guard for a series of days. The experiment had to be terminated prematurely because the subjects were developing physical and psychological problems characteristic of stress and trauma. In other words, they were *becoming* prisoners and guards, despite their knowledge of the role play. At the time Zimbardo wrote:

> The potential social value of this study derives precisely from the fact that normal, healthy, educated young men could be so radically transformed under the institutional pressures of a "prison environment." If this could happen in so short a time, without the excesses that are possible in real prisons, and if it could happens to the "cream of the crop of American youth," then one can only shudder to imagine what society is doing both to the actual guards and prisoners who are at this very moment participating in that unnatural "social experiment."
> **(Zimbardo et al., 1973)**

Thirty-four years later, in 2007, Zimbardo has again been speaking on this study which tells us so much about the human capacity for evil and torture, as witnessed in Abu Ghraib in Iraq. Such theoretical generalizability is the raison d'être of basic and applied research on social injustice.

On provocative generalizability

There is another form of generalizability I want to offer here, one inspired by Maxine Greene's writings on the social imagination where she argues for research, literature, art, music, dance . . . that "fight the numbness of oppression." Greene seeks aesthetic experiences that "awaken a sense of injustice," and create "openings" for what we do not yet know, have not yet experienced. She contrasts the creative provocation of an *esthetic* experience with its opposite, the numbing of pain produced by *anesthetic*. Working with John Dewey's quote that "facts are made and repellent things," Greene writes that without reflection, openings, and re-analysis, facts deaden us to what could be.

Drawing from Greene's inspiration, *provocative generalizability* refers to researchers' attempts to move their findings toward that which is not yet imagined, not yet in practice, not yet in sight. This form of generalizability offers readers an invitation to launch from our findings to what might be, rather than only understanding (or naturalizing) what is. Greene's desire for social and ethical imagination rises as a standard for social research: does the work move readers to act?

Susan Sontag, in *Regarding the Pain of Others*, speaks to the provocation of the photograph or the televised viewing of war abroad:

> The imaginary proximity to the suffering inflicted on others that is granted by images suggests a link between the far away sufferers—seen close up on the television screen—and the privileged viewer that is simply untrue, that is yet one more mystification of our real relations to power. So far as we feel sympathy, we feel we are not accomplices to what caused the suffering. Our sympathy proclaims our innocence as

> well as our impotence. To that extent, it can be (for all our good intentions) an impertinent—if not an inappropriate—response. To set aside the sympathy we extend to others beset by war and murderous politics for a reflection on how our privileges are located on the same map as their suffering, and may—in ways we might prefer not to imagine—be linked to their suffering, as the wealth of some may imply the destitution of others, is a task for which the painful, stirring images supply only an initial spark.
>
> **(Sontag, 2003: 102–3)**

Sontag is quick to note that although we cannot know the pain of others in our bodies, we must resist the temptation to distance or grow weary. We must view scenes of torture and ask how would this be? How could it be otherwise? And, as Greene asks, What can I do to repair the world? What else is possible? How could it be otherwise? And again, What Shall We Do?

Provocative generalizability, joined with strong objectivity, asserts that researchers and readers, performers and audience, victims, people of privilege and witnesses: we are all positioned in unjust settings. And such an existential truth obligates us to be present, feeling and thinking critically about how unjust distributions of resources and opportunities affect our comfort and discomfort, our dependencies, privileges, joys, our moments of shared pain and potential collective actions. We have no choice, but a certain obligation, to act. Carolyn Payton, psychologist and the first African-American director of the Peace Corps, argued years ago in the pages of the *American Psychologist*:

> I would suggest that it is absurd for us not to make our stand clear on matters of injustice, that failure to do so does grave image damage to us in the public's eye and that to continue to ignore damage done by social injustices that are readily apparent through use of our sense organs and consciences severely weakens our credibility.
>
> **(Payton, 1984: 392)**

The theater of *Echoes*, the sticker campaign of Fed Up Honeys, the protests of IDEA, the videos/national and local presentations of the SJEP demanding adequate facilities, urinals, culturally relevant curricula . . . and the ongoing organizing of CREDD bear witness to the possibility of provocation induced by collectives of participatory researchers.

On action

Today we face what French theorist Pierre Bourdieu has called "a crisis of politics . . . [in which we encounter] despair at the failure of the state as guardian of the public interest" (1999: 2). Locally and globally, the public sphere has walked away from the needs of individuals, families, and communities, particularly those who are poor, working class, and of color. Needs have been replaced by privileges as a mark of those who deserve; the state has been displaced by the market; entitlement occluded by "choice." The neo-liberal state and the encroaching privatization of public goods have been represented as natural, rational, and progressive, through

> symbolic inculcation in which journalists and ordinary citizens participate passively and, above all, a certain number of intellectuals participate actively . . . This kind of symbolic drip feed to which the press and television news contribute very strongly . . . produces very profound effects. And as a result neo-liberalism comes to be seen as an inevitability.
>
> **(Bourdieu, 1999: 30)**

Democracy has shrunk to voting, and those who are deemed *undeserving* are being escorted out of public schools, parks, public housing, healthcare . . . and into prisons and/or the military. Communities are dispirited; injustice feels inevitable and too heavy to move. It is a propitious time for participatory work to prick the anesthesia that is settling into our collective bodies.

PAR projects gather up social critique and outrage, ambivalence and desire, as forms of knowledge. Inquiry is valued as oxygen for democratic sustenance. Collaborations are forged as necessary for sustaining global movements of resistance. Participatory action research is a strategic tool anchored in some very untraditional formulations of some very traditional notions of objectivity, validity, and generalizability. With innovation and a proud legacy of activist social researchers, participatory research collectives can interrupt the drip feed, engage critical questions, produce new knowledge, provoke expanded audiences, and allow us to ask as scholars, in the language of the poet Marge Piercy (1982), how can we "be of use?"

~

And so, committee members, I hope this memo is sufficient to explicate the intellectual legacy and epistemological commitments of YPAR scholars. I am sorry but I just cannot bear to deal with questions like, "Why are these articles co-authored?" or "What percentage of the essay did she write?" as if writing collectively and democratically were easier than writing alone (try it and call me). I cannot dignify questions like, "Would you consider this researcher an activist or a scholar?" and finally I do not think anyone should entertain, in the twenty-first century, why collaborating with community youth and elders is considered "nice" while collaborating with middle-aged, balding White guys in a think tank is "science."

I certainly hope that the level of interrogation YPAR scholars endure is dwarfed by the level of scrutiny that befalls faculty who receive funding from pharmaceutical companies, oil companies, the Department of Homeland Security, and the Department of Defense, for example, those whose research findings are held exclusively and confidentially by corporations and the military.

Alas, if you have further questions—send them on. Perhaps soon, I will publish an update as YPAR comes to be recognized as a gift of critical pedagogy, deliberative public scholarship, and a delicious space for imagining multi-generational possibilities for a very different tomorrow.

Sincerely,

Michelle Fine
Distinguished Professor of Social Psychology,
Urban Education, and Women's Studies
The Graduate Center
City University of New York

References

Allport, G. (1986). *The Nature of Prejudice*. New York: Anti-Defamation League.

Bourdieu, P. (1999). *Acts of Resistance: Against the Tyranny of the Market*. New York: New Press.

Brydon-Miller, M. (2001). Participatory action research: Psychology and social change. In *From Subjects to Subjectivities: A Handbook of Interpretive and Participatory Methods*, ed. D. L. Tolman and M. Brydon-Miller. New York: New York University Press: 76–89.

Cherry, F. (1994). *The Stubborn Particulars of Social Psychology*. New York: Routledge.

Clark, K. (1963). *The Negro Protest*. Boston: Beacon Publishers.

Cook, S. (1984). The 1954 social science statement and school desegregation. *American Psychologist* 39(8): 819–32.

Cook, T., and D. Campbell (1979). *Quasi-experimentation: Design and Analysis Issues for Field Settings*. Boston: Houghton Mifflin.

De Jesus, M., and B. Lykes (2004). Racism and "whiteness" in transitions to peace: Indigenous peoples, human rights and the struggle for justice. In *Off White: Readings on Race, Privilege and Resistance*, ed. M. Fine, L. Weis, L. Powell Pruitt, and A. Burns. New York: Routledge: 331–44.

Deutsch, M. (2004). *Oppression and Conflict*. Plenary addresses at the Conference on Interrupting Oppression and Sustaining Justice, Teachers College, Columbia University, New York.

Deutsch, M., and R. Krauss (1965). *Theories in Social Psychology*. New York: Basic Books.

DuBois, W. E. B. (1990). *Souls of Black Folks*. New York: First Vintage Books.

Fanon, F. (1967). *Black Skin, White Masks*. New York: Grove Press.

Fine, M. (1991). *Framing Dropouts: Notes on the Politics of an Urban High School*. Albany: State University of New York Press.

Fine, M. (1994). Working the hyphens: Reinventing self and other in qualitative research. In *Handbook of Qualitative Research*, ed. N. K. Denzin and Y. S. Lincoln. Thousand Oaks, CA: Sage: 70–82.

Fine, M. (2004). The power of *Brown v. Board of Education*: Theorizing threats to sustainability. *American Psychologist* 59(6): 502–10.

Fiske, S., D. Bersoff, E. Borgida, K. Deaux, and M. Heilman (1991). Social science research on trial:

The use of sex stereotyping research in *Price Waterhouse v. Hopkins. American Psychologist* 46: 1049–60.
Gurin, P., E. Dey, S. Hurtado, and G. Gurin (2002). Diversity and higher education: Theory and impact on educational outcomes. *Harvard Educational Review* 72(3, fall): 330–66.
Haney, C. (1997). Psychological secrecy and the death penalty: Observations on the mere extinguishment of life. *Studies in Law, Politics, and Society* 16: 3–69.
Harding, S. (1987). Introduction: Is there a feminist method? In *Feminism and Methodology*, ed. S. Harding. Bloomington: Indiana University Press: 1–14.
Harris, A., S. Carney, and M. Fine (2001). Counter work: Introduction to "Under the covers: Theorizing the politics of counter stories." *International Journal of Critical Psychology* 4: 6–18.
Harvey, J. (1999). *Civilized Oppression*. New York: Rowman and Littlefield.
hooks, b. (1984). *Feminist Theory from Margin to Center.* Boston: South End Press.
Jackson, J. P. (2004). "Racially stuffed shirts and other enemies of mankind": Horace Mann Bond's parody of segregationist psychology in the 1950s. In *Defining Difference: Historical Perspectives on Psychology, Race, and Racism*, ed. A. S. Winston. Washington, DC: American Psychological Association: 261–83.
James, W., and B. Kuklick (1987). *William James: Writings 1902–1910*. Washington, DC: Library of America.
Jones, J. (2004). Whites are from Mars, OJ is from Planet Hollywood: Blacks don't Support OJ and Whites just don't get it. In *Off White: Readings on Power, Privilege and Resistance*, ed. M. Fine, L. Weis, L. Pruitt, and A. Burns. New York: Routledge: 89–97.
Katz, C. (2001). On the grounds of globalization: A topography for feminist political engagement. *Signs: Journal of Women in Culture and Society* 26(4): 1213–34.
Lather, P. (1985). Research as praxis. *Harvard Educational Review* 56(3): 257–77.
Lewin, K. (1946). Action research and minority problems. *Journal of Social Issues* 2: 34–46.
Lykes, M. B. (2001). Activist participatory research and the arts with rural Maya women: Interculturality and situated meaning making. In *From Subjects to Subjectivities: A Handbook of Interpretive and Participatory Methods*, ed. D. L. Tolman and M. Brydon-Miller. New York: New York University Press: 183–99.
Lykes, M. and Coquillon, E. (2007). Participatory action research and feminism. In *Handbook of Feminist Research*, ed. S. Hesse-Biber. Thousand Oaks, CA: Sage: 297–326.
Martín-Baró, I. (1994). *Writings for a Liberation Psychology.* Cambridge, MA: Harvard University Press.
Matsuda, M. (1995). Looking to the bottom: Critical legal studies and reparations. In *Critical Race Theory: The Key Writings that Formed the Movement*, ed. K. Crenshaw, N. Gotanda, G. Peller, and K. Thomas. New York: New Press: 63–79.
Matsuda, M. (1996). *Where Is Your Body?* Boston, MA: Beacon Press.
Mills, C. W. (1959). *The Sociological Imagination*. London: Oxford University Press.
Morawski, J. (2004). White experimenters, White blood and other White conditions: Locating the psychologist's race. In *Off White: Readings on Power, Privilege and Resistance*, 2nd edn., ed. M. Fine, L. Weis, L. Pruitt, and A. Burns. New York: Routledge: 215–34.
Mouffe, C. (1979). *On Gramsci and Marxist Theory*. London: Routledge.
Oakes, J., J. Rogers, and M. Lipton (2006). *Learning Power: Organizing for Education and Justice.* New York: Teachers College Press.
Payton, C. R. (1984). Who must do the hard things? *American Psychologist* 39: 391–7.
Piercy, M. (1982). *Colors in the Water*. New York: Knopf.
Rahman, A. (1985). The theory and practice of participatory action research. In *The Challenge of Social Change*, ed. O. Fals-Borda. Beverly Hills, CA: Sage Publications
Rahman, A. (forthcoming). The praxis of participatory action research. In *Handbook of Action Research*, ed. P. Reason and H. Bradbury. London: Sage.
Sampson, E. (1983). *Justice and the Critique of Pure Psychology*. New York: Perseus.
Sherif, M., O. J. Harvey, B. J. White, W. R. Hood, and C. W. Sherif (1954). *Study of Positive and Negative Intergroup Attitudes between Experimentally Produced Groups: Robbers Cave Study.* Norman: University of Oklahoma Press.
Smith, M. B. (1986). McCarthyism: A personal account. *Journal of Social Issues* 42(4): 71–80.
Sontag, S. (2003). *Regarding the Pain of Others*. New York: Picador.
Torre, M. E., and M. Fine (2006). Participatory action research (PAR) by youth. In *Youth Activism: An International Encyclopedia*, ed. L. Sherrod, C. Flanagan, and R. Kassimir. Westport, CT: Greenwood: 456–62.

Zimbardo, P. (2007). *A Simulation Study of the Psychology of Imprisonment*. Available online at www.prisonexp.org/ Accessed February 20, 2007.
Zimbardo, P., W. Banks, C. Haney, and D. Jaffe, (1973). A Pirandellian prison, *New York Times Magazine*, April 8, 1973: 38ff.

Contributors

Natasha Alexander is currently working in New York City. She has plans to return to her studies in marketing and public relations, and to attend culinary school with the goal of opening her own restaurant.

Jovanne Allen is a GED earner after being pushed out from her New York City public high school. Jovanne plans to attend college in New York City.

Maria Bacha graduated from an alternative public high school in New York after having been pushed out from her school in Florida.

Amir Bilal Billups is a senior majoring in history and education at Saint Peter's College. A proud father of a two-year-old daughter, he is pursuing his dream of becoming a high school history teacher. He co-facilitates the "chill-town researchers," a youth participatory action research team in a local high school.

Yasmine Blanding, a Brooklyn native, is enjoying every moment of motherhood with her two year old son Ame Divine, while studying psychology and education at York College and working for a Long Island-based heating, ventilating, and air-conditioning management company.

Caitlin Cahill is now living far away from the Lower East Side in Salt Lake City, Utah. Currently an Assistant Professor of Community Studies at the University of Utah, Caitlin received her doctorate in Environmental Psychology with a concentration in public policy and urban studies at the City University of New York. Caitlin's work focuses upon young people's well-being, racial equity, urban restructuring, critical race and feminist theory, participatory action research approaches, and social justice. She is interested in research at the intersection of theory and practice that contributes to social change and pushes scholarship in new directions. She has had the privilege to work collectively with the Fed Up Honeys, some of the most intellectually generous, honest, critical thinkers she knows.

Julio Cammarota is an assistant professor in the Bureau of Applied Research in Anthropology and the Mexican-American Studies and Research Center at the University of Arizona. His research focuses on participatory action research with Latina/o youth, institutional factors in academic achievement, and liberatory pedagogy. He has published papers on family, work, and education among Latina/os and on the relationship between culture and academic achievement. He has co-authored a seminal article on applying a social justice approach to youth development practices. Currently, he is the director of the Social Justice Education Project in Tucson, Arizona.

Chiara M. Cannella is a PhD candidate in the Department of Language, Reading and Culture in the College of Education at the University of Arizona. Her current research focuses on evaluating youth development programs. She is also working with the Research Collaborative for Youth Activism.

Kim Dominguez is a native Tucsonan, and a 2003 graduate of Cholla High School. She has been an active community member and Social Justice Education Project participant since the project began in January 2003. She hopes to receive her teaching credentials in the near future and implement the SJEP at Cholla High School.

Michelle Fine is Distinguished Professor of Social Psychology, Urban Education, and Women's Studies at the Graduate Center, City University of New York, and has taught at CUNY since 1990. A member of the CUNY, Graduate Center, PAR Collective (http://web.gc.cuny.edu/che/start.htm), her work focuses upon sexuality, critical race theory, critical methods, and mass incarceration. Recent publications include: M. Fine and S. McClelland, Sexuality education and desire: still missing after all these years, *Harvard Educational Review* (2006, fall); L. Weis and M. Fine (2004), *Working Method: Social Research and Social Injustice* (Routledge, 2004); M. Fine, L. Weis, L. Powell Pruitt, and A. Burns, *Off White: Essays on Race, Privilege and Contestation* (Routledge, 2004); M. Fine et al., *Echoes of Brown: Youth Documenting and Performing the Legacy of* Brown v. Board of Education (Teachers College Press, 2004); and M. Fine et al., *Changing Minds: The Impact of College in Prison*, www.changingminds.ws (2001), an executive report on the impact of college on prisoners post-release, conducted after *Pell.*

Emily Genao recently graduated with a degree in communications from Fordham University. After interning at various magazines in New York City, she is taking advantage of her newfound freedom to write and explore.

Shawn Ginwright is an Associate Professor of Education in the Africana Studies Department and Senior Research Associate for the César Chávez Institute for Public Policy at San Francisco State University. In 1989, he founded Leadership Excellence Inc., an innovative youth development agency located in Oakland, California, that trains African-American youth to address pressing social and community problems. In 1999, he received his PhD from the University of California Berkeley. His research examines the ways in which youth in urban communities navigate through the constraints of poverty and struggle to create equality and justice in their schools and communities. He is the author of *Black in School—Afrocentric Reform, Black Youth, and the Promise of Hip-Hop Culture* (Teachers College Press, 2004) and co-editor, with P. Noguera and J. Cammarota, of *Beyond Resistance!: Youth Activism and Community Change: New Democratic Possibilities for Practice and Policy for America's Youth* (Routledge, 2006). He has published extensively on issues related to urban youth in journals such as *Social Problems, Social Justice, Urban Review*, and *New Directions in Youth Development.* He is a highly sought-after speaker to national and international audiences.

Sandy Grande (Quechua) is an Associate Professor of Education at Connecticut College.

Maxine Greene is a professor of philosophy and education and the William F. Russell Professor in the Foundations of Education (emerita) at Teachers College, Columbia University, where she continues to teach a course in educational philosophy, social theory, and aesthetics.

Liz Hernandez graduated from Tucson High in 2006. She is currently attending Pima Community College and is a project coordinator for the SJEP.

Pauline Lipman is Professor of Policy Studies in the College of Education, University of Illinois-Chicago and Director of the Collaborative for Equity and Justice in Education. Pauline's research focuses on race and class inequality in schools, globalization and urban development, and the political economy and cultural politics of race in urban education. She is the author of *Race, Class, and Power in School Restructuring* (State University of New

York Press, 1998), *High Stakes Education; Inequality, Globalization, and Urban School Reform* (Routledge, 2004), and numerous articles on these topics. An advocate of activist and engaged scholarship, her current projects examine the relationship of school policy to neo-liberal urban development in Chicago, particularly gentrification and displacement of communities of color. She is also a founder and active member of Chicago-area Teachers for Social Justice.

Elinor Marboe is majoring in classical civilizations at Wellesley College, where she works at the Learning Center. She has studied in Greece and Israel and hopes to continue to travel after graduation.

Luis C. Moll (PhD, UCLA, 1978), born in Puerto Rico, is Associate Dean for Academic Affairs and Professor at the College of Education, University of Arizona. His main research interest is the connection among culture, psychology and education, especially as it relates to the education of Latino children in the United States. Among other studies, he has analyzed the quality of classroom teaching, examined literacy instruction in English and Spanish, studied how literacy takes place in the broader social contexts of households and community life, and attempted to establish pedagogical relationships among these domains of study. He is presently conducting a longitudinal study of biliteracy development in children and the language ideologies that mediate that development. He has served on the editorial boards of several journals, including the *American Educational Research Journal*, *Educational Researcher*, *Reading Research Quarterly*, *Journal of Literacy Research*, *Cultura y Educación*, and *Mind, Culture, and Activity*. His co-edited volume, *Funds of Knowledge: Theorizing Practices in Households, Communities, and Classrooms*, was published in 2005 by Lawrence Erlbaum. He was elected to membership in the National Academy of Education in 1998.

Alexis Morales was pushed out from her New York City public high school and earned her GED. She plans to enroll in college.

Ernest Morrell is an assistant professor in the urban schooling division of the Graduate School of Education and Information Studies at the University of California at Los Angeles. His work examines the possible intersections between indigenous urban adolescent literacies and the "sanctioned" literacies of dominant institutions such as schools. Particularly, he is interested in youth popular culture; adolescent literacy practices in non-school settings; critical literacy education; engaging youth and teachers in action research projects, and urban teacher development. He teaches courses on literacy theory and research, critical pedagogy, cultural studies, urban education, and action research.

Sarah Quinter graduated from an alternative public school in New York City and is a co-founder of the Misled Youth Network.

Grecia Ramirez has been involved in the Social Justice Education Project since her junior year in the 2004 summer. The following year she graduated early from Cholla high school. After her graduation, she continued her education at The University of Arizona, where she is currently attending. She plans on continuing her education and staying involved in the SJEP for as long as she can. She is hopeful that the project will expand and continue to influence the Tucson community.

Indra Rios-Moore was born and raised on the Lower East Side of New York to a strong, inspirational, and determined single Puerto Rican mother. She grew up in the Baruch Houses of the New York City Public Housing Authority, the largest project development in Manhattan. After attending public school until 6th grade, her mother pushed to get her free testing for admittance to a Manhattan private school. She attended private school until 9th grade when she decided to home-school herself so that she could concentrate and have more time for musical pursuits. In 2003, she graduated from Smith College with a Bachelor degree in American Studies and a minor in Spanish. She has a strong desire to continue working and studying in a way that will allow her to contribute to social justice and finds all of the members of the Fed Up Honeys to be continually inspiring.

John Rogers is an Assistant Professor of Education at UCLA and the Co-Director of UCLA's Institute for Democracy, Education, and Access (IDEA). He also serves as the faculty director of UCLA's Principal Leadership Institute. He studies strategies for engaging urban youth, community members, and educators in equity-focused school reform. He draws extensively on the work of John Dewey to explore the meaning of and possibilities for democratic education today. He is the co-author (with Jeannie Oakes) of *Learning Power: Organizing for Education and Justice* (Teachers College Press, 2006).

Augustine Romero is completing his first year as Tucson Unified School District's (TUSD) Coordinator of Ethnic Studies. During the previous four years, he served as TUSD's Director of the Mexican American/Raza Studies Department. He is also the Co-Director of the Social Justice Education Project. This project is a collaboration between TUSD, the University of Arizona's Mexican American Studies and Research Center and its Bureau of Applied Research in Anthropology.

Tahani Salah is majoring in English at Columbia University. A member of the Nyorican Poets Slam Team, she recently appeared on HBO's Def Poetry Jam. She is the author of the forthcoming *Respect the Mic*.

Jamila Thompson graduated from public school in Washington, DC, and attends Eugene Lang College, The New School

Tiffany Threatts is the only Fed Up Honey who still lives on the Lower East Side and she continues to be involved with her community. She was born and raised in the neighborhood to a single mother. She finished State University of New York Farmingdale with her Associates in Liberal Arts and is planning to continue college in the near future in New York City. She hopes to pursue a career in psychology.

María Elena Torre is Assistant Professor and chair of Education Studies at Eugene Lang College of The New School. Committed to participatory action research in schools, prisons, and communities, she is a co-author of *Echoes of Brown: Youth Documenting and Performing the Legacy of* Brown v. Board of Education, and *Changing Minds: The Impact of College on a Maximum Security Prison*, and has been published in *Urban Girls, Revisited* (NYU Press, 2007), *Handbook of Action Research* (Sage, 2007), *Qualitative Research in Psychology: Expanding Perspectives in Methodology and Design* (American Psychological Association, 2003), and in journals such as *Teachers College Record*, the *Journal of Social Issues*, *Feminism and Psychology*, and the *Journal of Critical Psychology*.

Eve Tuck is a doctoral candidate in Urban Education at the Graduate Center, City University of New York.

Melody Tuck is a graduate of Atlantic City High School and attends State University of New York Purchase College.

Kendra Urdang is double majoring in Creative Writing and Human Rights at Bard College. She is involved in the Bard Prison Initiative and runs weekly poetry workshops at the Beacon Correctional Facility for Women in Beacon, New York.

Luis Valdez graduated from Cholla High School in 2005. He is now attending Pima Community College and is a project coordinator for the Social Justice Education Project.

Index